SHREVEPORT MARTYR
FATHER LOUIS GERGAUD

SHREVEPORT MARTYR
FATHER LOUIS GERGAUD

IN HIS OWN WORDS

Very Reverend Peter B. Mangum, JCL.; William Ryan Smith, MA;
Cheryl H. White, PhD

Foreword by Archbishop Christophe Pierre, the Apostolic Nuncio to the United States

THE
History
PRESS

Published by The History Press
Charleston, SC
www.historypress.com

First published 2023

Manufactured in the United States

ISBN 9781467152204

Library of Congress Control Number: 2022947095

Notice: The information in this book is true and complete to the best of our
knowledge. It is offered without guarantee on the part of the authors or The
History Press. The authors and The History Press disclaim all liability in
connection with the use of this book.

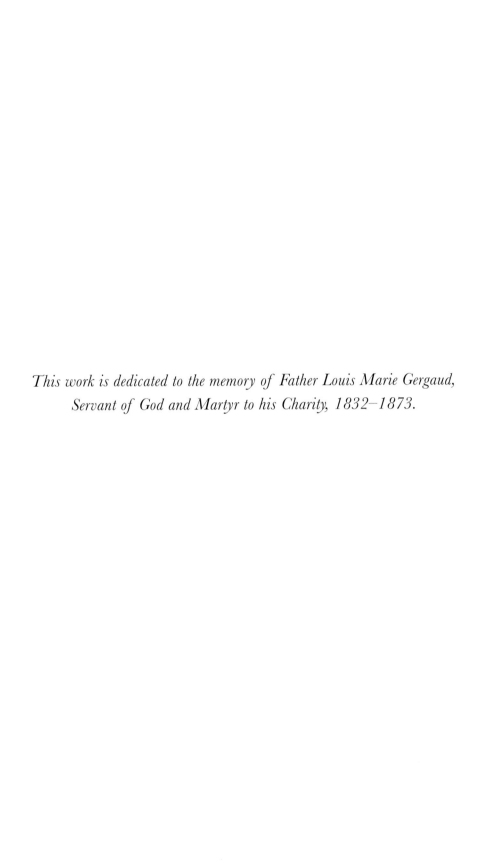

This work is dedicated to the memory of Father Louis Marie Gergaud,
Servant of God and Martyr to his Charity, 1832–1873.

CONTENTS

FOREWORD

The first priests I met at the early age of three were French missionaries from Brittany working in Madagascar, where my family had immigrated. A few years later, I came across Breton Franciscan priests in Morocco. Then when appointed Nuncio in Haiti, I learned that hundreds of missionaries of the Society of Priests of Saint Jacques, religious brothers and sisters from Brittany, had contributed to the evangelization of this land.

At many times, it could be said that the Catholic faith was the greatest export of my homeland. Within the passages of that rich history one can find many remarkable stories of the zeal and sacrifice of young men, but there are perhaps none as moving as that of the five heroic priests who gave their lives in the service of charity in Shreveport, Louisiana, in 1873. The five Shreveport martyrs—Father Isidore Quémerais, Father Jean Pierre, Father Jean Marie Biler, Father Louis Gergaud and Father François Le Vézouët—answered the summons of Bishop Auguste Marie Martin, a native of Saint-Malo, that led to their free and willing offering of their own lives to live out the Gospel among strangers in need. These inspiring Servants of God may indeed one day be raised to the altars of God as canonized saints.

Shreveport Martyrs of 1873: The Surest Path to Heaven, published in 2021, relates in full the story of all five of these virtuous priests. This volume, however, focuses on the life of just one: the newly ordained Father Louis Gergaud, from the small village of Héric near Nantes, who came to the new mission field of the Diocese of Natchitoches in 1854. The letters and papers edited and prepared for this collection relate, in his own words, the many joys and challenges of answering that missionary call in a most difficult period of American history: before, during and after the Civil War. Significantly, he reveals to all of us in our own time a model of charity that emulates that of Christ, a priest of Jesus Christ who saw neither blue nor gray, Black or white but fellow children of God. This is a story that has endured for nearly 150 years at the time of this writing and will continue to resonate with all who come to know it, for at its core is the profound truth of mankind realizing his own creation in the very likeness and image of God. We were created for love. And as Jesus Christ has told us, there is no greater love than this.

The human condition is always crying out for understanding. In the example of sacrifice found in Father Louis Gergaud and the other Shreveport martyrs, there is the universal and accessible truth that our lives have their greatest meaning when we offer them for others. In his own words, Father Gergaud shows us this truth with clarity, as he responded to God's call and followed it to its most ultimate expression.

Archbishop Christophe Pierre
Apostolic Nuncio
Washington, D.C., August 1, 2022

PREFACE

This book is a sequel of sorts, a follow-up to the book these authors published in 2021, *Shreveport Martyrs of 1873: The Surest Path to Heaven*. The 2021 publication chronicles the compelling story of five noble and heroic Roman Catholic priests who made a free offering of their lives during the 1873 Yellow Fever Epidemic in Shreveport, Louisiana—the third worst that United States history records. As a project rooted in friendship and reaching back several years, the research into the exemplary lives of all five priests (Father Isidore Quémerais, Father Jean Pierre, Father Jean Marie Biler, Father Louis Gergaud and Father François Le Vézouët) soon formed the basis of petitioning the Vatican's Congregation for the Causes of Saints for the necessary nihil obstat, that a canonization inquiry might begin. On December 8, 2020, Bishop Francis Malone of the Diocese of Shreveport acknowledged them as *Servants of God*. This marked the first step in what hopefully will be an ongoing cause for beatification and canonization that will extend beyond our own lives. The historical and theological work for the promotion of that cause continues, and will, no doubt, for many years yet to come. Some of the biographical narrative for Father Louis Gergaud, which proved to be foundational to both the previous book and the historical inquiry for sainthood, is therefore repeated herein. Not intended to be redundant, this vital information necessarily frames the context for his story across several works.

Through the process of ongoing research, we became aware of the existence of many of the personal writings of Father Louis Gergaud, who at the time of his death from yellow fever on October 1, 1873, had served as pastor of St. Matthew's Church in Monroe, Louisiana, for eighteen years. He also served as an energetic missionary priest to many small communities throughout the Ouachita region of northeast Louisiana and established what became lively Catholic communities that exist to this day. His zeal for the Catholic faith and his selfless and tireless work among the people of the region eventually endeared him to many, evidenced in the abundance of secondary source material about him, and more importantly for our purposes here, his life is equally well-chronicled in his own words.

In the archives of St. Matthew's Church, there exists a third-person narrative of "The Catholic Church in Monroe," compiled by Father Louis Gergaud. This beautifully written chronicle spans the years 1854 through 1871, and previous historians deemed it significant enough to have certified copies of it placed on file in at least two other major archival depositories: the University of Louisiana at Monroe and the Archdiocese of New Orleans. In fact, it was in a fortuitous misspelling of Father Gergaud's name in an internet search engine that this was fully realized. Father Gergaud documented the ordinary, sometimes mundane, day-to-day life of an emerging Catholic parish and its missions in northeast Louisiana.

However, this work also provides the current reader with some keen insights into other important historical vignettes, including the plight of the enslaved population during the Civil War and the effects of the conflict on the civilian populations. Father Gergaud perhaps unintentionally offers the contemporary reader a view of the economic conditions of the region and, indeed, the broader expanding United States. Important commentary on the life of the broader Catholic Church emerges in this work as well, making it useful for historians from a variety of aspects.

In the pages that follow, that chronicle is published in its entirety and forms the foundation and center of this work. The names of the baptized and confirmed are duplicated in the sacramental registers of St. Matthew's Church, including the lists of slaves who were baptized in the years before emancipation. The significance of Father Gergaud's ministry among the enslaved is such a striking commentary on his compassion and vision that the list of baptized slaves is included in an appendix, just as he composed it in his own hand, which he preserved as a permanent sacramental and historical record.

In addition to letters that Father Gergaud wrote to Bishop Antoine Jacquemet in his home Diocese of Nantes in France, where he was ordained a priest in September 1854, there is also surviving correspondence between

Gergaud and Bishop Auguste Marie Martin of the Diocese of Natchitoches. As appropriate, those are included herein as well, since these letters often provided further illumination to details chronicled in the third-person narrative. Father Gergaud related important and often quite personal observations touching on the historicity of the age in which he lived and the unique circumstances of his own life and ministry. Because this volume is not a comprehensive verbatim record of all of his letters, those selected for inclusion here are ones that offer the best insights into his personality and his ministry, or they provide important commentary that augments his canonization cause. In some cases, Father Gergaud referenced events or people who cannot be historically identified with certainty, and editorial commentary therefore cannot illuminate.

To be sure, what one clearly sees from the historical record is that a cult of devotion to Father Gergaud began to develop immediately following his death. This is evidenced in the outpouring of public reaction, the rivalry between two cities of Shreveport and Monroe as to which would retain his earthly remains, the veneration of those remains upon their exhumation and transfer and the memory of him that infuses many communities to this day. Along with the other four Shreveport martyrs, there is a sustained public record of remembrance of him across nearly 150 years, to the time of this writing.

Beyond his chronicle and correspondence, Father Gergaud gave voice to the age in which he lived, including fascinating insights forever captured in the public record. For example, the reader encounters his profound and intense intellect in a partially preserved newspaper record of a public lecture he once gave on papal infallibility in Bastrop, Louisiana. The acuity of his mind and his communication skills are especially recognizable in his critical and clarifying response to the newspaper coverage of his lecture. In his *Last Will and Testament* (of which there are actually two versions surviving), the final surviving primary document that we have written in his own hand, Father Gergaud provides an eloquent and concise closure to a life well-lived in the service of others. Intended of course to be a perfunctory and necessary legal document, even this manages to reveal much about his generous and giving character.

What emerges from all of these primary sources combined is a complex composite of Father Louis Gergaud—a man who was driven, committed and calm, with an obvious inherent personal dignity that marks every written word on the page. At the same time, there is a discernible aspect of him that was often impatient, especially regarding pastoral matters and the expansion of his ministry in northeast Louisiana. His humanity comes forth in all of its nuances, including occasional glimpses of anxiety and loneliness. However, the message that is clearest of all to the reader is his determination to plant the Catholic faith in the corner of the vineyard to which he believed God's Providence had assigned him. That overriding theme is paralleled only by the clarity of his resolve to respond to the crisis in Shreveport in 1873. To this final task, he turned with a familiar spirit of commitment, this time knowing it would be his last mission in this life.

The concluding portion of this manuscript contains several other important primary source documents that further illustrate the life and ministry of Father Gergaud. Among these are letters from Bishop Auguste Martin of the Diocese of Natchitoches touching on the events of Shreveport in 1873 as they specifically relate to Father Gergaud, as well as the official published resolutions of the Catholics of Monroe and Shreveport as each sought to lay claim to the saintly priest's mortal remains in the immediate weeks following his death. Many newspapers remembered him and recounted his sacrifice as well, noting so with great eloquence and respect. Two original letters from his successor at St. Matthews, Father Ludovic Enaut, shed light on Gergaud's tenacity and humility and are therefore included here. Together, these sources constitute an appropriate eulogy for a priest who was much loved in life and clearly venerated after his death—and not just by his own people of Ouachita Parish but by those who remembered well his sacrifice for strangers of Shreveport. There is a consistency and continuity to this early *cultus* of devotion apparent in what was immediately recorded about the life and death of Father Louis Gergaud.

There are many people we wish to thank who made this project possible, including Bishop Francis Malone of the Diocese of Shreveport and the Chancery of the Diocese of Shreveport. Also, thanks to Bishop Robert Marshall of the Diocese of Alexandria. We wish to especially thank Bishop Jean Paul James, formerly bishop of Nantes, now archbishop of Bordeaux, for his research assistance in opening the archives and his hospitality in welcoming our delegation to Nantes in February 2019. We also extend our ongoing gratitude to Archbishop Christophe Pierre, Apostolic Nuncio to the United States, who has taken a great interest in all five priests, including Father Louis Gergaud.

We are grateful to the University of Notre Dame Archives; the Archdiocese of New Orleans; St. Matthew's Church in Monroe, especially Jeanine Patton and Father Joe Martina; the Archives of the Diocese of Alexandria,

Louisiana; the Special Collections and Archives of the University of Louisiana; and the Noel Archives and Special Collections of Louisiana State University at Shreveport. These important historical depositories have diligently maintained the record that made this compilation possible. A special note of gratitude is reserved for the Louisiana State University at Shreveport Foundation, which has generously and enthusiastically supported the financial needs of ongoing research for this project, including the funding provided by the Hubert Humphreys Endowed Professorship in History, held by author Dr. Cheryl White and generously funded by its benefactors. Many thanks to Audrey Wulf, who provided great assistance with the transcriptions and English translations of original documents.

Most of all, we thank Father Louis Gergaud for offering his own words to us, which speak more powerfully than any we, or anyone else, could possibly write on his behalf.

Duty called him to Shreveport when the epidemic was at its worst; death met him at the gates, and the Christian soldier, in the vigor of his manhood, and in the height of his usefulness, laid down his armor forever.

—Ouachita Telegraph, *tribute to Father Louis Gergaud, February 6, 1874*

1

INTRODUCTION

The Yellow Fever Epidemic of Shreveport in 1873 brought death on an epic scale and proportion, generally ranking as the third worst recorded epidemic of its type in United States history. With approximately one-quarter of the population succumbing to the illness in just twelve weeks, the city was left reeling in its wake. Due to a merciful early frost in October of that year, followed by a hard freeze in early November, the mosquito population entered dormancy, and life returned to the prosperous riverport on the banks of the Red River in northwest Louisiana. The intervening weeks of turmoil and despair witnessed a scourge that did not discriminate, with death coming in such great daily numbers that the city opened a mass grave in its cemetery to provide for the efficient disposal of the dead. The Yellow Fever Mound, entombing more than eight hundred souls together, today remains the most visible and poignant reminder of the ferocity of the 1873 outbreak.

The 1873 epidemic therefore sharply punctuates the entire chronicle of Shreveport's existence, perhaps standing out as the most transformative and significant event in its history. From its earliest history as the Red River connector to the Texas Trail, Shreveport thrived on commerce and therefore experienced all of the population variables that characterized river ports during the great age of the steamboat. Every year on record, Shreveport reported a variety of communicable illnesses among its dense population, and yellow fever was certainly no stranger. William Bennett, one of the original founders of the Shreve Town Company and one of the

"Bird's Eye View" of Shreveport, 1872, drawn by H. Brosius. *Library of Congress Prints and Photographs Division, Washington, D.C.*

earliest commercial settlers in the area, died of yellow fever in 1837. Within just a few years of its establishment and incorporation, Shreveport became well acquainted with "the saffron scourge," also more commonly known as "yellow jack." A previous outbreak in 1853 also reached epidemic levels, but its impact paled in comparison to that of twenty years later.[1]

The medical science of the late nineteenth century was only beginning to discern possible connections between the illness and its true cause—the mosquito. The required vector of the mosquito was not fully realized until the early twentieth century with the groundbreaking work of Dr. Walter Reed, but the historical record indicates that in 1873, there was at least an awareness that the illness abated with cooler temperatures. For reasons not completely understood, the yellow fever outbreak that struck Shreveport in 1873 was particularly virulent and unrelenting. Among the factors influencing this were heavier-than-normal rainfalls throughout late summer and into early fall, an abundance of commercial activity on the Red River with its resulting transient populations and the density of population clustered near the riverfront in Shreveport. Added to this was the unfortunate reality that the daily newspaper, the *Shreveport Times*, was reluctant to name the illness as yellow fever, since such a public proclamation would mean cessation of river traffic, a federal quarantine, and the resulting economic blow would be severe. Among the equally reluctant were the city's most prominent and influential commercial brokers and businessmen.

The aggressive advance of the disease was simply yet eerily documented by mere lists of names and ages on a printed page. The *Times* began publishing just the year before the great epidemic. What began in 1872 as a robust daily publication that championed and promoted the successful commercial enterprise of Shreveport was by late September 1873 reduced to little more than a mere dispassionate death record. The newspaper effectively ceased to report news of any nature other than providing lists of the dead, and by the third week of the epidemic, the daily list began to number in the dozens. Many people who had the means chose to flee the fever-stricken city, while others had no choice but to remain.

In the darkest of times, it is quite often the discipline of history alone that can capture the rare glimpse of light, documented in the actions of others who choose to act and respond. The death toll in 1873 included five Roman Catholic priests, two religious sisters and one novice of the Daughters of the Cross convent, as well as others who volunteered to care for the sick and dying at the epidemic's peak. There were many more who fled the city for safer environs, but history most nobly remembers those who chose to remain and care for others. Yet even more remarkable are those who chose *to come* to the quarantined city, knowing that death awaited them on their arrival.

Such a person was Father Louis Gergaud, pastor of St. Matthew's Church in Monroe, Louisiana, some one hundred miles to the east of Shreveport and safely remote from the epidemic's reach in 1873.

Anyone approaching Shreveport from the Red River during the weeks of August 20–November 13 that year would have confronted visual confirmation of the strength of yellow fever's grip: shuttered storefronts, burning tar pits, muddy streets and the moaning of the sick and dying. The only sound of movement in the streets would have been hearses or carriages for the removal of bodies and the less obvious, but more important, movements of the volunteers who entered the homes of strangers to offer comfort and aid.

Among those volunteers were five priests who fell in succession in just three short weeks, each passing the baton of charitable sacrifice to the next and each making a willing choice to die in the service of strangers. Those priests, recounted in the order of their deaths, were Father Isidore Quémerais (died September 15), Father Jean Pierre (died September 16), Father Jean Marie Biler (died September 26), Father Louis Gergaud (died October 1) and Father François Le Vézouët (died October 8).

Father Louis Gergaud, date of photograph unknown. *Authors' collection.*

The fourth among these martyrs to their charity, Father Louis Gergaud of Monroe, approached the horrific scene of Shreveport in response to a plea for assistance that he would not deny. He surely carried with him on that final earthly journey the history of his own homeland, where plague scenes such as these were common. Periodic epidemics were a constant feature of life in his native France, including Nantes, a beautiful city in France's picturesque Loire River valley. In 1832, the year of his birth,[2] France had a cholera outbreak with a shocking mortality rate of 25 to 50 percent. Over five thousand people died in Brittany alone. When he was sixteen years of age, another epidemic of cholera broke out, followed by yet another the three years before his ordination in Nantes in 1854.

The rural environment of his childhood probably kept such outbreaks at a distance, as he grew up in a family of common laborers in the small village of Héric, sixteen miles north of Nantes. Héric was a hamlet born of the Middle Ages, a community clustered around farming of common lands. The sloping hills would have been verdant green in Father Gergaud's memory, due to an unusually rainy climate with mild summer temperatures. Louisiana had matched the rain, at least. This was perhaps never truer than in the summer and fall of 1873.

In Héric, the village cemetery reflected the town's medieval past, and among its dead were victims of historic plagues, including bubonic plague, which ravaged all of France from the fourteenth to the sixteenth centuries. The local church dedicated to St. Nicholas had original foundations old enough to have witnessed the medieval pestilence. It was there the parents of infant Louis Gergaud presented him for baptism on the day following his birth[3] in an eighteenth-century *église* that stood on those older stones. He entered the Grand Seminary of Nantes on October 8, 1851, at the age of nineteen.[4]

Nantes had visible cobblestone and concrete evidence of the fourth-century Roman presence, and Gergaud would have certainly known the edifice of the stately Château des Ducs de Bretagne, with its thirteenth-century foundations. The manorial home of the dukes of Brittany was a constant reminder of the unique geopolitical identity of Nantes, at once

Héric, France, with St. Nicholas Church on right. *Authors' collection.*

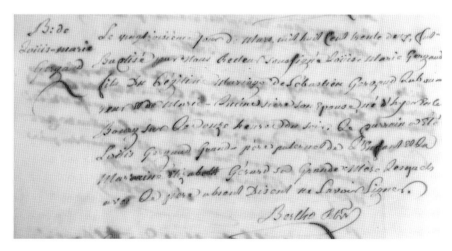

The baptismal record of Father Louis Gergaud from Héric, France. *Provided by the Archives of the Diocese of Nantes.*

The Grand Seminary at Nantes, updated nineteenth-century postcard. *Authors' collection*.

fully French yet independent by centuries of association with historic Breton culture. The Grand Seminary had a long history stretching back to the early eighteenth century, before French Revolutionary radicals shuttered the seminary doors in 1793 and executed one of its Sulpician instructors who refused to turn over the keys.[5] The seminary reopened with the Bourbon monarchy restoration, and the young Louis Gergaud, a teenager during the 1848 revolution, knew well the bloody and tragic history of the Church in France. In Nantes, the Catholic landscape was unmistakable, its Gothic cathedral with a nave higher than that of Notre Dame in Paris, and a cornerstone first laid in joint ceremony in 1434 by the Bishop of Nantes and the Duke of Brittany. Without question, Father Gergaud was steeped in this history and had assimilated its lessons into his life and ministry as a priest.

It was to this rich Catholic culture that the newly ordained Bishop Auguste Marie Martin of the Diocese of Natchitoches in Louisiana traveled in 1854 to find and recruit missionary priests who were willing to take on the adventure and challenges of a brand-new mission field. He knew well that the seminaries of Brittany were full of just such zealous young men, eager to help spread the faith in his new remote diocese. Bishop Martin went on three such trips to Brittany during his episcopate.

Bishop Martin was able to happily announce to Archbishop Anthony Blanc in New Orleans, in a letter dated July 14, 1854, that his first recruitment

Bishop Auguste Marie Martin of the Diocese of Natchitoches. *Courtesy of the Diocese of Shreveport.*

visit through France had been fruitful. Martin expressed his certainty that "beyond his hopes" he had found a sufficient number of young workers, drawing principally from St. Brieuc and Nantes.[6] Among the four he counted from the Diocese of Nantes was Louis Gergaud, soon to be ordained a priest.

It was in the chapel of the Grand Seminary in Nantes where the twenty-two-year-old Father Gergaud prostrated himself before Bishop Antoine

Ordination record of Father Louis Gergaud (and his friend Jules Janneau) on September 23, 1854, at the chapel of the Grand Seminary of Nantes. *Provided by the Archives of the Diocese of Nantes.*

Jacquemet and was ordained a priest of Jesus Christ on Saturday, September 23, 1854,[7] having said yes to Bishop Martin's request. Recorded in the register as having been ordained the same day was Father Jules Janneau, also destined for priestly ministry in Louisiana.[8] As Gergaud's family and friends kissed his anointed hands after he offered them his first priestly blessing, Father Louis Gergaud knew that in less than a month's time, on October 21, he would leave his homeland.

In the *Annals of the Propagation of the Faith* in 1855, an entry records and documents the historic departure of Gergaud and companions, two of whom (Pierre and Le Vézouët) would find their fates directly and inextricably linked to Gergaud many years later in Shreveport. Another aboard that ship from the port of Havre, Father Jules Janneau, would remain a lifelong friend to Father Gergaud:

> *On October 21, 1854, Msgr. Martin, Bishop of Natchitoches (U.S.) embarked at Havre, taking with him to new diocese the following persons: Messrs. Gergaud, Avenard, Janneau, priests of the diocese of Nantes; Chapin, deacon of St. Brieuc, Beaulieu, sub-deacon of Rennes, Levezouet, minor of St. Brieuc; Pierre, tonsured of St. Brieuc; Malassagne, a student of St. Flou; Sisters D'Avanzi of Rome; Mamo, of Malta; and a lay sister of the Sacred Heart.*[9]

Leaving behind the cultural and architectural riches of Nantes, Father Gergaud journeyed to the missionary territory of Louisiana with its small wooden churches that lacked ornamentation. He was a keen observer of such comparisons and contrasts, drawing on the memories of his homeland. Although he left behind a mild climate and magnificent cathedrals, Father Gergaud never ceased to find beauty and promise in his adopted Louisiana and reflected on that fact in a surviving letter that he wrote to Bishop Jacquemet in Nantes soon after he arrived in his new mission field. The letter is included in its entirety in this volume.

Father Jean Marie Biler, chaplain of the Daughters of the Cross convent in Fairfield and the third priest to die of yellow fever. Image from prayer card. *Authors' collection.*

When Father Gergaud set sail from his homeland, he may have wondered if he would ever return and could not know with certainty what fate awaited him in Louisiana. He was likely unaware of the open hostility and anti-Catholic sentiment he would face in his new mission field. However, he also could not yet have known how, by his constant presence, positivity and living the Gospel example, he would be able to win many hearts and grow the Catholic faith in what must have initially seemed to be rather fallow ground.

He also could not have known that on September 18, 1873, a telegram would reach his hands with a desperate and fateful plea from Father Jean Marie Biler, a friend in Shreveport. The plea came because the city was in the grips of yellow fever, and countless hundreds were suffering and dying. Two beloved priests of Shreveport's Holy Trinity Church had already given their lives in the service of others, and Father Biler knew that he might well be next. The request to Father Gergaud in Monroe was simple and to the point:

> *Louis Gergaud, I am alone here. Other priests of the city have died. Please come to my aid.*[10]

Father Gergaud did not hesitate. In fact, his response by return telegraph was immediate and just as direct:

> *Am leaving by the stagecoach this evening.*[11]

Original St. Matthew's Church, Monroe, Louisiana. *Archives of St. Matthew's Church.*

After nearly eighteen years as a priest, Father Gergaud had already demonstrated himself to be a man of just this type of deliberate and decisive action. In Monroe, he founded a parish among Catholics he described as "only in name and in Baptism." He came to an area of Louisiana heavily

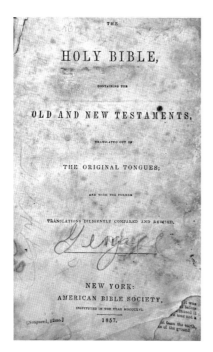

THE

HOLY BIBLE,

CONTAINING THE

OLD AND NEW TESTAMENTS,

TRANSLATED OUT OF

THE ORIGINAL TONGUES;

AND WITH THE FORMER

TRANSLATIONS DILIGENTLY COMPARED AND REVISED.

NEW YORK:

AMERICAN BIBLE SOCIETY,

INSTITUTED IN THE YEAR MDCCCXVI.

[Nonpareil, 12mo.]   1857.

Bible believed to have belonged to Father Louis Gergaud, in the library collection of St. Matthew's Church in Monroe, Louisiana. *Authors' collection.*

populated with Protestants, and his own accounts provide the evidence of the lack of charity shown to him as a Catholic priest. In his early days there, children pelted him with rocks in the streets. One anti-Catholic physician in Monroe went so far as to purchase land next to Father Gergaud's small church and then erected an office that doubled as a nightly saloon, right up to the property line, just to annoy the priest. Yet Father Gergaud reserved his anger from the young and adult anti-Catholics alike, using his considerable energy instead to turn a meager diocesan investment into a church, a school and a proper Catholic graveyard. Because of Gergaud's reputation, many expected he would be Bishop Martin's successor.[12]

Indeed, the record reflects that Father Gergaud was a capable, organized and conscientious administrator, a faithful steward of the resources entrusted to him. He was often frugal to the point of self-deprivation, and the financial record testifies to the gifts of his own money to further the work of the Catholic Church. His reputation as a man of integrity, ethics and dedication is the most obvious characterization of him that comes forth from history.

Bishop Martin knew of Father Gergaud's successful ministry and thus had appointed him *vicar forane* for "all the districts situated between the Mississippi and Red River valley."[13] Gergaud's efforts were tireless, and there apparently was no request of his time that was too small or insignificant, not when it came to pastoral care of others. By 1873, Father Gergaud had established missions at nearby Homer, Columbia, Harrisonville and Woodville, the seeds of which would later mature into full parish communities, and the ministry in Monroe had grown tenfold under his leadership. Fortunately for future historians, Father Gergaud recorded these mission activities with the same zeal and diligence he brought to documenting the larger community of Monroe.

Within a short period of time, his generosity became common knowledge to all in the area, whether they were personally acquainted or not. One especially telling vignette was recounted in a third-person narrative that herein follows and is attributed to him, *The Catholic Church in Monroe, Louisiana.* In 1871, Father Gergaud expressed a desire to return to France to visit his mother one last time, and the next week, prominent Monroe resident and former Civil War general John Frank Pargoud gave him a check for $500 to cover the cost. When a month passed and Father Gergaud had no travel plans, the general passed another check for the same amount, and this time, Father Gergaud agreed to spend the accumulated $1,000. He did not book an ocean voyage but instead purchased a square of land to begin St. Matthew's Cemetery.[14] Thus grew the reputation of the character of this priest from Nantes. Ironically, it was of course in this very cemetery that Father Louis Gergaud would have his final resting place after offering his life in Shreveport.

On that fateful September day in 1873, when the Western Union worker in Monroe also seems to have served as village crier, the news of Father Gergaud's imminent departure for Shreveport swept through the town. As he prepared to board the six o'clock stagecoach for Shreveport, the locals begged him to remain in Monroe. Robert Ray, a local judge, remanded Father Gergaud, anticipating the appearance of yellow fever at Monroe any day. He said Father Gergaud would only end up abandoning his people when they needed him most. The good priest replied to the judge, "It is my duty and I will go."[15]

Just a moment later, as he boarded the stagecoach, Father Gergaud spoke to his assistant pastor, the newly ordained Father Joseph Quelard: "Write to the Bishop. Tell him that I go to my death. It is my duty, and I must go."[16]

He then turned to the crowd and bade them all farewell. He told the coachman to drive on and looked ahead as the road drew him nearer to his final calling. As Mother Mary Hyacinth wrote from the Daughters of the Cross Convent at Fairfield just south of Shreveport: "The noble Father Gergaud answered: 'I take the stage tonight.' What courage! What heroic devotion to a confrere!"[17] This moving vignette, and its simple documentation in the historical record, succinctly summarizes the heart and mind of a priest who was not deterred from the gravity of the task before him.

Thousands of miles from the Diocese of Nantes, when Louis Gergaud boarded the stagecoach in Monroe bound for Shreveport, any memories of France would have yielded no comparison. The stage road crossed flat cotton farmlands and a network of small streams and bayous that cut through pine forests. The rolling hills and pleasant temperatures of his homeland were in stark contrast to the Louisiana wilderness and humidity. The Loire River

Left: Father Isidore Quemerais, the first priest to die of yellow fever in Shreveport. *Image provided by the Mouaze-Quemerais family, used with permission.*

Right: Father Jean Pierre, pastor of Holy Trinity Church in Shreveport, with an unidentified child, date of photograph unknown. Father Pierre was the second priest to die of yellow fever in Shreveport. Image from prayer card. *Authors' collection.*

certainly had no rival in the Red River, aptly named for the muddy red-brown clay of north Louisiana.

It was this muddy river that formed the eastern boundary of death-stricken Shreveport. When he arrived at the riverbank, what Father Gergaud saw was a town not unlike a medieval village in the grip of the Black Death, with the only major difference of a calendar year centuries apart. What must Father Gergaud have considered over the course of such a long journey across north Louisiana? With his own death a certainty to which he had already resigned himself, he surely spent some time reflecting on his many years of ministry, which he had regularly recounted in letters and papers. In the time between his priestly ordination in Nantes in September 1854, his subsequent departure for Louisiana in October 1854 with Bishop Martin and the very day he arrived on the banks of the Red River in Shreveport in late September 1873, there was indeed much fruitful work for him to reflect on, if he had only had but a moment to pause before he entered the quarantined city. Instead, he went straight to the duty for which he came, as the offering of his life was but days away.

2

SERVANT OF GOD
FATHER LOUIS GERGAUD

In His Own Words

SELECTED LETTERS

The following section includes selected translated letters of Father Louis Gergaud[18] in a chronological format beginning in early 1855, shortly after his arrival in Louisiana. Some editorial commentary has been provided as a header to certain letters, as appropriate and necessary. In some cases, historical references from Father Gergaud could not be clarified or verified, and these are either redacted or otherwise noted in the editors' text.

The first surviving letter is one that Father Gergaud wrote to Bishop Antoine Jacquemet of the Diocese of Nantes, with the original preserved in the diocesan archives. It was Bishop Jacquemet who ordained Louis Gergaud to the priesthood in the chapel of the Grand Seminary of Nantes, knowing that Gergaud was answering a missionary call to Louisiana—an arrangement secured with Bishop Martin of the Diocese of Natchitoches some three months before. Because he wrote this letter soon after his arrival in Louisiana, Father Gergaud gave many details about the state of the new Diocese of Natchitoches; the conditions of the churches, schools and missions; and, most remarkably, observations that underscored his concern for the enslaved population. The latter concern proved to be an ongoing focus of Father Gergaud's ministry, evidenced in the two hundred–plus slave baptisms he recorded during his years as pastor of St. Matthew's in Monroe.

Bishop Antoine Jacquemet of the Diocese of Nantes, who ordained Louis Gergaud to the priesthood on September 23, 1854.

Portrait of St. Peter Claver (Blessed at the time of Father Louis Gergaud's ministry). Painting in Cartagena, Colombia. *Public domain*.

The reference Father Gergaud made to "Father Claver" is more than just a bit remarkable to the time and place (pre–Civil War rural northeastern Louisiana). St. Peter Claver, beatified in 1850, canonized in 1888 (in a ceremony alongside fellow Jesuits St. Alphonsus Rodriguez and St. John Berchmans), was a Catalan priest from Verdú, Spain, who died in 1654

The third entry in the "Baptism of Slaves" registry maintained in Father Gergaud's own hand, beginning in 1857 until slavery ended in 1865. The entry poignantly documents a baptism in the Morehouse Parish jail, one day before the slave, Joseph, was hanged for the crime of "assault and mutilation of a white man whose finger he had bitten off." Father Gergaud probably regularly visited the jails of the area, to provide the sacraments to those imprisoned or, as in this case, already condemned.

in Colombia, South America, as a missionary to the New World. He was already known as the "slave to the slaves." The fact that Gergaud referenced him in this 1855 letter indicates a model of missionary priesthood with which he was obviously familiar and that he emulated among those otherwise so hopelessly and shamelessly "abandoned"—abandoned from decent human relations, prevented from forming lasting family units and abandoned from the Holy Sacraments. Ultimately, Father Gergaud would choose to minister to the enslaved, in a move that cost him social status and caused personal hardship. No doubt he saw these sufferings as insignificant when compared to those of the "abandoned" people of the cotton fields. The appendix to this book, containing the registry of slave baptisms, is itself a testament to the inspiration Father Gergaud took from then "Blessed" Father Claver and countless other examples within the Catholic faith, living the Gospel imperative of "making disciples of *all* men."

This also accents a noteworthy point of Old World–New World cultural history, which undoubtedly influenced the mind of Father Gergaud on this issue. The city of Nantes was a major center for the French slave trade during the eighteenth and early nineteenth centuries, with African slaves passing through there to begin forced transatlantic migrations to slave ports in the Caribbean and Louisiana. France first moved to abolish slavery in 1794 in the aftermath of the French Revolution, but Napoleon Bonaparte reinstituted it in 1802. Subsequent reform movements in France brought a final end to slavery in 1848, when Louis Gergaud was but sixteen years old, so he likely had good memory of this significant historical development. However, he

Above: Eighteenth-century view of Nantes port from l'ile Goriette, attributed to Nicolas Ozanne. Nantes was an important center during the era of French operations in the New World slave trade. *Public domain.*

Right: Pope Pius IX, photograph by Adolph Braun, 1875. *Public domain.*

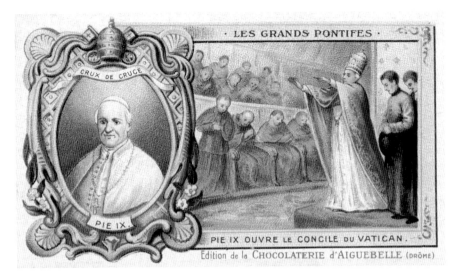

Pope Pius IX at the (First) Vatican Council. Chromolithograph, circa 1870. It reads, "The great pontiffs," (above), and "Pius IX opens the Vatican Council" (below). *Public domain.*

encountered a very different culture in Louisiana, and his personal position on the enslavement of peoples and their inherent human dignity cannot be understated. Again, this is illustrated well in the accompanying appendix to this book, which evidences his commitment to the enslaved populations of the region where he ministered.

Further important historical context can be found in Father Gergaud's reference and invocation of the Marian teaching of the Immaculate Conception, only recently dogmatized at the time of his writing this letter, so decreed by Pope Pius IX in his 1854 bull, *Ineffabilis.* Father Gergaud observed, with his characteristic fervor for the Catholic faith, that with her as patroness of the United States, the Catholic faith "may only advance." His reference to Protestant dislike of Catholics also serves as a reminder of the socioreligious divisions of the mid-nineteenth-century Deep South.

Interestingly, Gergaud opened this letter with a profound apology to Bishop Jacquemet for his delay in writing, but with a late October departure from the Port of Havre in France, and a subsequent ocean crossing, this letter of mid-April 1855 would have been written just a few months, perhaps mere weeks, after he settled in northeast Louisiana. As the reader will see in letters to come, Father Gergaud was otherwise conscientious of the timely correspondence etiquette of the period.

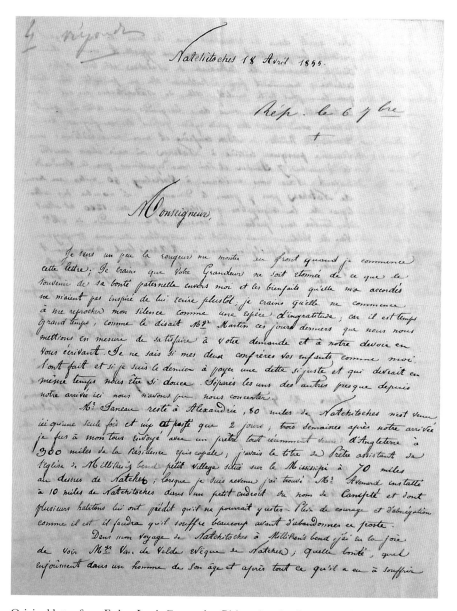

Original letter from Father Louis Gergaud to Bishop Antoine Jacquemet in France. *Provided by the Archives of the Diocese of Nantes.*

18 April 1855
Letter to Bishop Antoine Jacquemet, Diocese of Nantes

Monseigneur,

I feel redness from shame rising up my forehead as I begin to write this letter; I am afraid that Your Excellency may be surprised that the memory of his paternal kindness towards me and the good he gave me did not inspire me to write to him earlier. I am afraid that he may think of my silence as a sort of ingratitude, because it is time, as Msgr. Martin said recently, to please your request and our duty to write to you. I do not know if my two brothers, who are your children just like me, have done it, or if I am the last one to pay the fair debt....We have been separated here since our arrival and we have not been able to see each other.

Mr. Janneau who stayed in Alexandria, which is 80 miles away from Natchitoches, only came here once and stayed for 2 days; 3 weeks after our arrival, it was my turn to be sent with a priest who had recently arrived from England, 300 miles away from the episcopal residence; I had the title of Assistant Priest of the church in Milliken's Bend, a small village located on the Mississippi River, 70 miles north of Natchez. When I came back, I found Mr. Avenard settled 10 miles from Natchitoches in a little place by the name of Campte [Campti], where several inhabitants told him that he would not be able to stay. He is full of courage and self-denial and he will have to suffer much before he decides to give up his position.

In my travel from Natchitoches to Milliken's Bend, I had the pleasure to meet Msgr. Van de Velde, the Bishop of Natchez. There is so much kindness, so much passion in this man for his age, and after all the sufferings he went through, his taste for leisure that his pastoral load enabled him to take, reminds me of those of the beloved disciple. The Cathedral of Natchez is far from completion, the outer structure is completed but the inside sadly lacks signs of ostentation; the one in Natchitoches is the opposite, well maintained and during its grand church days it could compete with one of the small churches we have in countryside in the Diocese of Nantes.

My brother and I stayed for a week in Natchez, we arrived on Sunday, January 7, and left the following Friday. We stopped in Vicksburg, 50 miles north of Natchez to spend the Sunday. The number of Catholics reaches about 1,200 people, and there was going to be no priest, but at the advice and the request of Msgr. Van de Velde, but also at the instigation of my brother who was afraid of some difficulty in Milliken's Bend, I committed myself to staying there until Msgr. Martin asked me to return to him. While there, I performed many baptisms, blessed a few marriages, heard some confessions, and experienced some of the manners that our Protestant brothers use to address a Catholic priest, who must simply walk without taking into account the insults he is the object of and be happy in his heart to be a little despised for the love of Jesus Christ.

When I left Vicksburg, I missed by two hours meeting Mr. Guillou, which seeing him would have given me great joy, who Msgr. Van de Velde sent to replace me, and who had left on the same Sunday from Natchez, hoping to see me and talk about Nantes and those whom he cherishes and loves, but he came two hours after I left. If he was disappointed, so indeed was I.

There are seven churches in the Diocese of Natchitoches, among which are six led by their rector who usually lives there. The seventh one, lost in the swamps and away from any ecclesiastical residence, has had no priest for a long time. I saw all of these churches, except for two, and I have been able to work in some ministry. If we only needed to travel to earn the title of Apostolic Missionary, as one of the oldest priests of our mission used to joke, I would certainly be one of them.

There is only one house for education, the boarding school of the Daughters of the Sacred Heart in Natchitoches, and it is too small for the needs of the area. Monseigneur, who just began the visit of his churches is having to make decisions about creating other schools. The Daughters of Providence, which refused a building in one of the towns in South Louisiana, accepted one in Alexandria on the Red River, after Monseigneur Martin requested one, and under the order of their Superior, next year maybe the work will begin. The education of the boys is done outside because there is no college or school here.

The slaves are almost abandoned, and we cannot reach them now, either because of the distrust of their masters, or because of the corruption that is pervasive here which makes it impossible for us to get into their camps without losing our honor or reputation. This is what a rector from a church located 30 miles away told me. Negro missionary Mr. Avenard runs the risk of not having the opportunity to imitate the admirable devotion of Father Claver to these people. Most of these poor people are baptized, but for most of them, it is the only symbol they have of a Christian.

Monseigneur, the only difficulties that our ministry here encounters are indifference, the love for pleasures and luxury, and the lack of education, and all of this is enough to practice our zeal. In the north, the Catholic religion must face attacks that remind me of the diatribes from Luther against the papacy. Here is what an Evangelical Minister from Boston wrote to me last winter:

"We neither would like to exaggerate the harm or the strength or Romanism/Roman Catholicism, nor would we want to use one word of doubt.... We believe however that a system that prevails at the heart of our Republic, a system which is hostile to our churches, to our public schools, to our free institutions that have a total number of 3,000,000 members, and that is supported by 1,600 priests, 22 bishops, 7 archbishops, more than 100 schools and seminaries, and 1,700 churches, is a system that we should not let go with a disdainful smile or deal with a cold indifference. We do not declare the war to be against men, but against the principles that are subversive to our liberties, to our religion. We declared the war, and God helped, and we will continue waging it against a system that is, in the holy letters, called sin, the son of iniquity, the mother of prostitutes, an abomination. We want to break this system so that the victims can be delivered of its grip, and sheltered from its pernicious influences."

These diatribes only represent a fearful cry, an effort from Hell, that wants to stop the spread of Good, and wants to prevail over the decision of the dogma of Mary's Immaculate Conception, Patroness of the United States, and our religion can only advance. A few years ago, in Vicksburg, where I just spent seven days, the Catholics were seen as monsters and were represented as such. Today, people must begin to believe that we can be as honorable as anyone else and that our religion is not as detestable as they used to think.

Now, Monseigneur, my heart is satisfied, my duty is completed. I just need to ask on my knees for your blessing because your authority represents protection against all the dangers and all the difficulties that my ministry here faces.

It is in the greatest submission and the deepest respect that I have the honor, Monseigneur, of your Excellency.

Your very humble and respectful son,
L. Gergaud
Priest of Natchitoches

Father Gergaud's surviving correspondence with Bishop Auguste Martin of the Diocese of Natchitoches, with originals held in the archives of the Diocese of Alexandria, Louisiana, spans the years of 1862 to 1867. The first of the letters references two significant developments for the ministry of Father Gergaud in northeastern Louisiana: the assistance of Father Joseph Gentille (whom Gergaud references with a frequency indicative of his ongoing reliance on Gentille) and the arrival of the Daughters of the Cross to establish a Catholic school in Monroe. Interestingly, Father Gentille was destined to replace Father Jean Pierre as pastor of Holy Trinity Church in Shreveport in late 1873, following the yellow fever epidemic.

Archbishop Antoine Blanc of the Archdiocese of New Orleans (1835–1860). *Public domain.*

Although at times Gergaud's characterization of Bishop Martin is one of occasional neglect, there is no question that Martin highly valued and respected the work of Gergaud in the region of the Ouachita. Among Bishop Martin's correspondence can be found several references to just such admiration. In 1856, early in Gergaud's ministry, Bishop Martin observed that even in the absence of more priests for the young diocese, he would not remove Gergaud from Monroe, because "he will do well." Martin even referred to Father Gergaud in an 1860 letter to Archbishop Anthony Blanc in New Orleans as "the best qualified to care for the interests of the diocese."[19] It is perhaps Martin's complete trust of Father Gergaud that explained some of the lapse in correspondence.

In late 1872, less than a year before the yellow fever epidemic in Shreveport was to claim the lives of five of his priests, Bishop Martin wrote to the Propagation of the Faith in Paris, extolling all of the men who had answered his call to come to Louisiana, but in words that were especially applicable to Father Gergaud, Bishop Martin observed that they had fought to overcome "the hatred of slaves and the poor classes, against the prejudice of Protestants which are three-quarters of the total population....I would have failed as a bishop imposing on these apathetic peoples without the conquering priests who have served under my hands."[20]

Father Gergaud's ministry (and even plain sympathies) for the enslaved consequently put him at odds with the Confederate government in particular, and prevailing social dictums in general, during the ensuing and destructive war years.

5 June 1862
Letter to Bishop Auguste Martin, Diocese of Natchitoches

Monseigneur,

Mr. Gentille [Father Joseph Gentille] *has finally arrived in Monroe. I thank God who has sent him back to me. I count on him a lot to do good in this part of our diocese. I deeply regret that he did not practice more English during his absence, but he had every opportunity. However, I look upon his temporary absence as a source of blessing on my parish. He certainly contributed much after your instructions and decision that the Daughters of the Cross to come to Monroe. Their arrival was, in my opinion, most timely. They could not come later without suffering for their work, the providential moment of which had arrived, it seems to me. It is my ardent hope that they will be established here and provide their blessed influence on a great number of children. We put our trust in Divine Providence that empowers them.…*

I am, Monseigneur, the very humble servant of your Excellency.
L. Gergaud

As 1863 began, the Civil War was entering a crucial phase, with Union initiatives in the western theater of the war aimed at control of the ports on the Mississippi River. The proximity of Father Gergaud's geographic mission area in northeast Louisiana meant he was witness to some of the accompanying and related troop movements of both armies and was able to offer eyewitness accounts. In this letter, he singled out the destruction of the town of Milliken's Bend, where he had long had a mission established. His military observations were secondary to what he viewed as more pressing matters of eternal consequence. Significantly, Father Gergaud noted the numbers of baptisms that took place in battlefield hospitals of soldiers on their deathbeds. In addition to his ministry among the enslaved, the care of the war's wounded and dying was also a pressing urgency for Father Gergaud, as he responded to human need in whatever circumstances prevailed.

13 January 1863
Letter to Bishop Auguste Martin, Diocese of Natchitoches

Monseigneur,

For the beginning of the year, I wish you the best. May this year bring us the return of the peace that you undoubtedly want so much and more than anyone. For us, Christmas time has been a time of anxiety for us. Every day, we expected the enemy, who, after disembarking considerable forces above Milliken's Bend, marched with 7000 soldiers on the railroad. But we got off with no more than waiting. However, the enemy only withdrew after having burnt several bridges and made some damage. The village of Milliken's Bend was reduced to ashes. I did not hear anything about Mr. Chapin, except that he was then residing in Richmond at Mrs. Hines' house. Perhaps, since then, he has gone to Providence. When he came to Monroe, he asked me to lend him $250 to pay for a piece of land he had bought for the Providence church. But there is no other obligation from me except an acknowledgment through a receipt that the sum was given to him as coming from you. Since then, for my first term note for the property I bought in June last year for our little church, I had to pay $887.40; to provide this money I had to borrow something. Everything else is fine and I can now relax until June 1864, when my second note is due. I am attaching to this letter the Baptism registers for the year 1862. You will undoubtedly notice that half of the persons who have received this sacrament are soldiers who have since died at the hospital and that our Sisters of Charity had prepared. The Sisters join their wishes to mine, and ask that you accept our humble respect.

I am your most humble and obedient Servant,
Louis Gergaud

Father Gergaud suffered from dysentery, as he reported in the following letter to Bishop Martin. *Dysentery* refers to a common form of gastroenteritis, viral or bacterial, usually known by this name in the nineteenth century. The hygienic conditions of most populated areas during this era gave frequent rise to such illnesses and might be further explained by Gergaud's accompanying commentary on the rainy weather. Medical historians often cite the inadequate water drainage and poor sanitation of the time as contributing to ill health, a factor that would certainly again be in play in 1873 in Shreveport's confrontation with yellow fever.

25 February 1863
Letter to Bishop Auguste Martin, Diocese of Natchitoches

Monseigneur,

When I received your latest letter, I was in bed, as I was bedridden for about eight days because of dysentery. It has really been raining lately; but floodings, which last year at the same time seemed so favorable to the Yankees, do not seem to help them much. There is a lot of talk about peace, I believe the most favorable symptom is the desertion of soldiers both in the Federal armies and in the Confederate army. When the people causing war leave, the war has to end. Unless we force the soldiers, with the bayonet, it seems that they will not go, and this revulsion is found on both sides. Who will make peace? Can we get along? Will one side agree to give something and will the other side not ask for more than they should? I believe a mediation, done in good faith, would be the best chance of peace and of understanding that we have. But who will want it? As I haven't heard from Mr. Chapin since he got back to Natchitoches, I do not know where he resides. However, I believe that he is staying in Richmond at Mrs. Hines' house. That is where I sent guidelines for Lent. I know that the letters for Richmond are taken to Delhi by a special courier sent by a private company. In Providence, there may still be floodings in the whole region between the Mississippi and the Bayou Macon making any communication very uncertain. The Yankees are said to cut a canal of the Mississippi in the Providence Lake and the Lake in the Bayou Macon or Tensas with the intention of turning "Vicksburg by all means." God only knows what floodings these river-to-river communications along with almost continual rains will do to us this year. I will leave the $250 matter take its chance. A mortgage would not be very useful. General B. was just relieved of his military command of the post, and he remains "Superintendent of Conscript."...What politics, jealousy, stupidity and hatred can do to knock down a man was used against him. Fortunately, a man's popularity is not always based on his merit. Our Sisters of Charity offer their most humble respects. Best wishes to all my colleagues.

I am, Excellency, your most humble Servant,
Louis Gergaud

In the following letter of July 24, 1863, Father Gergaud offers some insightful commentary on the military and civilian situation in Monroe following the surrender of Vicksburg to Federal forces on July 4 after a siege of nearly two months. Gergaud observed that war often does not delineate clear moral good or rightness of conduct, as he blames both sides equally for the social instability among civilian populations. The "news from Virginia" that Gergaud referenced herein cannot be known with certainty; however, major news sources began reporting in mid-July with the optimism that conflict was shifting out of Virginia into "solely the enemy's territory" and indeed that the conflict would soon be over.[21] Interestingly, Gergaud made no reference to the July 1–3, 1863 Battle of Gettysburg—an equally significant turning point—though surely it would have been known by the dating of this letter. Perhaps this is an indication the shepherd's interest in the conflict was largely confined to the welfare of his local sheep (Black and white, enslaved and free, military and civilian). Clearly, he was not impressed with the Confederate government's ability to defend its citizens at this point in the conflict. Salvation from senseless violence and the ruin of towns, he mused, might be found in surrender without a shot fired. Regardless, Father Gergaud would remain at his post.

24 July 1863
Letter to Bishop Auguste Martin, Diocese of Natchitoches

Monseigneur,

Since Vicksburg was taken, we have been waiting here for the Federals. I do not believe, however, that they will come to Monroe before winter. [Confederate] *General Walker's troops are headed up the Red River….I believe the town of Monroe is doomed to burn, the preparations which our military authorities are making here, too insignificant to ensure its defense, will almost infallibly bring about its ruin. A pontoon* [bridge] *has been built but to get there it is necessary to cross the city. This pontoon must be defended by fortifications on the river….Our church is located almost at this point and will be one of the buildings most exposed to both parties. Unless it is razed in advance to give the brave defenders of the pontoon a larger battlefield. There is only one chance that could happen to us and that is that the arrival of the Federals before our authorities have time to build their fortifications. It is sad to have to wish for the arrival of* [Federals?] *to find protection. And yet, here is where the population of Monroe is now reduced to. We see it on all sides. Can the Yankees be more plundering and more desolating than our own Confederate soldiers?*

Two transports arrived on the river 15 miles from here all under the Confederate flag; they have on board nearly 300 wounded soldiers, many of them are Creoles from Red River and in particular from the parish of Natchitoches. They will be here today or at least in a few days; the transports could not yet come here because of the low waters. Our hospitals are full of sick people....The Daughters of St. Vincent de Paul are still here and beg us to accept their [help].

The news from Virginia is excellent if we are to believe it. What to believe…?

I stay here, at any event!
And I am Monseigneur, your very humble and obedient servant.
L. Gergaud

***

1 September 1863
Letter to Bishop Auguste Martin, Diocese of Natchitoches

Monseigneur,

Hoping that this letter will reach you, I offer some details on the excursion of the Yankees in Monroe. From the beginning of last week, we heard rumors that the enemy was charging. On the Bayou Macon and Rivière au Boeuf, we had a cavalry of about 1,000 men under Colonel Parsons' orders. On Thursday 27, troops were 4 miles East of Monroe intending to go up against the enemy when the mayor and some other citizens with the permission of our General P.O. Hébert crossed our lines with a diplomatic flag to communicate with the enemy. During that time, Hébert made his troops cross the Ouachita and destroy the bridge at around midnight. The next day at 10 a.m. sharp, an enemy cavalry battalion entered the town and started to take the horses. Citizens went in the stables to tell the owners to let them do what they wanted. This pillaging lasted until about eleven when an infantry regiment was established as guard of post; then the citizens who had their horses stolen were able to get them back with an order from the commanding General. However, several of them did not have the time or the presence of mind to make their claims and they lost their property.

That day and the following night, order was maintained quite well in the town but in the surrounding areas, robberies took place, worthy of the Huns and the Vandals. Private houses were visited during the night, the owners were threatened with guns, their gold and their money, their watches and their jewelry were taken, they were insulted with the worst insults in their own homes. God's eye saw all the abominations that were committed in the negros camp.…All of these affronts were committed by the cavalry, which is said to have been made up of Jayhawkers, the 4th Illinois Cavalry. The next day at 7 a.m., the Federals had left the town to go to Vicksburg, in a forced march. When will they come back? The Confederate post of Monroe was transferred to Vienna, 35 miles west. The town seems deserted and dismayed. The Confederate pickets pass through and keep pushing back to the Ouachita which is fordable. Respectfully, I am, Monseigneur, your most humble servant,
Louis Gergaud

Absent further context, Father Gergaud's reference to the hospital chaplaincy in the following letters from the fall of 1863 is obscure, its meaning lacking clarity nearly 150 years removed. Yet the question is at least partially resolved within the third person chronicle also included herein: *The Catholic Church in Monroe.* That chronicle clarified that the hospital in question was no longer necessary at this point in time due to troop positions. In keeping with his ongoing emphasis of the spiritual realities with less on the immediate military ones, Father Gergaud also noted many deathbed conversions to Catholicism that were made possible because of the hospital's proximity to him. Interestingly, there is a typed transcription on St. Matthew's Church stationery of a letter purported to date February 25, 1865, from Father Gergaud (the whereabouts of the original are unknown and therefore cannot be fully verified) that makes reference to Father Joseph Gentille as having assumed the role of chaplain of the Confederate hospital.

14 September 1863
Letter to Bishop Auguste Martin, Diocese of Natchitoches

Monseigneur,

This morning, I found a letter from the Dr J.C. Cummings, general physician of the subdistrict of Northern Louisiana, containing a proposal that I think I should submit to you. [Dr. Cummings] *had to transfer the hospital he had here at the time of the excursion done by the Yankees two weeks ago. He re-established it in Mount Lebanon. The Sisters of Charity were not able to leave Monroe for two reasons: the first because they were not allowed to do so by their Superior in Natchez, the second because in Mount Lebanon there is no Catholic priest. This is the offer from Dr. Cummings, he assures me that he can appoint me chaplain of his hospital if I want to accept. He probably thinks that it would be a way to make the Sisters of Charity come; and indeed, I believe that if this condition is met, he may obtain the approval of their Superior. Here is the proposal I wanted to submit to you, my lord. Now, it would be appropriate to tell you the conditions in which I could accept your approval.*

I absolutely need to be replaced in Monroe, where the mission has become too extensive to abandon it without any priest. My lord, you may remember that last year I bought land (and an office) adjacent to the church for the sum of $2,550.00. This land is in my name and I finished paying it last month, so my replacement will have no problems related to that.

I will need to go to Natchez to make sure the Superior allows it; our sisters here make me hope that there will be no problems since the Superior came here on a trip in July and promised Dr Cummings that if he changed his hospital, she would send sisters to him.

My replacement will have to agree to use my furniture and my personal effects and to take care of them. He can, as I did, take someone as a lodger, or if he prefers, he can take care of the home himself. I know that it will cost me to leave my congregation for some time, but if it may be useful for the good of the souls and of the country, I will accept to do it.

I wait for your decision, and I am, your most humble Servant,

Louis Gergaud

***

17 October 1863
Letter to Bishop Auguste Martin, Diocese of Natchitoches

I received at the same time both the visit of Mr. Avenard and your letter of October 2…. The health condition in which you find yourself and the news brought to me on this subject by Mr. Avenard, invites me to offer you my sympathy. I hope and pray to God that your infirmities are only temporary, and that your health will soon recover.

The issue of the hospital and my role as Chaplain has taken a turn that I think will save us all from embarrassment. The Daughters of Charity have returned to Natchez, and I think it more than probable that they will not return to the Trans-Mississippi....I have learned in the last few days that [Confederate] *General Hebert was thinking of returning to take up his headquarters in Monroe. Since the battle at Chickamauga, Yankee operations in Louisiana, Arkansas, and Texas appear to be suspended, and all reinforcements are being sent to Tennessee. If the hospital is re-established at Monroe and the Sisters return, things will remain as they were before the evacuation.*

I doubt that the few troops contained in the sub-district of north Louisiana, being scattered as it is, will provide the general hospital with large numbers of sick people. We have here only two cavalry regiments and they are very incomplete. They have a hospital a few miles from here with about ten patients.

The numerous and distant missions that I have do require the presence of another priest, and the difficulty of keeping house prevents me from asking for an assistant. Besides, it would be difficult for you to send one, since it is already so difficult to find a replacement for me if I were to accept the post of Chaplain for the sub-district of Louisiana.

And I am the most obedient servant of Your Excellency,
Louis Gergaud

At the resuming point in Father Gergaud's collection of letters, the war has now ended. President Lincoln has been assassinated and Reconstruction begun. Despite these monumental events, Father Gergaud's references are characteristically local. In his famous 1890 poem, "Tommy," Rudyard Kipling writes of the soldier's peculiar way of living: "An' if sometimes our conduck isn't all your fancy paints, Why, single men in barricks don't grow into plaster saints." From his observations at his humble church near the riverbank barracks of the Reconstruction soldiers in Monroe, it seems Father Gergaud would agree. Having himself baptized many of the recently enslaved, he now watched in trepidation as some of the newly freed citizens stumbled a bit on their earliest path to true equality.

Father Gergaud also referenced the happy occasion of a visit with a family member dear to him from his own flock that yields an easy chance at writing his own bishop. Father Gergaud would cross paths with James Muse Dabbs again many times, most notably in the last days of his life behind the quarantine line in Shreveport in 1873.

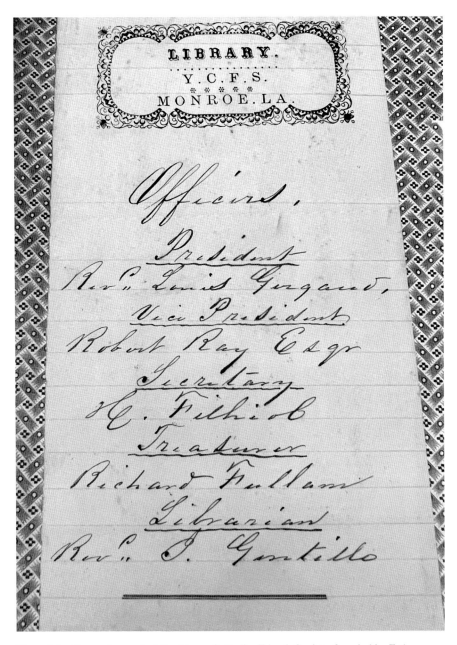

The original journal record of the Young Catholics Friends Society, founded by Father Louis Gergaud. *Authors' collection.*

Father Gergaud referred to "The Young Catholic Friends Society" in his correspondence, an organization he began in Monroe in July 1865 and served as its first president. The complete recorded minutes of this society have survived in their original written form and provide yet another rich testimony to Father Gergaud's dedication to growing and nurturing the seeds of the Catholic faith in the region. The stated objective, recorded in the first meeting of the society on July 9, 1865, was to devote themselves to "the education of Catholic and other indigent children in the Parish of Ouachita, the establishment of a Catholic library in the town of Monroe, the title of which shall be vested in this society, and promote religious and intellectual culture."[22] At the organization's first annual meeting on July 1, 1866, Father Louis Gergaud was recorded as having made a comprehensive report to those gathered, including the notation that he had paid for the printing of a report to be forwarded to Bishop Martin in Natchitoches, along with one hundred copies for "distribution to each of the clergymen of the Diocese." Clearly, he saw this intellectual and cultural vision as significant enough to share as a model for others.

7 August 1865
Letter to Bishop Auguste Martin, Diocese of Natchitoches

I am taking advantage of a trip by Mr. Dabbs to Natchitoches to write to you. It has been more than six months since I last heard from you. I have written to you several times in this interval. Mr. Gentille and I are enjoying good health today.

Catholic affairs are going on quite well and we have two societies opening, one of the Ladies, "The Altar Society," the other of gentlemen, "The Young Catholic Friends Society." We have begun a Catholic library and our school is going to start again. The sessions in the academy begin the first days of September. We have four schoolmistresses, not counting the music schoolmistress who has her own branch and is separate from the teaching staff. Mr. Gentille will continue to give French lessons. I believe that we have a good chance of succeeding. If I had a religious order in a house that he owned, I would be sure to have a permanent Catholic school in Monroe....

We have here some companies of negro soldiers. Their presence has brought about an almost complete erosion of the morals of the black population, which now follows them entirely into laziness and debauchery. Nothing seems to be organized by the civil government. We have only [little communication] between here and Shreveport.

The shipments of cotton have been very numerous the last few days, but the river is so low now that we can hardly expect any navigation until winter. Mr. Gentille joins me, Monseigneur, in offering you our humble respect.

I am the very humble servant of Your Excellency,
Louis Gergaud

The following letter references Bishop Martin's second trip to France to recruit more seminarians and priests for the Diocese of Natchitoches. Poignantly, Father Gergaud also expressed his disappointment at the removal of Father Gentille again and offered some insight into his feelings of isolation in his ministry at times. His loneliness expressed but then set aside, Father Gergaud was concerned about the practical and logistical ability to provide the Holy Sacraments to so many of his scattered sheep in a timely, realistic manner. He did not hesitate to use some honest examples to illustrate his point to his bishop.

3 September 1865
Letter to Bishop Auguste Martin, Diocese of Natchitoches

The reading of your letter announcing the need to take Mr. Gentille away from me shows me that I have only to bow my head and say "non mea voluntas sed tua fiat!" I will not say anything about the monetary harm that the absence of Mr. Gentille brings to my small enterprise; you have foreseen it and you are obliged to allow it. However, there is another consideration which you have not expressed; it is the isolation of all my colleagues, where the departure of Mr. Gentille will leave me. Your parishes in Red River are so close together that their respective parish priests, although each one alone in his parish, do not consider themselves and cannot consider themselves isolated from their colleagues, as a few hours of travel are enough to bring them together. As for me, the case is quite different. I have to sacrifice the ordinary wishes to see a colleague for the extraordinary needs. . . . The odds are ninety-nine to one that I will not be able to see them.

I assure you, Monseigneur, that this is the consideration which strikes me the most and which makes me regret even more the departure of my friend. Mr. Gentille had come here under the impression that he would have difficulty living with me. I hope that after his departure he will have nothing bitter in the memories he brings from his residing in Monroe. I will remain here alone, Monseigneur, as it is the order of Providence, for the six months that Mr. Gentille is away.

I do not know, Monseigneur, if it will be possible for me to go to your invitation for September 25, and between now and then, illnesses and an absence of ten days that I would have to be away, many things can happen. If I am not allowed, Monseigneur, to wish you a happy journey in person, allow me to express my wishes to you in this letter and to wish you an abundance of good health and all the best that you have at heart as goals and objectives of your undertaking.

And I am, Monseigneur, the very humble servant of Your Excellency,
Louis Gergaud

Postscript: May I assume, Monseigneur, that you will grant me the permission indicated…to receive and retain the securities until now, or that I could be entrusted with in the future and to go and make the loans that my situation here may require?

In the next letter, Gergaud referenced Father François Le Vézouët, a priest of Natchitoches and the fifth and final one to offer his life in Shreveport during the 1873 epidemic. This aligns with the third-person narrative account that also references visits from Le Vézouët to Monroe. Meanwhile, Father Gergaud continued to face harassment and discrimination from the Protestant majority of the region.

7 March 1866 [INCOMPLETE]
Letter to Bishop Auguste Martin, Diocese of Natchitoches

I am taking advantage of the departure of Mr. Le Vezouet, who must return to Marksville, to write to you. The needs of the Catholic population of Monroe have compelled me to do my best to establish a permanent school here. The Daughters of the Cross have accepted the proposals I have made to them, certainly counting on the approval of Your Excellency. I gave them the use of my house, kitchen, and essential furniture. I had to occupy the office which is next to the church. I propose either to take board in the city or to have my meals, prepared in the Sisters' kitchen, served to me in the office. I will perhaps have some inconveniences to undergo, but it was necessary to act. The Protestants were agitated, and the use of the Academy was being taken away from me. The time was right for the establishment. I am

Father François Le Vézouët, image from prayer card. *Authors' collection.*

happy to have finally been able to realize one of my main wishes, that of establishing a good school for girls. Offering you my congratulations on the success of your journey.

I am, with respect, your most humble and obedient priest,
Louis Gergaud

***

12 March 1866
Letter to Bishop Auguste Martin, Diocese of Natchitoches

I am hoping that this letter will reach you on your arrival in New Orleans. I hasten to announce that I have placed my girls' school under the management of the Daughters of the Cross, and that of the boys under that of Miss Springers, in the Sacristy. The Sisters have 41 pupils. They still have only one boarder. The boys' school has about 20 children. I hope, Monseigneur, that your trip was a happy one; my brother the Abbot wrote me that you were pleased with it. I offer you, Monseigneur, my sincere congratulations.

We are all waiting here, my congregation, the Sisters and I, for the next return of Mr. Gentille, whose services are becoming more and more indispensable to us here. I have given my house to the Sisters. I am living in the office. I hope that Mr. Gentille and I will be able to live with this for the time being.

I am, Monseigneur, the very humble servant of Your Excellency,
Louis Gergaud

In the following letter, Father Gergaud noted the recent death of his "brother," apparently a seminarian at the time. It is unknown if this is a true sibling or someone of close acquaintance, since Father Gergaud frequently uses the term to describe fellow priests and missionaries. Interestingly, he wrote of death as having spared his brother from the "prolonged exile" and "dangers" that Father Gergaud knew in his own ministry.

7 April 1866
Letter to Bishop Auguste Martin, Diocese of Natchitoches

I have filled in the numbers requested in the circular you sent me, and am sending it back to Your Excellency. I returned this morning from a trip I made to Avoyelles to bring back the Sisters we had in Monroe.

Our plans to provide the Sisters with a large house are not yet carried out. Perhaps they will be when school starts. If not, they will certainly be carried out during the course of the year. Our main support, Mr. Ray, will receive $12,000 in the fall from his wife. He proposes to apply it to the purchase in question, and no capital interest until such time as the Sisters are able to repay it. The interest in the meantime can be applied to the payment of four children for whom he is responsible, and whom the Sisters count among their pupils. The arrangement is most advantageous for both parties.

Whatever the opinion of the Sisters regarding their purchase in Shreveport, I regret it, because it takes them away from this city and will force them to keep a double house, because at the moment they can only get a sale barely sufficient to cover the interest on the sum paid by them, and certainly too insignificant to compensate for the inevitable damages that a property always experiences from unconcerned tenants who are not faithful custodians of what they have only the momentary use of.

I am leaving for Bastrop tomorrow, where I am called to celebrate a wedding.
I am in perfect health, as is my colleague, Mr. Gentille. A few weeks ago, I had the pain of learning of the news of the death of my poor brother. The poor child suffered 18 weeks, but he died, as one would not expect at his age and in the circumstances in which he left, during the most fervent years of the seminary, with his mind and heart all for God. If our God had shown him mercy, might he have prayed for his brother whose prolonged exile exposes him to dangers that he himself did not face.
Mr. Gentille joins me in offering you our most humble respect.

I am, Monseigneur, the most obedient servant of Your Excellency,
Louis Gergaud

The variable weather conditions of Louisiana often affected travel and communications, evidenced in Father Gergaud's commentary on the rains. He spoke again of the remote isolation of his missions, far from the See of Natchitoches and lacking ongoing communication from Bishop Martin. Meanwhile, the seeds of a proper education for youth have been firmly planted in remote Monroe, and Father Gergaud does not hold back from challenging his bishop to remember him and the peripheral sheep.

26 April 1866
Letter to Bishop Auguste Martin, Diocese of Natchitoches

Since your letter from New Orleans I have remained very worried, first because of the fever that you complained of, and then because of the fear that you might not be able to send Mr. Gentille back to Monroe. If I had thought I could leave my parish for a few days and if I had not feared that the heavy rains would have intercepted communications and made the trip from here to Natchitoches impossible, I would have gone in person to pay you my respects.

Our schools continue to thrive. The Sisters have 50 pupils, five of whom are boarders. They are very well set up and all expenses paid. Some of my influential Catholics with me have formed a larger place where they could hold a large boarding school of at least 50 pupils. If we could succeed, I would have reached one of my most ardent wishes. It would then become easier to take care of the boys. The school that I maintain for them is in the Sacristy, where we have 25 pupils crowded together under the yoke of a lady recently converted, and whose occupation has always been teaching. Of these 75 students, both boys and girls, two-thirds are Catholic.

I am almost tempted sometimes, Monseigneur, to think that you are neglecting us a little. Your presence and cooperation would be of immense benefit to us here. Perhaps we step a little over Providence and press by our desires, by our human movements, but the moment has proposed itself.

I received a letter from Bastrop informing me that a piece of land had been bought to build a Catholic church. It is a German who proposes to introduce a colony of Catholics of his nation to cultivate a vineyard which he has planted and wants to enlarge. I was invited to go to Bastrop last Sunday. The absence of assistance in Monroe forced me to decline the invitation. My zeal, I fear, Monseigneur, refuses to extinguish the limits of its action. Remote missions that require a week or two to be properly cared for at each visit have little appeal to me when I see myself obliged to leave Monroe, my primary town and residence.

If I am unable to obtain the Holy Oils within three weeks, it will undoubtedly be necessary for me to go to Natchitoches to get them myself, a long and arduous journey by land, and at a time when I will have to think about giving some precious care to the children of age to make their First Communion.

Please, Monseigneur, receive the assurance of the respect with which I am the very humble and obedient servant of Your Excellency,
Louis Gergaud

The *Morehouse Weekly Dispatch* article that Father Gergaud referenced in the next letter was appended to the original letter and is therefore reproduced herein. Once again, Father Gergaud emphasized his need for the assistance of Father Joseph Gentille. He would not see Father Gentille again until sometime after mid-May.

2 May 1866
Letter to Bishop Auguste Martin, Diocese of Natchitoches

I am writing to you on my return from Bastrop. Please find attached an excerpt from the "Weekly Dispatch," the Morehouse newspaper.

Last Friday, I had a meeting with those who are interested in the Catholic Church. I offered them my congratulations on their undertaking. They

Our Catholic friends propose building a Roman Catholic Church in Bastrop, and the building committee have requested us to state that sealed proposals for building the church will be received until the 25th of May next, and will be directed to Prof. J. J. Shardt, who is chairman of the committee, and left at the Drug Store of Messrs. Traylor & Bro. A plan of the edifice will be found at the latter place on next Monday, when all mechanics interested can have an opportunity of examining it.

Article from the *Morehouse Weekly Dispatch* announcing plans to build a Roman Catholic church in Bastrop, Louisiana. Father Gergaud was closely involved in this project, as he had established a mission there.

had already been established a committee…[names not all legible]. A subscription list was presented to me containing already 2000 dollars. The plan of the church is done. The lot purchased. It is hoped to begin the work in a short time. The wood will be provided by the vice-president.

I told them that the ownership of the church should be vested in you as bishop of the diocese. It was agreed to make the shell of the church and only then, when the lot is all paid for and the main work of the church is done, we will have it registered in our name.

The Catholic Church cannot fail to flourish in Bastrop, where the population is generally more educated than elsewhere. Catholic schools have reputation in Morehouse. This parish has sent more than a dozen pupils to Sacred Heart this year. We have a boarder from Morehouse among our girls of Monroe. Next year we can expect many more. Monroe definitely cannot do without another priest. If it were possible, please send Mr. Gentille to us. Everyone here wants him, and I believe it would [damage] the confidence of my parishioners if I did not make every effort to obtain for them the return of Mr. Gentille.

I am, Monseigneur, the very humble servant of Your Excellency,
Louis Gergaud

***

16 May 1866
Letter to Bishop Auguste Martin, Diocese of Natchitoches

Monseigneur, It is impossible for me to go to Natchitoches at the present. The rains have been so heavy that I have every reason to fear that the bayous, creeks, and swamps will make the road by land impracticable. As for the journey by water, I lack the time and finances to undertake it. The expenses that I have had to make on my own account, for the establishment of the Sisters and the repairs to the church and the diocesan property, amount to nearly one thousand dollars since last January 1. Thanks to the strictest economy and to the assistance of three of my friends, I am keeping out of debt.

I have here 67 dollars in Jubilee alms which I was unable to send to Natchitoches, having forgotten to give them to Mr. Le Vezouet after having offered him to do so. If you allow me to use them here, I assure you that they will not fail the purpose for which they were given: "spreading the Faith."

If it was possible for me to recover the $250 that I loaned to Mr. Chopin for the church at Providence, and which have not been returned to me, I would find a way to use that properly for the good of my church.

We have in view a beautiful property, a whole square with a beautiful house, across from the church, the Sisters have spent all on the purchase of Shreveport and I fear we cannot do everything by ourselves here.

Our schools are doing very well, but the locations and houses are too small I fear that a double school in Shreveport, in the city and in the country, require too many Sisters, and that the community will be obliged to make Monroe what they call "a little house." This will happen as Providence wills.

Monseigneur, you have certainly decided not to send Mr. Gentille back, since I have received nothing since your letter from New Orleans, in which you wrote to me that in Natchitoches you would "see what could be done."

I do not know, Monseigneur, when I will be able to obtain the new holy oils. I will use the old ones until then.

I am, Monseigneur, the very humble servant of Your Excellency.
Louis Gergaud

***

26 June 1866
Letter to Bishop Auguste Martin, Diocese of Natchitoches

Monseigneur, we are seriously thinking of buying for the Sisters in Monroe, opposite the church, a beautiful property consisting of a new and spacious house, very well adapted for a boarding school. We are being asked for $12,000. I am writing today to New Orleans to Mr. Lafite Dufilno & Company, bankers and agents for Mr. J.F. Pargoud. I propose to make a loan payable in four years, and I believe there is not the slightest fear that the Sisters, once in possession of the property, will not be able to make the payments in due time and thus acquire one of the most beautiful properties in Monroe.

If my project receives your approval, Monseigneur, I will not fear to put the matter in motion and to conclude it as soon as possible.

The Sisters are well, and always do well; they will close their school for vacations on July 21.

Mr. Gentille joins me in offering you our most humble respects.

I am, Monseigneur, the very humble servant of Your Excellency.
Louis Gergaud

In the final surviving letter currently known to exist, Father Gergaud speaks of an illness that, from its description, could possibly have been yellow fever. He also referenced this illness in the third-person narrative account of *The Catholic Church in Monroe*, after having visited someone in Arkansas who had what he termed "the swamp yellow fever."

27 September 1867
Letter to Bishop Auguste Martin, Diocese of Natchitoches

The Daughters of the Cross arrived here last Sunday on board the Homer. *Before and since your visit, the river has been so low that no boat could get up to Monroe. They found me recovering from an attack of bilious fever tending to congestion that I had probably contracted during my unfortunate trip to Arkansas. Mr. Gentille was also sick with a fever that he brought back from Boeuf River. I recovered but Mr. Gentille is still suffering.*

Our schools will begin again on Tuesday the 1ˢᵗ. The "Ouachita Female Academy" remains closed, so that St. Hyacinth Academy will be the only girls' school in Monroe for some time.

I am, Monseigneur, the very humble servant of Your Excellency.
Louis Gergaud

CHRONICLE: *THE CATHOLIC CHURCH IN MONROE, LOUISIANA*

From the original handwritten document located in the Archives of St. Matthew's Church in Monroe and certified copies of the same located in the Archives of the University of Louisiana at Monroe and the Archives of the Archdiocese of New Orleans, the following is a verbatim transcription of a third-person narrative about the Catholic Church in and around Monroe, Louisiana. The accounting of the past by oral history begins in 1800 but is detailed more greatly by 1855, the time of the arrival of Father Gergaud to Monroe. The transcription is as it was handwritten, and only a few portions have been redacted due to lack of clarity or duplicative lists existing in the sacramental records of St. Matthew's Church.[23]

The Catholic Church in Monroe, Louisiana
As Recorded by Father Louis Gergaud, Pastor of St. Matthew's Church,
1854–1873

1800

In the beginning of the nineteenth century, the banks of the Ouachita River and Bayou DeSiard were inhabited by a large population of Canadians and Frenchmen and by a large population of Choctaw Indians. At the spot where Monroe now stands a fort was erected by the Spanish government and called Fort Miro. The oldest inhabitants remember that a Franciscan [edited/corrected to "Carmelite"] friar, the Rev. Father Brady (Juan) resided there until Louisiana passed in the hands of France to be sold afterwards to the United States by Napoleon. Then the Catholic population was deprived of pastors for upwards of forty years and received but occasional visits from priests residing elsewhere. The Rev. Father Martin residing in Avoyelles baptized many in his travels and some records of Baptisms in his hand writing are still extant at the church in Monroe, others are from the hand of J. Timon, afterwards Bishop of Buffalo, New York (in 1842).

1851

In the year 1851, the Rev. Patrick Canavan was sent to Monroe by the Most Rev. A. Blanc, archbishop of New Orleans. The Catholic population was thinned by emigration and death, and with the exception of a few families, was composed of new-comers. A lot of ground was secured in the town of Monroe, a building committee appointed, a subscription taken up and a small church commenced under the direction of the Rev. P. Canavan, Dr. C.H. Dabbs, and G. Filhiol, the building committee.

Obstacles of more than one sort prevented the immediate construction of the building. The Catholic population was small, the subscribers were slack in giving their contributions, the contractors failed, and the Rev. P. Canavan left with a great deal of dissatisfaction after a residence of about eighteen months. Honest and straightforward but irritable, he offended many who could never justify the irascibility and the eagerness of the zealous man.

1852

The vacant mission was immediately conferred to another pastor, the Rev. J.J. O'Dougherty, a native of Ohio and formerly a priest of the Diocese of Toronto…a very polished gentleman and an excellent lecturer. However, his brilliant qualifications did not prevent his having to leave his mission at the end of two months, after only completing a set of pews in the church. Unfavorable to him and to the Catholic Church were the circumstances which brought about his departure.

The Diocese of Natchitoches was formed in 1854 [* actually 1853] and the Right Rev. A. Martin appointed to the new see, which comprised the whole of Louisiana north of the 31° of latitude, north. Four priests composed the whole clergy of the diocese; they had their respective parishes and the church of Monroe remained without a pastor until the year 1856.

In the meantime, the political Know Nothing party was organized and developed great prejudices against the Catholic Church. A Union church was built conjointly by the Free-masons who had their hall in the upper story and all the Protestant sects who held their meetings in the lower part of the building.

1856

The new bishop of Natchitoches visited Europe in 1854. In several dioceses of France, his mother-country and especially in the dioceses of Nantes, Rennes, and St. Brieuc, he obtained some

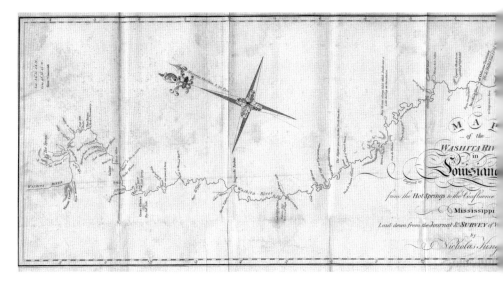

Nicholas King, *Map of the "Washita" River from the Hot Springs to the Confluence of the Red River with the Mississippi River.* London, 1804. *Library of Congress, Washington, D.C. Collection: U.S. Presidents (1801–1809), Thomas Jefferson.*

young missionaries, whom he brought to labor in his own dioceses. Among these the Rev L. Gergaud of the Diocese of Nantes was appointed in 1856 to the mission of the Ouachita. In March, he visited Monroe and returned in April to take his residence; he was enabled to do so by the kindness of Dr. C.H. Dabbs and lady, with whom he took board, having fitted a little room behind the church as his lodgings.

The situation was one of peculiar embarrassment for a young clergyman yet unable to preach with any ease the language of his parishioners, isolated from his fellow priests, countenanced only by a very small number of Catholics....Men who considered that the human means of success in his hands doubted whether he could remain here more than a few months.

The church was unfinished, although it had no debt, yet there was no means at hand to prosecuting the work, a subscription was proposed, the proceeds of which ($185) were spent in erecting an altar-piece to replace the shelf on which the Holy Sacrifice was offered heretofore.

In the following June, the church building yet unfinished was dedicated, under the patronage of St. Matthew (Festival

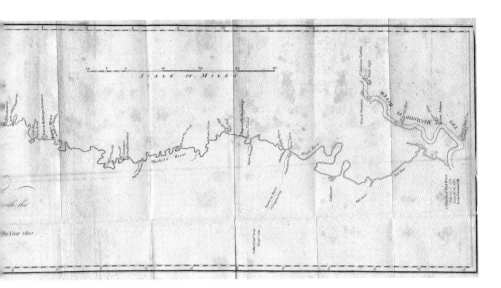

21 September) by the Right Rev. A.M. Martin, during his first episcopal visit. The Rev. H. Figari, pastor of Alexandria, and the Rev. L. Gergaud were present and assisted the bishop, the former preached the dedication sermon. After the ceremony and the celebration of Mass, the Right Reverend Bishop administered Confirmation to seven candidates. In the evening, he addressed the congregation in a short discourse, he departed the following day for the parish of Avoyelles in company with the Rev. H. Figari.

A law suit was pending in the parish of Caldwell against the contractor of the church building, as having failed to comply with his obligations. The Rev. L. Gergaud chose to compromise with him upon receiving the sum of $800....He dismissed the suit and undertook to finish the building as best he could. That money was spent in erecting a choir gallery and painting the entire building outside.

The congregation counted that year very few over a dozen communicants.

1857

In the following year (February) with the hope of adding to the solemnity of the celebration of Mass, a melodion was bought for the sum of $200 by the Rev. H. Figari the pastor of St. Theresa's New Orleans and sent to Monroe at the request of the pastor.

On the 5th of June of the same year, the Rev. L. Gergaud by virtue of his letters of faculties erected the Stations of the Way of the Cross (Via Crucis) after the celebration of Mass.

The children of the French who formerly dwelt on the banks of the Ouachita River and in Prairie De Lait, a few miles west of Columbia, had gathered themselves on the right bank of the Boeuf River, partly in Ouachita, partly in Caldwell parish. Catholics only in name and by baptism, they retained but little else of Catholicity. A regular mission was established among them and they continue to be visited from Monroe during the dry season. Separated from the Ouachita Valley by a swamp impassable in winter, the Lafourche, they cannot be attended at that time but by a resident pastor.

1858

In the month of November 1858 a small property was donated by one of them for church purposes to the Bishop of Natchitoches. It consists of a house and two acres of ground at the sound end of the land owned by J.B. Baillargeon who gave it. The house is used as a chapel by the missionary.

The church building in Monroe was painted inside for the sum of 200 dollars. Now it might be said to be completed as it will probably remain as it is now until a new church may be needed and built.

1859

The pastor has hitherto continued lodging in the sacristy, it is time he should think of building himself a residence. The lot of ground on which the church is built being only 60 ft by 120 is insufficient, another lot is secured in the same square for the sum of $200 by purchase from Mrs. B. Ludwig and fenced in (March 1859). More than a year must yet pass before he can think of building.

In August the first Mass ever said in Winnsboro was celebrated at the house of L. Sims where it was celebrated afterwards upon every visit to that place. Sermons were preached at that house and in the courthouse to a numerous and attentive audience. Three converts, and old gentleman and two married ladies, soon rewarded the first efforts of the missionary.

1860

The Second Provincial Council of New Orleans was assembled in that city in the month of January 1860. The Rev. L. Gergaud attended as theologian of the Bishop of Natchitoches. He then bought for his little church a fine gilded chalice and two chasubles. A collection is being made for the purpose of building a priest house, it yields but little comparatively yet lumber is bought, the work commenced and a year afterwards in February, he will be able to exchange his modest room with the more commodious parsonage.

In February, a first Mass was celebrated in the town of Bastrop at the residence of W. Prather, editor of the Morehouse Advocate. Eight persons communicated.

(March) The Rev. L. Gergaud received the sad news of his father's death in France and the pressing invitations by which his widowed mother entreats him to return for a while to his country. Moved both by filial love and the advice of his bishop, he resolved to undertake the voyage and left in the month of June. After an absence of 6 months, having visited several bishops and the officers of the Association for the Propagation of the Faith at the request of the Right Rev. A. Martin, he returned to this country accompanied by the Rev. J. Gentille, his former fellow student, who consented to come and devote himself to labor in this part of the field.

1861

(June 1861) An altar society is established composed of the ladies of the congregation with this motto: "O Lord, I have loved the beauty of thy house." Their object being to promote the cleanliness and ornamentation of our little church building. Fifty ladies became members of the association and nominated Miss Mary Henrietta Hankins as first president. The contributions for the Propagation of the Faith are discontinued on account of the difficulty of corresponding with officers of the Society.

A small lot separating the church from the priest house yard is secured to the church by purchase.

Altar cross belonging to Father Louis Gergaud, hand-carved ivory, mid-nineteenth century. Collection of St. Matthew's Church, Monroe, Louisiana. *Authors' photo*.

1862

June 1862. A physician, through opposition to the Catholic Church, purchased a lot of ground adjoining it and built an office as near to it as he could and kept disorderly company even during the hours of public worship. This however did not last long, a short and fatal disease soon carried him to the grave. His property was purchased by the Rev. L. Gergaud for the sum of $900, which was paid during the year 1863. A war existed then between the United States and the Confederate States of America. Many Irish Catholics sold their services in the army to men otherwise obliged to military service. Now as ever liberal towards their church, they opened their hands and purses and with a lavishness peculiar to that generous race, they soon enabled the Rev. L. Gergaud to pay as large an amount as the price of his last purchase.

During the first and second year of the war, Monroe became a place of some importance, for it was successively the headquarters of the recruiting department in North Louisiana and of the Sub-District of North Louisiana. The presence of troops necessitated the establishing of a general hospital. Gen. A.G. Blanchard, a Catholic, requested the Rev. L. Gergaud to make some efforts to procure Sisters of Charity. Three were obtained from the Orphan Asylum in Natchez, Mississippi, and took charge of the hospital in September 1862. Here as everywhere the works of charity dispelled many prejudices and upwards of fifty soldiers were received into the Catholic Church on their death bed. Monroe was evacuated by the Confederates in August 1863, the hospital transferred to Mount Lebanon and the sisters returned to the asylum with the blessings and good wishes of all who had known them and witnessed their daily works of love.

1863

(October 1863) A first Mass was celebrated near Woodville, Jackson Parish, at the house of Philip Maher, a refugee from the Mississippi Valley which he had to leave in consequence of the depredations of the enemy (the Yankees).

The same cause forced the removal of the Rev. M. Chapin from Milliken's Bend and Lake Providence, missions of the Mississippi, and the Rev. L Gergaud of Monroe was now the only Catholic priest in Louisiana north of the Red River. He then applied to the Bishop of Natchitoches with the request that an assistant priest might be sent to him. On Christmas Eve, the Rev. J. Gentille arrived with faculties as assistant priest and special missionary of the Boeuf River population and immediately entered upon the discharge of his duties.

The Catholic Church had now attained the developments as to require the establishing of a Catholic school, where the children of the Church being gathering around their pastor, might get into early relations with him, to take from him the first impression of religion. Fifty children were counted between the ages of five to twelve years. No delay was now justifiable, and in the beginning of December 1863, the school was opened with Mrs. J.W. Dabbs and Miss Moran as teachers. Three months later it numbered more than 60 pupils. The Female Academy buildings were offered to us by the trustees and accepted. The pastor retains the charge of Superior of the School and teachers are employed only upon his recommendation.

1864

March 1864: General Price's Division of the Confederate States Army is camped in southern Arkansas. The Rev. L. Gergaud, upon an invitation from some of the officers, visited the troops at their winter quarters, preached and celebrated Mass and administered Communion. He visited at the same time some of the Louisiana Catholic refugees at Camden.

In that year, the numbers of communicants at Monroe during Easter time was about sixty.

April 10: the Yankees arrived in Monroe; they had two gunboats (ironclad rams), four armed transports, and two lighter and very small steamers for landing purposes. They anchored in front of the town, landed a company of marine[s], and proceeded to search for Confederate stores. On the following day, they took aboard a number of negro men to load in the cotton bales. On Monday, a great many slaves came to the landing place to await the departure of the expedition and leave the country. They were persuaded to that course by the fear of subsequent ill treatment which was held out before them by men of mean character.... On Tuesday morning at the hour of Mass (6 o'clock AM), fire was set to the courthouse, jail, railroad bridge, R.R. depot, and the R.R. office by the enemy. They departed the same day.... Agriculture on plantation, situated on the Ouachita River, was thereby very seriously damaged.

A few days before that expedition, the Rev. J. Gentille went to Natchitoches for the purpose of renewing the oils used in the administration of Baptism and Extreme Unction. He unfortunately fell among the Federals who took possession of the town on the day of his arrival. His horse was afterwards stolen from the Bishop's stable; this event detained him two months, after which he gladly returned to the great joy of friends.

Natchitoches is situated on Red River [edited to Cane] about half way between Alexandria and Shreveport. The object of the Federals was to get possession of the latter place, and thereby insure the undisturbed control of the states of Arkansas and Louisiana. On their way from Natchitoches to Shreveport, the Confederates met them at Mansfield on the 8th of April and defeated them; a month afterward they had abandoned the Red River country, not however without devastating it. Plantations, towns, houses, and churches beheld the scenes of robbery and destruction worthy of the Huns, or the Gothic Barbarians of Europe in the Middle Ages.

The May devotions in honor of the Blessed Virgin were performed this year for the first time in the church at Monroe, and regularly attended by the children of the Catholic school congregation. The season during this month was excessively dry, only one day's light showers interrupted the drought which lasted over two months.

In the latter part of August, the Rev. L. Gergaud visited a few Catholic families living on the Ouachita River near Bambrick's Ferry, 12 miles above Harrisonburgh [*sic*].

Stations occasionally visited from Monroe:

I. Bastrop

II. Winnsboro, Franklin Parish

III. Woodville, LA Jackson Parish

IV. Near Columbia

V. Bambrick's Ferry

VI. Boeuf River

1865

[This is the final year of the Civil War. This year's notation in the diary begins with a terse list of bullet point/questions:]

First Sunday in Lent
- Unpaid pew rent
- Easter duties
- Regulations of Lent not yet received.
- What fasting is according to our present customs?
- Who is exempt from fasting?

Children two or younger—hard working colored—the poor—the soldiers who draw their rations from the government—delicate persons—pregnant and nursing women.

[Next paragraph not fully legible]

Surrender of Confederate Forces

On the 4th day of June 1865, all the forces of the Confederate States having surrendered in the different military departments, two federal gunboats made their appearance off Monroe and anchored out in the river. They were followed on the same day by a transport, the White Cloud, carrying negro troops, a portion of which was left to garrison that place under the command of Col. Dockery.

Negro troops appear well trained and in the perfect control of their officers.

Cleanliness and order in camp is remarkable—country negros leave the plantations and come to town but are sent back by the officers who advise them to go and work and stay with their former owners whom they style now their employers.

July 6

The second exhibition of our Catholic school took place on the 6th day of July. The audience was numerous. The children did remarkably well in music and in rendering a little play which had been composed expressly for their benefit.

July 16

By invitation from the Rev. L. Gergaud, the Catholic gentlemen of Monroe met at the priest home for the purpose of organizing a Young Catholic Friends Society to promote the education of indigent children and found a Catholic library of moral and intellectual culture. This meeting was attended by 23 gentlemen who, after discussing the Constitution, signed it and elected the officers of the society for the present year. The Rev. L Gergaud was elected 1st president of the society.

September

The Rev. J. Gentille received a communication from the Right Rev. Bishop of Natchitoches, ordering him to repair to Cocoville in the parish of Avoyelles. He was to replace the Rev. J. Janneau as pastor and director of the motherhouse of the Daughters of the Cross situated in that parish, during that gentleman's absence from the country. This assignment could not but grieve his friends in Monroe, where his worth has won many hearts to him. No time being left to discuss with his Bishop, the Rev. Gentille left for Natchitoches on the 4th day of September.

On the same day the Catholic school resumed its sessions in the buildings of the Ouachita Female Academy, but the Rev. L. Gergaud was notified by the president of the Board of Trustees that he could not remain in possession of these buildings any longer than it was necessary for them to make arrangements to have a school under their own direction.

On the 26th of September, Right Rev. A. Martin, Bishop of Natchitoches, being about to depart from his diocese for Europe, convened the majority of his priests in Natchitoches and apprised them of his arrangements respecting the administration of the diocese during his absence. He gave the Rev. L. Gergaud his instructions and pastoral letter related to the Jubilee granted by our Holy Father upon the occasion of the condemnation by the Apostolic See of the errors of the XIX century, generally known as the -isms of the age and the different propositions set forth by the enemies of the Church and of Christianity. This pastoral document was read in this church on the 2nd Sunday of October, and the month of December appointed for the district of which Monroe is the center, to comply with the necessary conditions to gain the Indulgence.

The decrees of the Provincial Council of New Orleans held in 1860 were also published in what regards the laity of the Church.

One decree condemning secret societies, and another announcing the penalty of excommunication applied to Catholics who would contract marriage before the ministers of Protestant sects.

In the month of December, the Daughters of the Cross, at the request of the Rev. L. Gergaud, consented to establish a branch of their institution in Monroe, and to take charge of the Catholic school. Three sisters were dispatched to come to this place. In January 1866, the Rev. L. Gergaud went to New Orleans to buy furniture for the proposed establishment, after calling upon the generosity of his congregation. H. Filhiol contributed $150 dollars. The sisters were expected to arrive in Monroe toward the end of February.

1866

On the 6th day of February, the Young Catholics Friend Society signed an instrument before the Recorder of the Parish of Ouachita, forming themselves thereby into a body politic, and praying to be considered as a corporate society.

On the 20th day of February 1866, three Daughters of the Cross, Sister Theresa of Jesus, Sister St. Joseph and Sister Loreto arrived, accompanied by the Rev. F. Le Vezouet, reached Monroe on the steam boat Nicholas Longworth, commanded by Capt. J.W. Tobin. They were installed in Father Gergaud's house and upon the very next day took the direction of the female portion of the Catholic school of this place. The male children were removed and placed in the Vestry, which was selected as their school room [under the supervision of Miss __]

[Editor's note: portion of this text redacted]

Rev. J. Gentille after an absence of eight months returned to Monroe, where he came to reside with the title of assistant priest as formerly.

At a visit from the Rev. L. Gergaud to the town of Bastrop, several Catholic gentlemen called upon him. They had formed a committee for the building of a Catholic church in the place. A lot had been purchased, a list of contributions made, a plan drawn and they proposed to go immediately to work upon said building. This came to no practical results on account of the failure of the cause by overflow and excessive rains.

1867

Up to the month of June, different improvements were made on the property belonging to the church—new fences—stable—kitchen. In the church confessional, choir gallery—painting—to the amount of about $1,000.00.

Three sets of vestments (white silk) (red damask) (imitation of cloth of gold) and (a cope of white silk) were imported from France at cost of $107.00.

A statement of the foundation, present state and prospects of the Catholic schools was furnished by the Rev. L. Gergaud to the Superintendent of Public Education for the State of Louisiana [ ] upon his request, made in a circular of May 19, 1867.

The superintendent, expecting to have a share of the Peabody Fund for the benefit of the Southern schools, allotted to Louisiana to distribute, asked for the above statement to guide him in the proper distribution of the share mentioned.

The second pastoral visit of the Right Rev. A.M. Martin, bishop of Natchitoches, having been postponed from the 19th day of May, on which he was previously expected, and on which the First Communions for this year took place, was made on the 28th day of June. That year it concurred with the Solemnity of Corpus Christi. The Bishop arrived on the steamer Idaho Sunday morning accompanied by the Rev. J. B. Avenard, pastor of Campti on the Red River. The same day the bishop celebrated Mass at 6-1/2 o'clock and administered Communion. High Mass was sung at 9-1/2 o'clock by the Rev. J.B. Avenard. Confirmation was afterwards administered to 36 candidates whose names are registered in the Record Book of Baptisms. In the afternoon, the Bishop addressed the Ladies of the Altar Society and the children of the catechism class.

The next day, the Young Catholics Friends Society met at their rooms and were presented to the Right Reverend Bishop, who made them an address in praise of their efforts for the education of indigent children. The Society was then placed by a unanimous vote under the patronage of the Bishop of Natchitoches and the Rev. J.B. Avenard elected an honorary member.

On Tuesday, the Right Reverend Bishop dined at the residence of Col J.F. Pargoud, 1-1/2 mile from Monroe. He departed the next day on the steamer *Homer* for Red River.

The impression made by the Bishop's visit was one of the most favorable to himself and to religion.

At Bastrop, the Rev. L. Gergaud bought in the month of July a lot for the use of the Catholic church, the title was vested in him and he paid towards the purchase $150.00 cash. The lot, 80 feet by 800, is the upper end of a square belonging to J. Skinner.

August 16, the Rev. L. Gergaud is called to visit that part of Chicot County state of Arkansas lying on Boeuf River by P.C. Perret. After a journey of two days and one night with short intervals for rest, he reached the house of P.C. Perret in the afternoon of the 18th. On the 20th he went to Eudora 12 miles beyond and four miles from Grand Lake on the Mississippi River, to visit Mrs. Adelaide Thompson who lays dangerously ill with swamp yellow fever, and returned the same day to P.C. Perret's. The next day he celebrated Mass and entered into marriage James Johnstone and Alice Perret, and returned to Monroe after an absence of 8 days.

September 4, the Rev. J. Gentille visit Boeuf River station—J.L. Perrins, Mrs. Barry's, baptized the family of John Ferrand (6 children).

8th—Rev. L. Gergaud taken sick with bilious indisposition, sick 12 days

12th—Rev. J. Gentille returns—14th taken sick with fever and subsequently with sore eyes

22nd—The Daughters of the Cross return to Monroe from the mother house at Marksville.

1868

Vestiary made at the expense of Rev. L. Gergaud at the cost of $50.00.

May 4—Rev. J. Gentille departure for France, where he intends to remain for five months. He is enabled to make the voyage by the generosity of our friend J.F. Pargaud, who after paying his passage gave him an order on his bankers in Paris for $600.00.

Repairs of the Sisters enclosure at the expense of Rev. L. Gergaud ($77.00).

June 28—Arrived here, the Rev. L. Enaut, a young priest recently ordained at Natchitoches by the Right Rev. A.M. Martin. He is to minister here during the absence of the Rev. J. Gentille.

August 1ˢᵗ—the vestry was enlarged, to make a suitable room for the male school. Porch so constructed as to be afterwards closed and made into a vestry. Cost of $550, all at the expense of Rev. L. Gergaud.

September 19—Arrival of the Daughters of the Cross to reopen St. Hyacinth's Academy for the session of 1868–1869, with Sister Mary Seraphina as Superior. Teaching to commence Monday September 28ᵗʰ.

December 1—Rev. J. Gentille returns to Monroe as Missionary priest to the stations of Milliken's Bend and Lake Providence.

December 27—Exchange of lots in Bastrop for the use and benefit of the church – a whole square acquired.

1869
Feb—Rev L. Gergaud and Rev. L. Enaut go to Natchitoches to attend the ecclesiastical retreat and 2ⁿᵈ diocesan synod. Decrees of the 2ⁿᵈ Plenary Council of Baltimore promulgated. Rev. J. Gentille remains in Monroe.

March—Rev. L. Enaut goes to Bastrop and takes steps to have a Catholic church built, prospects are very encouraging.

Rev. J. Gentille goes to Natchitoches to receive his mission to Lake Providence, Milliken's Bend, and St. Joseph.

March 28—Easter Sunday. Solemn Mass with Deacon and Sub-deacons. First collection for the seminarians $45.65. Mission announced to open next Sunday, and to be conducted by the Redemptorist Fathers from New Orleans. Rev. Joseph Gentille departs for Milliken's Bend and Lake Providence – sincere regrets of his friends at parting. A purse of $123.00 contributed by the Catholics of Monroe and presented to him in their name by H. Filhiol, Esq.

April 13—A great blessing has the Good God conferred upon this parish. The Redemptorist mission closed after 10 days of the most happy efforts on the part of the Rev. Father Burke and _____, to instruct and convert the souls and hearts to God. The success is complete. 165 confessions were heard. The number of communions by adults reaches 130. The general communion on Tuesday morning of about 120 persons was the most touching and edifying event. To feel the mental recollection, to witness the outward piety, the calm step to and from the communion table, of all these communicants was enough to make one shed tears of joy. This mission distinguishes itself among others by the signs of deep conviction penetrating calmly into the very souls, by the deliberate and therefore quiet earnestness of all in returning to God. No attempt was made to produce excitement and none took place. The intellect and free will were addressed. All who returned to their God or entered the true fold acted in doing so with a coolness of conviction and a set purpose, which bespoke the sincerity of all.

  18 years ago when this parish was formed, the number of paschal communions did not exceed 10 or 12, so the fruits of the goodness of the word of God are literally now a hundred fold, for they were received in a good heart, a very good heart, that is to say the one heart and one mind of this little parish.

   May our Good God preserve forever the fruits of this mission, and pour his choicest blessings upon the faithful, zealous Fathers Burke and… [ ].

   12 adult persons were baptized, others are preparing for baptism.

   The Redemptorist Fathers left for Shreveport on the 15th of April.

May 23—First Communion was administered to 19 children, all of whom except two, frequent the Catholic schools of this place.

June 9—The property formerly known as the Louisiana Intelligencer's Office was bought by the Young Catholics Friends Society for $1200—paid cash on the 7th day of this month. This property consists of a large room 50 feet long and becomes the meeting room of the YCFS. It is also applied to the purposes of the Catholic male school, which is being taught in it by Rev. Father Gergaud and Father Enaut. The school numbers 32 pupils.

A new vestry was built behind the Catholic church at the expense of $150 and preparations made to turn the former school room for boys into the church and thereby enlarge that building 18 feet in the length.

An exhibition and public distribution of premiums took place in the new boys' school apartment – the boys of the Catholic school numbering thirty. It was attended by at least 100 persons who take an interest in the school.

The Sisters gave also premiums to the girls of their institution on the 15th of same month. Music and recitations and distribution of nearly 80 beautiful volumes filled the two hours of pleasant entertainment. The public was not however admitted.

August 8—Rev. L. Enaut started for Winnsboro—work commenced to enlarge the church by the addition of a new sanctuary—new pedestals—painting—cost of $587.00.

September 15—Sisters opened the academy for the fall session, Sister Seraphina, Superior.

Rev. L. Gergaud goes to Milliken's Bend and Lake Providence to visit the Rev. J. Gentille, whom he finds sick in the latter mission—he brings him back to Monroe, where his old friends were happy to welcome him. Father Gentille is to stay here about three weeks to recover his health.

Rev. L. Enaut visits Bastrop. Receives Mr. J. Biggar into the Church, in presence of a large congregation assembled in the courthouse.

October 3—Boys Catholic school reopened for the fall session.

The sum of $100 is sent from here to the Right Rev. Bishop Martin to contribute towards his expenses to Europe where he goes to attend the 19th Ecumenical Council at Rome.

[Editors' Note: The First Vatican Council, convened from 1868 to 1870, is technically numbered as the Twentieth Ecumenical Council of the Church.]

Attached to this page of the journal is a newspaper clipping, publication unknown, that is titled "Protest of the Catholics of Monroe," which merits inclusion here:

> *At a meeting of the Catholic laity of St. Matthew's Church, in the town of Monroe, Parish of Ouachita, and State of Louisiana, on the 6th day of November, 1870, H. Filhiol, Esq. was called to the Chair, John L. Moore appointed Secretary, and a number of gentlemen Vice-Presidents. The object of this meeting was explained by Judge Robert Ray in a few appropriate remarks to be for the purpose of protesting against the unwarranted and unlawful action of Victor Emmanuel in taking possession of the State of the Church by force of arms, and on his motion, the following protest was adopted, being the same adopted by the Catholic laity of New Orleans.*

The protest was a direct response to the seizure of the Papal States in 1870 and is similar to the response found in many Catholic communities in the United States.

December 8—First celebration of the Feast of the Immaculate Conception as a feast of obligation, and concluding of the exercises of the Jubilee granted by the Holy Father upon the occasion of the Ecumenical Council. Jubilee alms distributed to the Altar Society and Young Catholics Friends Society ($110).

1870
March—Cloth (carpet) for the sanctuary bought by the Ladies of the Altar Society $125.00.

Easter—About 50 or 60 communions at Easter. The renewal of the Redemptorist mission being announced to commence Sunday after Easter. Several wanted to make their Easter duties at the time of the Renewal—collection for seminarians $52.00.

April 24—Renewal of the mission conducted by Fathers Burke and Neithart, CSSR—it closed on Tuesday May 3rd. The renewal was even more successful than the mission itself had been. The number of confessions was near 200, that of communions amounted to 165. During the confessions were 19 persons who had for many years neglected their religious duties and even seldom in this life been at church. There were 5 converts, who make their abjuration and were conditionally baptized. The sermons were very impressive and drew large audiences. Only about 35 Catholics in the whole congregation, or persons who have the name of Catholics did not go to confession or communion, three-fourths of these are either French or of French descent, the remaining fourth comprises Germans, Americans, and Irish. Father Neithart's oratory is very striking. The voice is fine—the delivery full of life—the subject matter handled clearly and conclusively. His sermon on the true Church was excellent and were in fact all his instructions. The fathers left for Shreveport Thursday morning, 6:00 a.m. 5th day of May.

June 5—The First Communion took place on the Feast of Pentecost. Nine children.

July 2—Exhibition and distribution of premiums at the Catholic Boys' school. Recitations by the children. We had the Monroe Brass Band to play for us at the ceremony—number of children during the year 42, at the close 35.

July 15—Exhibition and distribution of premiums of the Convent of St. Hyacinth's. Charade by the girls. Recitations. The mothers only were permitted to be present. Sisters left for Shreveport on the stage on Monday 18th. Jerome Bres sent to St. Charles College, Ellicott, to study for the priesthood.

August 13—Dining room and cellar built cost $800.

September 15—Girls school reopened under Daughters of the Cross.

October 5—Boys school reopened. Rev. L. Gergaud and L. Enaut, teachers.

1871

February—Ecclesiastical retreat commenced on Sunday, February 5 at Natchitoches, ended on the 12th by the ordination of five priests and 2 deacons. One of the ordinands the Rev. E.

Duclercq was sent to Monroe as Assistant Priest. Rev. L. Enaut to remain here until ready to go to Bastrop, rector of which place he was appointed by the Right Rev. Bishop of Natchitoches.

April 22—A square of ground was purchased (326 feet x 265) for the purpose of establishing a Catholic cemetery in the town of Monroe. Mr. H. Filhiol was the vendor and received $1000 dollars for said land—Title deed made in the name of Rev. L. Gergaud. Land to be used for a Catholic graveyard and for church purposes generally.

June 2—Trinity Sunday—First Communion administered to fifteen children.

June 16—Our Holy Father the Pope's 25th anniversary. Feast of the Sacred Heart. 40 communions for the Pope. High Mass at 9 o'clock—Benediction at 8:00 p.m.

July 25—Visit from the Right Rev. Bishop of Natchitoches accompanied by the Rev. J. Gentille of Lake Providence. 75 communions at the Bishop's Mass. Grand High Mass with Deacon and Sub-deacons, Rev. J. Gentille celebrant. Confirmation of 17 persons by the Right Rev. A.M. Martin, who afterwards made an address to the congregation.

July 29—Rev L. Enaut goes to Bastrop to reside, with the expectation of building a church there, building materials already purchased and paid for, and ready to use.

August 1—Rev Father Garasche, S.J. from St. Louis University—the first of his order—visits Monroe.

August 29—Rev. E. Duclercq departs for France.

October 2—Boys school reopened.

October 7—Rev. Joseph Quelard, a newly ordained priest, is sent here to replace the Rev. E. Duclercq as assistant priest to St. Matthew's Church, Monroe, La.

LECTURE ON PAPAL INFALLIBILITY

Although the text of the chronicle *The Catholic Church in Monroe, Louisiana* concludes abruptly with the October 7, 1871 entry, affixed to the bottom of the original final page are two newspaper notices, one reporting the death of Sister St. Vincent de Paul at St. Hyacinth's Academy, noting she "was much beloved by the scholars and those connected with the school." Also affixed was this "Religious Notice," announcing the opening of St. Joseph Catholic Church in Bastrop:

> *Next Sunday, February 4, solemn opening of the Catholic Church. At 10 o'clock A.M. benediction of the church, High Mass; sermon by Rev L. Gergaud of Monroe. At 3 p.m., a lecture on the infallibility of the Pope will be delivered by the same reverend gentleman. After the lecture, solemn benediction of the Blessed Sacrament. A collection will be taken up at both services for the benefit of St. Joseph Church, Bastrop, La. [signed] Rev. L. Enaud [Enaut], Pastor of St. Joseph Church.*[24]

Father Gergaud wrote to the editor of *The Conservative* with some corrective comments on the coverage of his lecture, hand-dated as February 16, 1872. The text is not fully legible; therefore, what follows is a partial transcription only from a degraded copy of the newspaper article:[25]

> *At three o'clock in the evening of the same day, Father Gergaud delivered a lecture on THE INFALLIBILITY OF THE POPE. The doctrine set forth in this proposition has long been a debated question among the Christians…[unreadable]…The Roman Catholics themselves have been to some extended divided on the subject. Doubtless there was not a person who went to hear the lecture who, as he understood the doctrine, had not already made up his mind on the question. The Roman Catholic believing implicitly in it as the true doctrine, as the Protestant nursing his disbelief as one of the cardinal tenets of his Protestant faith.*
> *The first point of the lecture was made in reference to the dual character of the Pope. Father Gergaud proceeded to say that in one sense of the term the pope was but a man; in another and higher sense he was the grand official head of the Church, the Vice-Gerent of Christ upon earth. That as a man he was not exempt from the frailties incident to his human nature. That some occupants of the Papal office had led such immoral lives that the church was in doubt whether these had ever attained to salvation. But in his official*

capacity as the successor of St. Peter, and the great head of the church, the Pope was under the guidance of divine inspiration and he could not err—he was infallible. That to the Pope was committed certain powers, that his jurisdiction extended to all matters involving questions of Christian faith and practice, that his authority in regard to these matters was supreme and exclusive, and that when his decisions were rendered they were and ought to be final. In other words, the errors of the Pope were to be charged to the Pope as a man, and he was accountable for them in his individual capacity, but in his official character as the sublime judicial head of the church he could not go wrong. In this sense he was infallible and in no other. An apt illustration was made on this point of analogy to temporal government. In every stable government among men there is a supreme power. To this power appeal may be had as in the last resort. But when this power decides, the contested question is settled forever—it can no longer be agitated. The principle upon which the decision is made must be taken as true and the judgment itself as just. In this sense infallibility is synonymous with finality.

Such a liberal construction is very different from the view usually taken and taught by Protestants of this doctrine. As thus expounded, the infallibility of the Pope is not such a horrid dogma as many imagine, but on the contrary it is not unreasonable nor inconsistent with sound religion.

The point was also made that St. Peter was constituted by Christ himself the chief of the Apostles and the head of the Church. This high honor first being promised and afterwards actually conferred. The exposition of the scriptural texts quoted in support of this historical fact was fair and seemingly reasonable. Not so in some other discourses we heard on the same passages in which both the spirit and the sense of the language was distorted in order to argue to a very different conclusion. The lecturer proceeded to say that St Peter, as the first bishop of Rome, was succeeded by some two hundred and sixty other bishops, each of whom in his turn inherited the sacred mantle and discharged the office of his great predecessor as the Vice Gerent of Christ upon earth. That such a succession was required because the church was not intended to continue only during the natural life of St. Peter, but was established to be maintained till the final consumption of the world.

Now whether this view of the historical facts is the true one or not—whether the Pope is really the head of the church as the successor of St. Peter—there is one thing evident, and that is that the Roman Catholics are not without argument to support their convictions. Their position means to work out the cultivation of the good principle in the man, and that a preference as to them is a mere matter of taste. That set of means is best suited to that man *upon whom it will have the greatest influence for good. Sectarian controversy at least should not be permitted to disturb the harmonies, the fraternal relations which should exist among the different denominations, each and every one of which bears inscribed on its banner, "Peace on earth and good will to men."*

Temporal dominion was especially disclaimed by the lecturer for the Pope. If the Pope, he said, exercised temporal power even in the semblance in any particular instance, this resulted from the fact that jurisdiction of the temporal and ecclesiastic sovereignties were often join over the same subject matter. That in every act of man was involved the question of religion, and to this extent, that the act was religious or moral—and no further did the jurisdiction of the church extend. That every man, high or low, from the prince to the peasant, was the subject of the moral law and thus owed fealty to the church.

It cannot be seen from such a view that the Pope claims any greater power than is exercised by all the Protestant churches each over its own membership.

What Father Gergaud said claiming divine inspiration for the Pope, this is a position upon which all Protestants will take leave to differ from him. His remarks, also showing that the jurisdiction of the Pope extended into heaven and hell is one part of his lecture upon which no comments can be made, for who are afraid to follow him into those misty regions.

The Papal office, considered simply as an element of complete organization—of administrative strength, giving unity and consistency to the religious faith and stability to the church establishment itself—cannot but be appreciated by every thinking mind which has not been closed by bigotry and fanaticism, again the light of reason.

The lecture of Father Gergaud will not fail to remove much prejudice from the minds of many who heard him against the Roman Catholic Church and teachings. As a cultivated gentleman and a Christian divine, he stands high in the esteem of all who know him, and he has many friends in our community outside of his own church.

Father Gergaud's reply to the editor of *The Conservative*, noted to be February 16, 1872:

The kind and considerate notice which your correspondent took of my lecture on the infallibility of the Pope calls for a few observations, which in justice to myself, I beg to submit.

I did not claim inspiration for the Pope as your correspondent thinks, nor does the Catholic Church teach that he is inspired in the exercise of his

85

role as an infallible teacher. We only claim for him divine assistance, which prevents him from committing an error in his official and authoritative teaching of religion, and this claim is supported by the words of Jesus Christ to St. Peter (Luke XXII, 32), "I have prayed for thee that thy faith fail not," the prayer of Christ which can never be rejected—which the Father always grants. The sacred writers of Scripture were inspired, but the Pope is only assisted into infallibility.

As for the jurisdiction of the Pope in heaven and hell, I am at a loss to know what that can possibly mean, and I could certainly not assert anything on the subject. Jurisdiction means authority vested in a person or inherent to an office, to govern, judge, or direct subordinates. Now surely the Pope exercises no jurisdiction in heaven or hell, for his office was established here on earth, and his jurisdiction does not reach beyond its limits. But that the exercise of his jurisdiction on earth is approved of and ratified in heaven appears from the words of Christ (Matthew XVI, 19), "whatever thou shalt bind on earth shall be bound in heaven, whatever thou shalt loose on earth shall be loosed in heaven."

The act of faith is not only, as your correspondent affirms, a necessary act of the intellect driven to conviction—it is also an act of the will adhering to the known truth, and therefore a free and moral act with its responsibilities. It can be made or refused at will, otherwise the Lord would never have affirmed, (Mark XVI, 16), "He who will not believe shall be condemned." Conviction was not wanting to the contemporaries of Christ; his Godhead was proven to them by overwhelming evidence, but the perverseness of their will prevented them from surrendering to evidence. The same thing happens in all functions of life, where both mind and will are often in desperate conflict.

The fine liberal opinion put forth [by the newspaper] that all contending sects contradicting one another and the Church make a one great whole under the benign approval of God, is really too much to swallow and digest by any sober-minded logician. It is one of those opinions the falseness of which is so glaring that a smile is the only answer to be indulged in. Ask any man whether yes or no mean the same thing, great or little. Really, softness can entertain as dangerous an opinion as rigorism, and to direct us among the breakers and quicksand bottoms, we need, alas, nothing short of an infallible guide.

L. Gergaud
Catholic Priest
February 16, 1872

Wall painting in St. Laurentius Church in Voorschoten (Netherlands) to commemorate the dogmatic constitution *Pastor Aeternus* (papal infallibility). Painted in 1870, this artwork was rediscovered in 1996 and restored as much as possible. Depicted from left to right: flock of sheep (symbol of the Church), St. Thomas Aquinas holding the Summa Theologica; Christ (with St. Peter); Pope Pius IX. Artist is unknown. *Public domain, licensed under Creative Commons Attribution International.*

Editors' Note: The dogma of Papal Infallibility was decreed at the First Vatican Council of 1870, as expressed in a Dogmatic Constitution of that Council, *Pastor Aeternus*. The idea that there is an infallible (unfailing) teaching authority in the Pope as the successor of St. Peter is an ancient one, based in Sacred Scripture and in Sacred Tradition of the Roman Catholic Church. Father Gergaud's rigorous defense of this dogma appears to have been primarily in response to Protestant criticism, as it is framed in theology and apologetics. This is perhaps the reason his lecture was publicly announced and open to the general public.

LAST WILL AND TESTAMENT

Father Gergaud's *Last Will and Testament*[26] poignantly makes reference to the "square of ground" he purchased on the date of this document, to be used for a Roman Catholic graveyard. It was to this same "square of ground" that his mortal remains were returned in February 1874, what is today the St. Matthew's Cemetery in Monroe.

April 22, 1871
State of Louisiana
Parish of Ouachita
Town of Monroe

I, the undersigned priest of the Holy Roman Catholic Church, and pastor of St. Matthew's Church, Monroe, Louisiana, after recommending my soul to God, do make this my last will and testament, written with my own hand, dated April the twenty-second, one thousand eight hundred and seventy one, and signed by me.

1st—I bequeath to the Right Reverend A.M. Martin, Roman Catholic bishop of Natchitoches or to his successor in office, for the use of the Roman Catholic Church, all my real estate and property, consisting of lot No. seven in square No. five in the town of Monroe, Louisiana, with the buildings and improvements therein, it being the property now occupied by St. Hyacinth's Academy.

Of a square of ground three hundred and seventy five feet by two hundred and sixty five, bought by me from H. Filhiol for the sum of one thousand dollars as per deed of April 22, 1871 to be used for a /R/Catholic graveyard.

Of a plot of ground in the town of Bastrop, Morehouse Parish, Louisiana, bought by me for the use of the Catholic Roman Church, from J.J. Schardt.

2nd—I bequeath all my personal effects and property, furniture, moneys, and so forth, to the same Right Reverend A.M. Martin, Roman Catholic Bishop of Natchitoches, or his successor in office for the benefit of the Roman Catholic Church in Monroe, La., except what may be otherwise disposed of…

7.
Julia
Fields.

On the 22ᵈ day of June 1873 I have baptized Julia aged 3½ years, daughter of Harvey Fields & Rose Williams. Sp. Thomas
Books room

L. Gergaud Mᵉ

8.
Washington
Joseph
Guiffot.

On the 6ᵗʰ of July 1873 I have baptized Washington Joseph son of Emma & Joseph Guiffot. Spons: Fannie Wilson.

Spr M.C. Ouéllard

9.
Lula Reid

On the 4ᵗʰ day of July 1873 I have given private Baptism to Lula Reid, daughter of Georgia Reid aged about 4 weeks. —

L. Gergaud Mᵉ

10.
Julia
Farmer.

On the 9ᵗʰ day of July 1873 I have given private Baptism to Julia, aged about 4 years, daughter of Thomas Farmer & Maria, r.

L. Gergaud Mᵉ

1874.

1.
Henry.

On the 11ᵗʰ day of August 1874, I have baptized conditionally Henry aged about 70 years

L. Enautz

2.
Joseph
Enoch
Hopkins

On the 12ᵗʰ day of August 1874 I have baptized Joseph Enoch born on the 14ᵗʰ day of October 1873 of Hiram Hopkins & Sophie Steward. Sp. Mʳ & E. Jack

Last sacramental registry entry for Father Gergaud, July 9, 1873, the baptism of a four-year-old girl, Julia Farmer. *Archives of St. Matthew's Church, Monroe, Louisiana.*

The last marriage recorded by Father Gergaud, November 26, 1872, Joseph Roth to Wilhelmina Worth. *Archives of St. Matthew's Church, Monroe, Louisiana.*

In consideration of the foregoing legacies and bequests, I charge the Right Reverend A.M. Martin, Roman Catholic Bishop of Natchitoches, or his successor in office.

1st— To send to the Superior of the Theological Seminary of Nantes, where I was ordained, the sum of one hundred dollars to be used by him as he thinks proper for the benefit of said institution.

2nd—To send to the pastor of the parish church in Heric, Loire Valley, France, where I was born and baptized, the sum of one hundred dollars to defray the expenses of funeral services, for me, parents and relatives deceased, to be celebrated in the church of said parish.

3rd—To have Mass celebrated in his cathedral fifty times and in St. Matthew's Church of Monroe, La. fifty times for the repose of my soul, said Masses to be announced from the pulpit.

Done at Monroe, parish of Ouachita, state of Louisiana, this twenty-second day of April, A.D. one thousand, eight hundred and seventy one, and signed with my own hand.

Louis Gergaud
Roman Catholic Priest

Editors' note: This *Last Will and Testament* represents the final surviving document, currently known to exist, written in Father Gergaud's own hand.

Shreveport 1873 and Beyond

Father Louis Gergaud Remembered

F ather Louis Gergaud responded to the plea from his friend Father Jean Marie Biler to come to his aid in Shreveport as the yellow fever epidemic raged. From the time of his arrival in that city, Father Gergaud worked tirelessly in the service of others. Father Gergaud went to find Father Biler and the sisters healthy enough that he took on other relief duties. He found the deathbeds of two former lay assistants of Father Pierre's parish and provided them with their Last Rites.[27] Father Gergaud's presence dispelled any fear that they would die without the sacraments. Certainly, they invoked the day's (September 23) martyred saints, especially St. Eustace, one of the Fourteen Holy Helpers frequently invoked in medieval plagues.

The confrere who summoned him to Shreveport, Father Jean Marie Biler, initially seemed to be improving upon Gergaud's arrival, but such was the deceptive pattern of yellow fever.[28] Father Gergaud next turned to care for strangers. High on the list of victims were most certainly the volunteers themselves. He probably visited Otto Schnurr, the dry goods store clerk who worked with Father Jean Pierre and the first Howard volunteers in Fever Ward 1 of the city. Otto died the next day, having just reached his eighteenth birthday.[29]

In Shreveport that September, rain was a familiar constant companion, as unceasing as the grip of death around Father Gergaud. He splashed through the muck in his cassock, ministering to the sick and the grieving, and soon saw a member of his own home parish among the victims. James Muse Dabbs, residing at the Southern Hotel, on the south side of Milam Street between Market and Spring Streets, and now under the care of Dr. J.L.

Brooks, worked in the stage office at the time of the outbreak and was now trapped by the Shreveport quarantine.[30]

Dabb's parents, Dr. Christopher Hunt Dabbs and Julia Washington Bourgeat Muse Dabbs, were among the closest friends Father Gergaud had in Monroe, sharing a close hospitality building St. Matthew's Church. They, like so many others, were moved by his generous heart, energetic nature, cultivated spirit and prudent, reserved manner.[31] Julia had taught in the Catholic school that Gergaud founded in Monroe, St. Hyacinth's. Father Gergaud baptized their two grandchildren, one of whom died hours after birth. Now, Father Gergaud visited with their son James, sharing the hope of Christ and as much time as he could at his bedside.[32]

With the course of his earthly life nearing its end, Father Gergaud most certainly offered Mass on the anniversary of his priestly ordination on September 23. He surveyed the face of the fever's latest victim, Sister Mary Angela, and was able to administer the final sacraments in time. She died at St. Mary's at four o'clock in the afternoon on Tuesday, September 23, having answered the call from Father Pierre and her final calling in service to God. Father Gergaud paused in his relief efforts to accompany her mortal remains, with the customary psalms on his lips, back to St. Vincent's that evening.[33]

Sister Mary Angela was laid to rest in the convent cemetery, spared from the mass grave of the city. Sister Mary Angela (née Marie Angèle Le Nédélec, circa 1835) came to Louisiana just four years prior and had only taken her final vows in August 1871, with Bishop Martin of Natchitoches presiding. Mother Superior assigned her to St. Mary's Day School in Shreveport for but a few months and later transferred her to Monroe. She then volunteered to come to Shreveport. Her course was typical, as she first exhibited signs of yellow fever on September 19 and died four days later.[34]

Father Gergaud, "a torch spreading light and heat around him,"[35] buried Sister Mary Angela himself, commending her soul to the Almighty at ten o'clock in the morning on Wednesday, September 24, a day in honor of Our Lady of Mercy. He then moved on to his next work of mercy, visiting the mourning sisters and Father Biler, who was in the "calm stage" and hopeful of recovery. His condition had worsened since the day before, when he was able to sit up, write a few letters and "relish" the chicken prepared for him. When Mother Hyacinth checked on him at five o'clock in the morning, she found him with high fever and restlessness and sent for a doctor right away.[36] On the same Wednesday afternoon, September 24, both Fathers Biler and Gergaud took dramatic turns.

Father Gergaud suddenly collapsed about five o'clock that evening while caring for others, and at least two physicians tended to him. By then, the two priests were miles apart, and without the ability to offer each other last sacraments. Father Biler passed through his "calm stage" and resigned himself to death. They could only await the arrival of the next priest to step into the breach. Father Gergaud could no longer continue; his body was already spent. He relinquished his earthly struggle around half past three in the morning on Wednesday, October 1.[37]

The letter Bishop Martin hastily wrote the day before was too late. Having learned of Father Gergaud's decision to go to Shreveport, he urgently penned the following:[38]

Natchitoches
September 30, 1873

Father Gergaud, V.F.

On Sunday 28, dear friend, I wrote you by two friends…sent a letter to you by them.…I am afraid my letter never reached you.

Father Biler gave up his life. I have sacrificed dear Father Le Vezouet. That is enough, my God! That is enough!

I renew my recommendation. It is most important. It is that no priest be in Shreveport after sundown, and that he not enter there before breakfast time except if it be necessary, on Sunday, to say only one Low Mass.

He should visit only the sick people who are Catholics and there is one exception: he may visit Protestants or infidels who ask for a priest.

I have appointed Father Enaut to Shreveport, but only for after the cessation of the epidemic in the middle of November. The plague leaves with the cold weather (yellow fever).

I would like to send Fr. Quelard to Bastrop if you think this be proper in which case I would give you Father Simon who as for assistantship in exchange for his position as a pastor in Bayou Choupique.

Give me some advice on the subject. I wrote to you in Monroe; perhaps you did not receive my letter. The yellow fever has been in Campti and I the

*neighboring area now for several days. There have already been 12 deaths.
I have had no news from my confrere. Here the quarantine is rigid. Father
Le Vezouet was in Shreveport providentially, where he was to have spent
only a brief time.*

*Adieu, dear son. May the Lord keep you always.
Custodiat te Dominus semper!*

Auguste Martin, Bishop

Father Gergaud would not read this last imperative from his bishop. By
the time the letter reached Shreveport, this *homo dei* had already sacrificed
his life to charity. Shreveporters buried the beloved Monroe pastor near
the young Father Isidore Quémerais, the first of the five priests to die, on
September 15, in the City Cemetery.

On October 3, 1873, the *Ouachita Telegraph* published an obituary, reprinted
here in its entirety:

Death of Rev. Father Gergaud
A few days ago [on the eighteenth], *Father Gergaud left Monroe, in
vigorous health and at the meridian of his life, to minister to and aid the
suffering people of Shreveport. The mission was one of extreme hazard and
certain danger, but was undertaken, and voluntarily, by Father Gergaud,
in pursuance to solemn convictions and an earnest desire to be of service
to the afflicted. Four days after Father Gergaud reached the scene of his
self-imposed and arduous labors, he was seized with the fever which has so
terribly scourged the people of Shreveport. Dr. Chopin, of New Orleans,
gave the Reverend Father the benefit of his great skill and learning, and it
was hoped he would recover. But the malady steadily increased, and at 4
o'clock Wednesday morning the faithful priest and servant of God passed
to the Better Land, of whose beauties, joys and holy peace he had so often
fervently proclaimed.*

*Louis Gergaud was a native of Brittany, France, where he was born in
the village of Heric, on the 22nd of March 1832. He was educated for the
ministry at the celebrated seminary of Nantes, under the direction of the
priests of St. Sulpice, and was ordained priest 23rd September 1854, at the
age of 22 years. He followed the Right Rev. Bishop Martin to this state
in 1854, sent to Monroe in 1856. He was yet unable to speak English,
found here a very small congregation, of which there was only one male*

communicant, and was isolated from his fellow priests. He set vigorously to work, and as the result of his zeal and labor, St. Matthew's now has 150 members, with a convent, boys' school, and in connection with the church is a benevolent society of Young Friends with a library and building. Father Gergaud extended his efforts to other parishes, and was largely instrumental in setting up churches of the Roman Catholic faith at Bastrop, Delhi, and Lake Providence.

The entire community has heard the sad tidings of the holy man's death with genuine sorrow. The loss of such a man not only is keenly felt and appreciated, but that he should have received, in his noble mission, the fatal shaft so soon—as if he passed over to Shreveport only to close his earthly journey—adds poignancy to the general sorrow and has called forth words and tears and sighs where perchance they had not been.

In a later letter he wrote to the Propagation of the Faith in Paris, and believed to be dated late November 1873, Bishop Martin properly remembered all five of the martyr priests, including Father Gergaud, and in the interest of providing complete context, it is included in its entirety here:

Gentlemen:

You may have learned from the Paris newspapers that a pestilential fever, with a deadliness heretofore unknown in Louisiana, broke out about the end of August in Shreveport, a commercial city of ten thousand, in the extreme northwest of my diocese. There it caused and continues to cause dreadful ravages, the extent of which we will not know until later. That which the newspapers could not tell you, gentlemen, is of the irreparable losses to my diocese and my pain as bishop, in seeing fall, in the space of three weeks, five of my priests and among them, the three most eminent members of my clergy. In a rare assemblage of priestly virtues, of science and of talents, three had joined the Mission in 1854 and had reached maturity while producing an apostolic career filled with work and rich in the fruits of life which will live after them.

The first victim chosen by God was Mr. Isidore Quémerais, age 26, from the Diocese of Rennes, vicar in Shreveport. Mr. Father Quémerais was one of the seven young Bretons who followed me to Louisiana on my return from the Vatican Council. The piety, the gentleness, the unselfish dedication of this young priest, his filial affection for his bishop and the ease with which he mastered the difficulties of the English language permitted me to place great hope in him for the future. This was a flower; the angels gathered him for heaven. After two years of his ministry and while practicing the charity that immolates, he died on September 15th.

The next day marked the death of one of the most saintly priests that I have known in my long career: Mr. Father Pierre, founder of the missions in Bayou Pierre, Minden and Shreveport, whom you will learn more about from the account of his life and work, published in the Catholic Propagator, which I have the honor of sending you. Long since, his excellent reputation had reached past the limits of my humble diocese and to keep such a treasure, it was necessary, more than once, to defend him against the truly justified esteem of several of my venerable colleagues, who saw in him a worthy candidate for the episcopate. The good Lord had given us this treasure; he has taken him away: may his Holy Name be blessed.

On the 26th Mr. Father Biler died. He was chaplain of the novitiate and boarding school of the Daughters of the Cross at Fairfield. This excellent priest, 33 years old, from Diocese of Saint-Brieuc et Tréguier, had been in our mission only two and a half years. He had given up everything in Brittany, through the entreaties of Rev. Mother Le Conniat, his relative, to dedicate himself to this establishment to which it was impossible for me to provide a priest. At the first news of the illness of his confreres, he went to them, appointed himself their guardian, assisted them in their last moments and blessed their tombs. Left alone at the height of the plague, he called upon the charity of Messrs. Father Gergaud and Father Le Vézouët. The first arrived only a few days later to see him fall in his turn and to provide him with the consolations which he had given to the others at the expense of his own precious life.

Mr. Father Gergaud, from the Diocese of Nantes, ordained a priest for the diocese of Natchitoches in 1854, founder and pastor of the mission of Monroe for eighteen years, Vicar Forane, appointed by the bishop, for all of the districts situated between the Mississippi and the Red River valley, was a true "Homo Dei." Endowed with a very energetic nature, an elevated and cultivated spirit, patient and ardent zeal, a tender and generous heart protected by a prudent and reserved manner, Mr. Father Gergaud was a torch spreading light and heat around him. In a place where never before had a priest resided, where I had nothing to offer him but the unfinished skeleton of a chapel and a few diffident Christians, and where I doubted that he could live, Mr. Father Gergaud founded and leaves behind him a flourishing mission: church, presbytery, convent, Catholic school for boys, a large cemetery for the exclusive use of the faithful—he created it all;

and in a period of eighteen years, his expenses for the honor of the religion exceeded two hundred thousand francs, of which I had allocated him barely ten thousand from the society. It is because his faith, while giving him the courage for any undertaking, also gave him the power to open the hearts and instill some of the generosity of his own soul. Through his outstanding talents, his priestly virtues and his work, Mr. Father Gergaud was a veritable power in Monroe: and because of his incontestable superiority, he was the leader of the diocesan clergy. At the time of the last Provincial Council, to which he accompanied me as a theologian, I nominated him to my venerable colleagues and he was readily accepted as my successor to the see of Natchitoches. Such a great consolation was to be denied me.

Upon receiving Mr. Father Biler's letter calling him to his aid, Mr. Father Gergaud left without a moment's hesitation. His only directive to his assistant, Mr. Quelard, was: "Write to Monseigneur at once; tell him that I am going to my death, that it is my duty and that I am leaving." He lived only ten days in Shreveport. Welcomed by all as a Godsent angel, he over-extended himself during one week to satisfy all the needs; he exerted himself beyond measure. There were more than one thousand sick people, of that number, perhaps fewer than twenty-five were Catholic but, in the presence of death, it was the priest that everyone called for; and God alone knows how many souls owe their salvation to the heroism of the Catholic priest. Meanwhile, Mr. Father Biler was stricken; he died on the 27th, assisted by Mr. Father Gergaud. The following day Mr. Father Gergaud was also mortally stricken and he died on October 1st, consoled and purified by the ministrations of one of his holiest and best-loved confreres, Mr. Father Le Vézouët, who, like the others, was a victim destined for death.

Mr. Father Le Vézouët, from a very Christian family of wealthy farmers of the Diocese of Saint-Brieuc et Tréguier, was endowed with a wide-ranging intelligence and a keen imagination. He had completed a brilliant course of classical and scientific studies and passed, with distinction, the examinations then required by the university for almost all of the liberal arts. Among all the careers open to him, he chose the serious and dedicated life of the priesthood and had completed his theological studies when, in 1854, he asked to follow me. After eighteen months of strengthening himself in his studies and in learning English, which he mastered easily, his talent for drawing young people to himself and his remarkable aptitude for teaching made me decide to entrust to him very particularly, the religious instruction and spiritual direction of St. Joseph College which I was establishing at Natchitoches in 1856 and in which, at the same time, he was teaching *several classes. Shortly after, the president having retired, he succeeded him and with great zeal and success he directed, until 1862, the establishment which in that disastrous time, was completely devastated and ruined by the successive invasions of two belligerent armies. Hardly had he been relieved of the direction and his teaching at the college, when I entrusted him with the evangelization of the poor and degraded Mexicans, spread out between the Red River and the Sabine, whose language he spoke with ease. Although he usually resided in Natchitoches, where his presence had become indispensable to me, he regularly fulfilled this difficult Mission with the dedicated zeal that he brought to everything that he undertook; he did this as an apostle for nine years, instructing the people, validating marriages, building and furnishing churches and by the Divine Word and the grace of the sacraments, he elevated these unrefined people to the dignity of Christians. Finally, as his crowning achievement in this work, in 1871 he founded a permanent mission in Many, at the very center of this population. There he constructed a church with its presbytery, its cemetery, the lands necessary for the residence of a priest and he even installed, in the same year, a young confrere, successor of his zeal. Here Mr. Father Le Vézouët was one of the three members of the episcopal council, diocesan director and zealous promoter of the works of the Propagation of the Faith and the Holy Childhood, chaplain of the convent of the Sisters of Mercy and director of a day school which he founded for boys; responsible, moreover, for several small missions at a short distance from Natchitoches, for preaching in English at the Cathedral and for a large number of penitents. But, above all, Mr. Father Le Vézouët was the friend, the consoler, the priest of the children, of the afflicted, and of the poor. Whatever time these rigid demands left to him, he used for them, he spent with them; going from cabin to cabin, bringing encouragement, consolation and alms to all.*

On September 19th, Mr. Father Le Vézouët returned to Natchitoches after an eight day mission on the left bank of the Red River. After having told him of Mr. Father Biler's request to me that he be sent immediately to Shreveport, I asked him, "What would you like to do, my son?" He replied, "Monseigneur, if you tell me to leave, I leave; if you leave it up to me, I stay." He realized that I was searching his eyes for the real meaning of his response, and he added: "I want to go so much that if you left the decision up to me, I would believe that in going, I was acting according to my own will and I do not want to do anything but the will of God." "If it is so," I replied to him, "go." He spent one more day to put his affairs in order and to visit several families for the last time. The news of his imminent departure spread quickly and to those who said, "You are going to your death." He replied: "I believe it, but I know that I am taking the surest and the shortest path to heaven." Because other means of transportation were lacking, Mr. Father Le Vézouët had to undertake the 110 mile journey to Shreveport on horseback. He arrived there to find Mr. Father Gergaud mortally ill and gave him the assistance and consolations of the Holy Church. Shortly after, he began to sink under the inexorable attacks of the plague. He had foreseen this and had telegraphed the Archbishop of New Orleans, requesting two priests. A Jesuit father and an assistant from the cathedral left on October 3rd; they arrived soon enough to console him in his last moments and to open heaven to him. He died on the 8th, having completed his fortieth year in the eighteenth year of his priesthood.

Gentlemen, I have often spoken to you of the growing prosperity of my mission and its hopes for the future. Today I have told you of the losses and the sorrows. The hand of God has struck me and with these priests, pride of the priesthood, the crown of my old age has fallen. Inscrutable, truly, are the ways of the Lord. I adore them and I accept them with my whole soul, and I can only say: Happy is the diocese that could lose such men, happy is the earth watered by their sweat and sanctified by their death. Martyrs to charity or martyrs to persecution, in their venerated tombs will grow the deepest roots of the Holy Church of the One whose death was our life.

Pray, gentlemen, that before my own death, I may find worthy successors to the ministry and the admirable virtues of these saintly priests.
Aug. Marie, Bishop of Natchitoches

The bishop was not the only one to eloquently mourn the loss of Father Louis Gergaud. The heroic priest who had endured harassment from hostile non-Catholics in Monroe was never to know of an unsolicited remembrance published by a local Methodist pastor in the Monroe newspaper. It too illustrates the deep admiration for the French priest:

He left Monroe, where he was in perfect safety, against the remonstrances of his friends, to go to Shreveport on a mission of mercy....He knew his danger, but he knew his duty....He fell in the battle—he fell as a noble man and Christian hero....We can but love and admire a great man who adorns the Gospel as much as this man, and we sincerely hope, if we ever reach the Better Land, to find and know him there.[39]

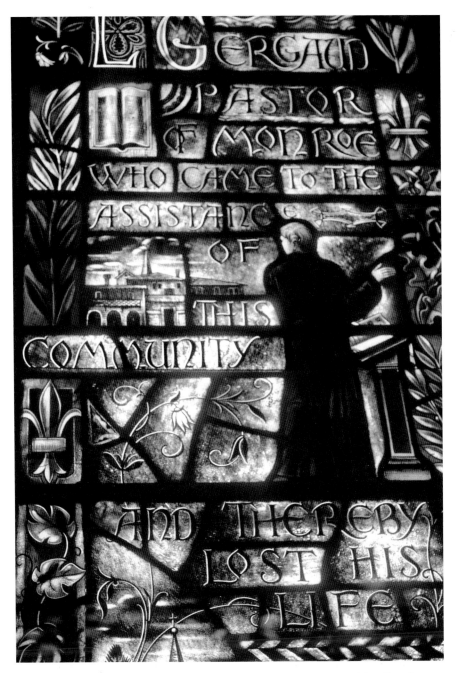

Father Louis Gergaud. Commemorative stained-glass window at Holy Trinity Church, Shreveport, Louisiana. *Authors' collection.*

SHREVEPORT, November 30, 1373.

At a meeting of the Catholics of Shreveport, held this day, John J. Horan was requested to act as President and William Kinney as Secretary.

The President, in a feeling manner, stated the object of the meeting, and the following gentlemen were appointed to draft suitable resolutions expressive of the feelings of this meeting: Messrs. T. A. Flanagan, as chairman, F. N. Sanchez, Joe. L. Moore, Wm. Hardrick and M. A. Walsh, who reported the following which were unanimously adopted:

RESOLUTIONS:

Whereas, It has pleased Almighty God to visit upon us during the past two months or more, an epidemic of Yellow Fever, more virulent in its type, more malignant in its attack and more fatal in its effect than any perhaps ever before known or met with on this or any other continent, bearing, as it did, death and desolation, sorrow and distress, to the homes and hearts of almost every household here; and,

Whereas, It pleased the same Omnipotence to remove from us, even in the midst of his ministering to the sick and dying about him, our late beloved and esteemed pastor, Rev. Jean Pierre, who, fatigued, heart-sore and worn with waiting and watching, himself fell an easy prey, succumbing to the fatal fever on the 16th of November, A. D. 1873. And,

Whereas, The same omniscient and inscrutable God saw fit to take also, forever from his vineyard, and in quick succession, the co-laborers of our late lamented pastor, to-wit: Rev. F. J. Quemerais, assistant pastor, who died on the 15th of September ult.; Rev. J M. J. Biller, chaplain of St. Vincent's Academy who died on the 26th of September, ult.; Rev. Louis Gergaud, parish priest of Monroe, and Vicar Foreign, of our diocese, who died on the 30th of September, ult., and Rev. Father Le Vezuet, Episcopal Secretary of our Diocese, the two latter of whom came amongst us facing pestilence and death to fill the places of the faithful fallen before them and minister to the wants of a stricken flock:

Left: Grave of Father Louis Gergaud, St. Matthew's Cemetery, Monroe, Louisiana. *Authors' collection.*

Right: Newspaper announcement of the "Meeting of the Catholics of Shreveport," as an attempt to retain Father Gergaud's body in Shreveport following his death. The Catholics of Monroe passed a competing resolution and eventually claimed Gergaud's earthly remains in February 1874.

The aftermath of Father Gergaud's death moved many to extraordinary memorials. The *Shreveport Times* reported that the District Court of Monroe, Louisiana, closed "out of respect to the memory of Father Louis Gergaud, the Catholic priest of Monroe, who lately died here of yellow fever, a volunteer nurse to the sick and dying of our stricken town."[40]

The body of Father Gergaud was later reinterred in St. Matthew's Cemetery, which he founded in Monroe. The wording on his gravestone was chosen with precision, to ensure that all who saw it would know that "he fell a martyr of his charity during the epidemic of Shreveport."[41]

The removal of Father Gergaud's body from the City Cemetery in Shreveport caused some disagreement among Catholics of northwestern and northeastern Louisiana, in a preserved record that is indicative of the devotion to him shortly after his death. Because of the significance of the record in demonstrating the early cult of devotion, not only for him but also for the other four priests who martyred themselves to charity, that public record is reprinted here in its entirety:[42]

Meeting of the Catholics of Shreveport
Shreveport, Nov. 30, 1873

At a meeting of the Catholics of Shreveport, held this day, John J. Horan was requested to act as President and William Kinney as Secretary.

The President, in a feeling manner, stated the object of the meeting, and the following gentlemen were appointed to draft suitable resolutions expressive of the feelings of this meeting: Messrs. T.A. Flanagan, as chairman, F.N. Sanchez, Joe L. Moore, Wm. Handrick and M.A. Walsh, who reported the following, which were unanimously adopted:

Resolutions:

Whereas, it has pleased Almighty God to visit upon us during the past two months or more, an epidemic of Yellow Fever, more virulent in its type, more malignant in its attack, and more fatal in its effect than any perhaps ever before known or met with on this or any other continent, bearing, as it did, death and desolation, sorrow and distress to the homes and hearts of almost every household here; and,

Whereas, it pleased the same Omnipotence to remove from us, even in the midst of his ministering to the sick and dying about him, our late loved and esteemed pastor, Rev. Jean Pierre, who fatigued, heart sore and worn with waiting and watching, himself fell an easy prey, succumbing to the fatal fever on the 16th of [September] A.D. [1873], and

Whereas, the same omniscient and inscrutable God saw fit to take also, forever from his vineyard, and in quick succession, the co-laborers of our late lamented pastor, to-wit: Rev. Quemerais, assistant pastor, who died on the 15th of September, Rev. Biller [sic], chaplain of St. Vincent's Academy, who died on the 26th of September, Rev. Louis Gergaud, parish priest of Monroe and Vicar Forane of our Diocese, who died on the 30th of September [October 1], and Rev. Levizouet [sic], Episcopal Secretary of our Diocese, the two latter of whom came amongst us, facing pestilence and death to fill the places of the faithful fallen before them, and minister to the wants of a stricken flock.

BE IT RESOLVED by us, the Catholics of Shreveport, Louisiana,

That, recognizing the Divine Author of our beings the source of our afflictions and knowing that He who "doeth all things well" does naught in vain, we bow in meek and humble submission to the almighty hand of him who smites us.

That, in the death of our late lamented and esteemed pastor, Rev. Jean Pierre, North Louisiana has lost a pioneer missionary; the Catholic Church has lost a zealous, true and unswerving standard bearer; Shreveport has lost one of her best, earliest, and most earnest citizens; society has lost a most exemplary member; the poor have lost their open-handed, best and warmest friend; and we, his congregation, have lost a kind adviser, an indulgent and forgiving father.

That, as our late pastor, Rev. Jean Pierre, was the founder of the Catholic Church in, and the first parish priest of Shreveport, it behooves us to pay a more durable tribute to his works and his memory than these mere verbal expressions of our esteem and sorrow, and therefore that, at as early a date as possible, we organize ourselves into a Memorial Monument Association, whose object it will be the erecting of a suitable marble monument as a worth memorial both to our late pastor and to the other devoted Fathers, who fell as martyrs, ministering to our wants.

Resolved further, that we deeply and heartily console with the distant families and friends of these deceased Fathers in this, their great sorrow, and we assure them, knowing that their hearts of faith will be consoled in the knowledge that the lives of the deceased have been such that their good works, living after them, tell of the rewards that awaited them; and these good works living on, will still add jewels to their crown.

Be it Resolved further, that appreciating the severe and almost irreparable loss to the diocese in the death of these five zealous and devoted priests, and the poignant grief to his own paternal heart, in his now declining years, is the loss at once of these his devoted sons in the Faith, we must sincerely sympathize with our esteemed Rt. Rev. Bishop Martin, and venture to console him with the hope that He who sent and has taken them away, will send other and as able workers to the Vineyard.

Resolved further, that, whereas the Catholics of Ouachita Parish resolved at their meeting held in Monroe, on the 5th of October, ultimo, to remove to Monroe the remains of their late pastor, Rev. Louis Gergaud; and whereas, we feel that we also have a claim to his ashes, as it was in our cause, and amongst us, and for us, that he died, and we wish his name and memory to fully share whatever honors and tribute we may pay to those, the other lamented Fathers who died as he did; that the Chairman of this meeting appoint a committee of three to communicate with both our Rt. Rev. Bishop and with the Catholics of Ouachita Parish, through the Chairman of their meeting…enclosing them a copy of these resolutions, and requesting them to permit the remains of Rev. Father Gergaud to rest here by the side of those who fell with him in the same holy cause and labor, in order that the same monument may equally honor, and the shadow the same cross equally hallow them all; and that the Catholics of Ouachita Parish, in particular, and those of the State of Louisiana in general, be urgently invited to unite with us in heart, effort, and purse in erecting a suitable and worthy monument to the honor and memory of the above mentioned deceased Fathers.

Be it resolved further, that the printed copies of these resolutions be forwarded by the Secretary of this meeting to the Rt. Rev. Bishop, with the respectful request that he have them sent without delay to the families of the above deceased Fathers, we not knowing their whereabouts.

Resolved further, that the Shreveport papers and the Morning Star *and* Propagateur *of New Orleans, and the* Western Watchman, *St. Louis, be requested to publish these resolutions.*

Resolved, that the thanks of the Catholic congregation be tendered to the Howard Association for their uniform kindness shown to us on all occasions during our late disastrous epidemic.

On motion, Messrs. Handrick, Walsh, Kelly, Moore, Flanagan, Horan, and Rev. Father Duffo as Chairman, were appointed a committee to devise the best means to establish in our city an Orphan Asylum. The meeting then adjourned.

John J. Horan, President
William Kinney, Secretary

Father Gergaud's remains were indeed removed from Shreveport in late January 1874, by resolution of the Catholics of Ouachita Parish, as recorded:[43]

Rev. Louis Gergaud

On the 1ˢᵗ day of October 1873, the soul of this Reverend Priest took its flight for that unknown sphere for which he had so rigidly prepared it. Duty called him to Shreveport when the epidemic was at its worst; death met him at the gates, and the Christian soldier, in the vigor of his manhood and in the height of his usefulness, laid down his armor forever. To the five brother martyrs in that fearful plague—for courage, faith, and devotion—the great heart of the American people must ever rise in admiration.

The congregation Father Gergaud had clustered around him in his ministry of this division of the Diocese, inspired by love of the shepherd and the heroism of the man and brother, claimed his remains for interment in the cemetery of his creation and his gift. On Tuesday, the 27ᵗʰ of January, they were disinterred from the Shreveport cemetery, and "Requiem Mass" was celebrated by Father Martin, Chancellor of this Diocese, delegate of his Grace the Right Reverend Bishop Martin, assisted by Father Enaut. Wednesday they were followed by a large concourse to the steamer Texas, and on Monday the 2ⁿᵈ, they arrived here by the cars from Delta.

The body remained in the church Tuesday. Wednesday, after solemn and impressive ceremonies at the church, in the presence of the largest gathering have ever witnessed on such an occasion, they were carried to their last resting place in the following order:

Grand Marshal, on horseback, opening the procession.
Monroe Silver Cornet Band.
Monroe Fire Department.
Members of the Bar.
School girls with their banners and young ladies dress in white.
Sisters of the Convent.
Ladies of the Altar Society with their badge.
School boys with their banner; young men and citizens, and members of the Memorial Association.
Young Catholic Friends' Society with their badge.

In the middle of the ranks of the Y.C.F., the clergy, preceded by the choir boys who serve at the altar.
The Hearse—horses led by two members of the Y.C.F.S.
Carriages.

At the grave, Judge Ray eulogized the deceased.
"Earth to earth," and the good Priest was at rest in the place of his choice. Father Gergaud's thorough education, coupled with executive ability, engaging manners and dignified presence, would have made him a man of mark in any vocation. His devotion and the unobtrusiveness of his faith upon others brought, as in evangelical alliance round his tomb, mourners of every sect and worshippers of every creed, in heartfelt supplication that for the good deeds done in the body, he may enjoy in perpetual youth the beauties of his hope and the felicities of his teachings.
Priest, brother, friend, farewell—rest in peace!

The written primary source record regarding the life and legacy of Father Gergaud concludes with references in letters from one of his successors at St. Matthew's in Monroe. Father Ludovic "Louis" Enaut, who of course knew Father Gergaud well and was the one to accompany Gergaud's remains when they were removed to Monroe in February 1874. Enaut was also a native of Brittany, France; studied at the seminary in Rennes; and came to Louisiana at the behest of Bishop Martin in 1868. He served as Father Gergaud's assistant until 1871, when Bishop Martin moved him to Bastrop, Louisiana, where he supervised the construction of St. Joseph's Church in that community.[44] On Father Gergaud's death in October 1873, Bishop Martin appointed Father Enaut as pastor at St. Matthew's in Monroe. As both personal friend and immediate successor to Gergaud, Father Enaut is an important eyewitness to history.

Father Enaut wrote of the exemplary mission work Gergaud began and its remarkable growth under his leadership, to which Enaut was of course the immediate beneficiary. Enaut witnessed Father Gergaud's dream of more land and a larger church coming to fruition in the time immediately following Gergaud's death of yellow fever in Shreveport, as recorded in a partial letter surviving from December 1873.[45]

In a second letter of 1880 to Bishop Francis X. LeRay of the Diocese of Natchitoches (Martin's successor), Father Enaut recounted the death of Gergaud's assistant pastor, Father Joseph Quelard. It was Father Quelard who heard and reported Father Gergaud's final words as he boarded the

Left: Father Ludovic Enaut, successor to Father Gergaud as pastor at St. Matthew's in Monroe. *Archives of St. Matthew's Church, Monroe, Louisiana.*

Below: The present St. Matthew's Church in Monroe, Louisiana. *Authors' collection.*

stagecoach in Monroe to go to Shreveport: "Write to the bishop and tell him I go to my death. It is my duty and I must go." In the letter excerpt printed here, Father Enaut made a poignant eyewitness observation to Bishop LeRay regarding Quelard's deathbed moments.[46]

Letter from Father Ludovic Enaut to Bishop Auguste Martin
5 December 1873
From Monroe, Louisiana

Bishop:

In Monroe, my predecessor accomplished much, but according to him there is still much to be done; I shall die content if I can acquire a larger lot and more suitable quarters for the church. Later there will be, in the very distant future, a larger and more substantial church. But where to build it?

Father Gergaud came to see me in Bastrop and he pretended to envy my lot. He said, "at least, Enaut, you have four good acres. Oh, if I had that in Monroe! If I had that instead of thirty-six little corners of land, thirty-six small pieces which I had to buy piece by piece and pay for with the eyes out my head! I could have built, but no…and the Sisters, that is my greatest embarrassment. Their house is too small. They have no place for the children to have recreation!"

So, at that time before his death, Father Gergaud and myself went through the different quarters of the city of Monroe, looking for a convenient and suitable location to establish our Catholic institutions and our church. But the circumstances were not favorable. There was not a single chance of buying without paying a fools' price.

A little while before his death, we were together looking at that wonderful cemetery which he laid out (a cemetery which cost him a great sacrifice, that of not seeing his mother again—a poor mother who was only asking to kiss him once more). Father Gergaud showed me two squares of 300 square feet. Both were empty and near each other. "This," he pointed out, "is what you need, but Filhiol, the proprietor, does not want to hear of selling or giving." "Don't despair," said I, "Filhiol is a man of faith, a good Christian, and will understand some day how necessary it is to be accommodating."

Bishop, today Filhiol remembers the words of Father Gergaud during one of their last conversations. "Remember, you cannot take this land to heaven with you, and to sell it to the church will never harm your children, but may lessen your purgatory." I knew all this because Father Gergaud kept no secrets from me, so the first thing that I did was to get after Filhiol. I talked, I prayed, and I succeeded.

"Filhiol," said I, "we must prepare for the future. The congregation is growing. The large number of young people coming up will soon be the adults of the next generation. They will be too confined in our little church. Besides, our church is becoming a fire hazard, or it may well fall upon us one day (as you know this wooden frame building is not well built and may not last long). Then, we will have to build another church. Shall we build a brick building on this niggardly piece of land? Truly, that would be pitiful. To avoid all this the things necessary, dear Filhiol, the permission of the bishop, the active cooperation of the pastor, and your own good will, dear friend."

Bishop, God blessed my designs. I like to believe that from heaven the former pastor of St. Matthew's played his part in this because Filhiol accepted my proposition, subject to your consent, Bishop, to your approval, with the following conditions:

For the greater glory of God, the honor of our Mother, the Church, for the expiation of our sins, and for the salvation of his soul, and in respect and memory of his dear friend, Father Louis Gergaud, Filhiol made a gift to the church of a lot measuring 300 feet. But...

In view of the fact the lot he donated is not the most desirable, and that the neighboring lots are exactly what we need, in view of the fact that the site for a church and rectory, a school for boys, a social hall, or assembly place for Catholic associations, etc. is too small, we must get the more desirable location with the understanding there will be on the other side a convent, a hospital, perhaps, and later, maybe an orphanage. All this would enter into future plans for building. So, another lot was precisely what we wished, and it would be most essential that we get the Sisters interested in owning their own convent. Filhiol consented to let me have both squares which Father Gergaud had chosen, one as a donation and the other for $5000.

Now, I propose this plan to you. Filhiol has signed it...lock, stock, and barrel. I shall have to give the title of one of the lots in your name, the title to the other in the name of the Sisters, the Daughters of the Cross, for the sum of $5000. I shall share the expense in paying for the convent. I should say, the parish will share the expense.

During five consecutive years I will pay $500. The Sisters will pay as much, the same amount. That will be $2,500 for each and five years from now, the church and the Catholic institutions will, without too much pain, be proprietors of a property which is worth $8000....I happen to know that Filhiol refused $4000 each for these lots.

As regards the parish, I know that I can save $500 each year. In that case, I do not have to mortgage any of the buildings occupied at present on parish property. If it should be necessary that you should come to the aid of Monroe or one of the missions, I have not the least doubt that in order to help so noble an enterprise, I know you would do this.

Let me have, if this need arise, the $75 or $80 which we collect each year for the Propagation of the Faith. (When this would be only a gesture of approbation and encouragement).

Now, for the Sisters, will good Mother Hyacinth understand the importance and necessity of the expenditure when she finds out that she must pay $500 per year to own the property in Monroe and be assured of having it always? The money trouble of today should not make her think that we can not have any more collections. In any case I do not have to ask for the $500 until January 1875.

After all, Bishop, it should be easy for the Sisters to pay this amount, then, every year, except last year when they were not able to collect their pensions from France, but today they can collect them. Every year, I know, that they take with them from Monroe, to Avoyelles and Shreveport, some money. I wish they would spend in Monroe the money they make there. They would never regret this. Their pastor would not be unmindful of this, and the people seeing the Sisters giving a helping hand to the good works of Monroe, the people, I say, would remember in six or eight years when the question of building for them will come up.

Build, Bishop! Do not let this word trouble you at this point. I am as patient as I am enthusiastic. I know it will take much time and money and it will give me and my successor much worry before we see the two lots with their buildings on them, but how shall we ever build if we do not possess the land? In five years, we can pay the amount and during that time, we will find out how to build.

If you accept my plan, Bishop, please write immediately to the Superior of the Daughters of the Cross so that they let me know if they too accept this contract with me having power of attorney to act their name and in the name of the Convent. Please send me, Bishop, yourself this power of attorney to act in your name also in order to buy. Then, I shall act at once to accomplish this work. The sooner the titles are cleared, the sooner we will save Filhiol the taxes on the land. When the time to build comes we will have to sell the land we occupy now.

***

Letter from Father Ludovic Enaut to Bishop Francis X. LeRay, Diocese of Natchitoches
14 October 1880
Monroe, Louisiana

Right Reverend Father, I remained with Father Quelard to the last. For a month, I had been going to and from Monroe to Vicksburg, but after the arrival of Father Mahe, I made it my duty to remain constantly by the bedside of our dear patient. It would take a volume to relate to you all the particularities of his sickness, of his agony, and of his death. Poor Father Quelard, if he had any imperfections to atone for, he paid for them bountifully for he suffered much and most patiently. His death was the death of a saint and all Vicksburg was edified. Last Saturday morning, I gave him viaticum, and after the communion, he asked me to read him the Gospel of the day—that day, he offered his suffering for the Diocese of Natchitoches, for every day I suggested to him an intention for the purpose of making his pain not only profitable for him, but meritorious for others. Saturday evening he appeared to be speechless, when about one o'clock Sunday morning he aroused our attention by reciting with a strong and powerful voice the Lord's Prayer. I stood by his bedside and was much astonished, then he said with a very distinct voice, "Oh my God, assist me in my last agony! I suffer for the love of thee, I offer thee my suffering for the good Doctor O'Leary, for my nurses, for my parents, and for all my fellow priests of the Diocese of Natchitoches,—where is my mother? I want her to kiss me goodbye." Taking me by the hand, he said, "and you, dear Father Enaut, oh, pray for me…I go to my Creator. Father Gergaud is coming for me!" These were his last words.

Accounts of the work of Father Louis Gergaud in the Catholic missions of the surrounding regions of the Ouachita River, along with important observations about his memory and legacy, all from primary source accounts, provide a rich collection of insights into the life of this virtuous and heroic priest. In a way that only such sources can provide, the narrative of his life takes on the unique perspective of those who knew him best. From his own correspondence, we get intimate glimpses of his personality, which comes to life with equal measures of impatience and determination. More than a mere accounting of events, the third-person chronicle attributed to him offers insights into the Catholic Church, the American Civil War and the communities to which Father Gergaud gave so much of himself to establish and nurture. Although he is best remembered and most beloved as the pastor of St. Matthew's Church in Monroe, a survey of the record reveals that Father Gergaud was an energetic and enthusiastic source of life for the smallest of Catholic communities. Indeed, there was no request or expressed need for him that was too small. Excerpted from *The Catholic Church in Monroe* is the following synopsis of the missions Father Gergaud undertook, a list that provides in itself a fitting tribute to the fruits of his labor, as many of these went on to build Catholic churches that remain in the communities to this day. It is a simple summary but a nevertheless important notation to include in this work.

THE MISSIONS OF FATHER LOUIS GERGAUD

1857   Father Gergaud established a mission at BOUEF RIVER (French descendants living on the banks of the Ouachita River just a few miles west of Columbia).

August 1859   Father Gergaud celebrated the first Mass at WINNSBORO at the home of "L. Sims." He also "preached a sermon" at the courthouse to a "numerous Protestant audience."

February 1860   Father Gergaud celebrated the first Mass at BASTROP in the Prather residence (he notes that this was the editor of the *Morehouse Advocate*), with eight persons in attendance.

October 1863   Father Gergaud celebrated the first Mass at WOODVILLE at the home of Philip Maher.

October 1863   Father Gergaud noted that Bishop Martin removed Father Chapin from serving the communities of MILLIKEN'S BEND and LAKE PROVIDENCE and that he (Gergaud) took over the pastoral care of those areas until December of that year, when Father Joseph Gentille was assigned there.

March 1864   Father Gergaud was invited to CAMDEN, ARKANSAS, to "celebrate Mass and administer Communion" to Confederate troops of General Price's division, still in winter quarters there.

August 1864   Father Gergaud celebrated the first Mass at BAMBRICK'S FERRY.

August 1867   Father Gergaud responded to a call "to visit that part of CHICOT COUNTY, state of Arkansas, lying on the Boeuf River for a small community of Catholics."

APPENDIX

I n the pages that follow, the scanned images of Father Louis Gergaud's original sacramental registry documenting the numerous baptisms of enslaved peoples testify to the fervor of his commitment to serving all. In a time when institutionalized slavery dominated the economic system of the Deep South, Father Gergaud responded in the manner appropriate to his calling as a Roman Catholic priest—he performed baptisms of all of those he could reach. The record begins in 1857 and concludes in 1865, with the simple but poignant notation at the conclusion: "Slavery Ended." Because of their great historical significance, these records are included here in their entirety, although their legibility has faded. To merely transcribe this record would fall short of the honor due them and obscure the human element of devotion captured in Father Gergaud's own handwriting.

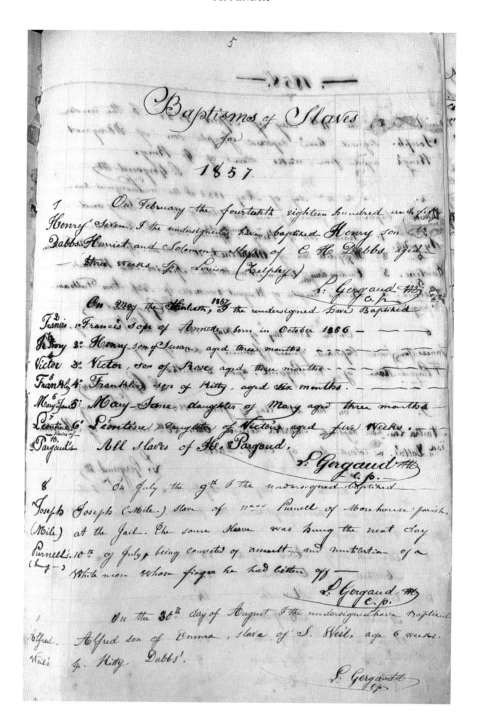

5

Baptisms of Slaves

for

1857

1. On February the fourteenth eighteen hundred and fifty
Henry / Seven, I the undersigned have baptized Henry son
Dabbs. Harriet and Solomon ———— of C. H. Dabbs aged
—— three weeks. Sp. Louisa (Zelphey)

L. Gergaud
c. p.

On May the tentieth, 1857, I the undersigned have Baptized

2. Francis / 1. Francis Son of Annette born in October 1856 ————
3. Henry / 2. Henry son of Susan, aged three months.
4. Victor / 3. Victor, son of Rose aged three months ————
5. Franklin / 4. Franklin son of Kitty. aged six months. ————
6. Mary Jane / 5. Mary-Jane daughter of Mary aged three months
7. Leontine / 6. Leontine daughter of Victoire aged five weeks.
Pargoud's — All slaves of H. Pargoud.

L. Gergaud
c. p.

8. On July the 9th I the undersigned baptized
Joseph / Joseph (Mile.) slave of Mrs Purnell of Morehouse parish,
(Mile) at the Jail. The same Slave was hung the next day
Purnell's. 10th of July, being convicted of assault, and mutilation of a
(hung —) White man whose finger he had bitten off ————

L. Gergaud
c. p.

9. On the 30th day of August I the undersigned have Baptized
Alfred. Alfred son of Emma, slave of S. Neil. age 6 weeks.
Neil's / Sp. Kitty Dabbs'.

L. Gergaud
c. p.

— 1858.—

1. On the 11th day of April 1858 I the under
Joseph. signed have baptized Joseph son of Margaret
King's aged four weeks. slave of J. King.
L. Gergaud M
C.P

2. On the 16th day of May 1858 I the undersigned have
Francis. baptized the following persons all slaves of Mr. F. Pargoud.
3. 1. Francis son of Kitty 5 months old. Sponsor Mrs M. Fulham
Hyppolite. 2. Hyppolite son of Madeleine, 10 months old. Sponsor Mrs M. Fulham
Cardine. 3. Cardine dang. of Cesarine, 11 months old. Sponsor Mrs Kline. —
Rebecca. 4 Rebecca daughter of Margaret 5 months old: Sp. Miss Ann Fulham.
F. Pargoud's.
L. Gergaud M
C.P

6 — On the 23d day of May 1858 I the Pandersigned
James (Jamy) slave baptized James (Jamin) son of Augustine
F. Pargoud's slave of F. Pargoud, aged 2 months
L. Gergaud M
C.P

7. On the 21st day of June 1858 I the undersigned
Martha Lou. have baptized Martha Louisa born 20th instant of Martha
isa Dabbs's. a colored slave of Cpt H. Dabbs.
L. Gergaud M
C.P

On the 15th day of September 1858 I the
undersigned have baptized the following slaves of Mr.
F. Pargoud:

8	Edmund	son of	Ann	aged	15 years
9	Matthew	son of	Christine		14 years
10	Emile		Melinda		14 years
11	Francis		Mary ann		13.
12	Jeremiah		Polly ann		12.
13	Julius.		Polly ann		8.
14	Antoine		Melinda		9
15	Jeff.		Melinda		5.

1858.

16.	Robert son of	Mélinda	aged 3 years	
17	Pinkney	Melinda	1 year	
18	Goldman	Martha	7 months.	
19	Milton	Louise	3 years	
20	Louis	Patsey	8 months	
21	Solomon	Julia	12 years	
22	Willis	Juliet	13 years	
23	Stephen	Maria	8 months. (dead	
24	Jordan	Maria	3 years	
25	Smith	Caroline	5 years (dead	
26	William	Virginie	5 years	
27	Gilbert	Virginie	4 years	
28	Carter	Virginie	2 years	
29	Bernard	Ann	4 years	
30	Samson	Lucindy	7 months (dead	
31	Cooper	Martha	3 years.	
32	Amos	Natalie	11 years.	
33	Jesse	Charity	7 years.	
34	Martin	Charity	6 years	
35	Hobines	Hortense	4 years.	
36.	Leonie daughter of	Ann	age 11 years	
37	Laura	Caroline	15 years.	
38	Lauras	Enés	12 years	
39.	Hannah	Polly Ann	11 years	
40	Louisa Ann	Polly am	6 years	
41	Rosine	Mary. am	6 years	
42	Esther	Mary	13 years	
3	Emelie	Mary	9 years	
4	Sally	Mary	2 years	
5	Sarah	Catherine	2 years.	

1858.

46.	Félicité daughter of Catherine	aged	3 years (dead)
	Félicité		
47	Henriette	Louise	6 years
48	Rosetta	Louisa	1 year
49	Elisabeth	Maria	6 years
50	Jenny	Maria	18 years
51	Makeiley	Ann	11 years
52	Nancy	Ann	8 years
53	Amanda	Malinda	10 years.
54	Grace	Caroline	2 years.
55	Susan	Virginie	7 years
56	Josephine	Virginie	7 years
57	Lisette	Annette	5 years
58	Fanny	Flora	8 years
59	Jeannette	Flora	7 years
60.	Hellen	Julia	2 years
61	Elise ann	Charity	3 years
62	Diana	Ombrosine	4 months.

L. Gergaud †††
c.p.

~~~~~~ 1859 ~~~~~~

1. On the 10th day of April 1859 I the undersigned
Julius, of have baptized: Julius, son of Annette, aged about
Pargoud's six months: slave of Mr. F Pargoud.

2. And Hellen daughter of Jeannette aged
Hellen. about four months. Slave of I.F Pargoud.
.F Pargoud's

L. Gergaud †††

3. On the 17th day of April 1859 I the undersigned
Mary. have baptized Mary. daughter of aged 8 months.
F Pargoud's
Laura slave of J. F Pargoud.

F Pargoud's And Laura daughter of aged 8 months
slave of J. F Pargoud.

L. Gergaud †††
c.p.

119

9

5
Monette   On the 24th day of May 1859 I the undersigned
J.F.Puryoud's have baptized Monette aged 2 months daughter
slave of Selina. Slave of J.F.Puryoud. Sp. Mrs Dalts.
                                            L. Gergaud M.
                                                c. p.
6.   On the 31 day of May 1859 I the undersigned
Nathan have baptized Nathan. 7 months son of Mary
J.Ray's Slave of Mrs Jesse Ray. Sp. mrs K. Ray
                                            L. Gergaud M.
                                                c. p.
7.   On the 26th day of June 1859 I the undersigned have
Pauline baptized. Pauline daughter of Rosa aged 2 months.
J.F.Puryoud's slave of J.F. Puryoud. Sp. mrs Nolan.
                                            L. Gergaud M.
                                                c. p.
8.   On the 26th day of June 1859 I the undersigned have
George baptized George aged three weeks son of Caroline
Hemphen slave to the Hemphen Estate. Sp. Mary Anne.
Died July 12th 1861.
                L.g.g.
11.   L. Gergaud M.
        On the 15th day of September 1859 I have baptized
        the following Slaves.

No.	Name		Mother	Age	Slave of
9	Benjamin	son of	Liza	aged 1 year	Slave of G. Filhiol.
10	Joseph		Lucette	3 years	do
11	Henry Holmes		Louise	3 years	do
12	Lizzie		Liza	3 years	do
13	Clemence		Lucette	2 years	do
14	Lucette		Mary	2 years	do
15	Milinda		Mary	3 years	do
16	James	son of	Betsey	11 months	Slave of Jerome Bre
17	George		Betsey	11 months	do
18	Henry		Mary	14 months	do
19	Alfred		Liza	10 years	do
20	Richard		Liza	11 years	do
21	Lucy	daughter of	Betsey	3 years	do
22	Jane		Liza	7 years	do

23.   Nancy daughter of Mary aged 11 years slave of Jerome Bro...
24.   Rose   Betsey   12 years   do
25.   Emily   Liza   15 years   do
26.   Virginia   Cicily   16 years   do

L. Gergaud ptr

27.   On the 28th day of October 1859 I have
William   baptized William Henderson born 1st day of July setting
Henderson   of Betsey, slave of Mrs O'Neill (Honore)
o'neill's

L. Gergaud ptr

—— 1860. ——

On the 13th day of February 1860
I the undersigned have baptized the following slaves
1.   belonging to J. B. Filhiol to wit viz.
Corinne.   Corinne (Mary) daughter of Sally, aged 5 months
2.   sponsor: Mrs N. Filhiol.
Cheney.   Cheney (Mary) daughter of Margaret, aged 2 years.
3.   Sp. Mrs N. Filhiol.
Norma   Norma (Mary) daughter of Sarah, aged 5 years
4.   Sp. Mrs N. Filhiol.
Josephine.   Josephine (Mary) daughter of Sally aged 3 years
5.   Sp. Mrs N. Filhiol.

L. Gergaud ptr

Mary Magdelen   On the 26th day of February 1860 I the under-
6.   signed have baptized the following slaves of Henri Bry &c
   Mary Magdelen aged 10 months, daughter of James
6   & Vicey. Spons: Zelphy Louisa Dabbs's.
Martha ann/   Martha Ann Susan aged 18 months daughter of
Susan,   James & Vicey. Sp. Zelphy Louisa Dabbs's.

L. Gergaud ptr

7.   On the 8th day of April 1860 I have baptized
Joseph   Joseph aged six months born of Kitty slave of Mrs Francis
Pargoud's   Pargoud. Sp. Edward (curon's)

L. Gergaud ptr

121

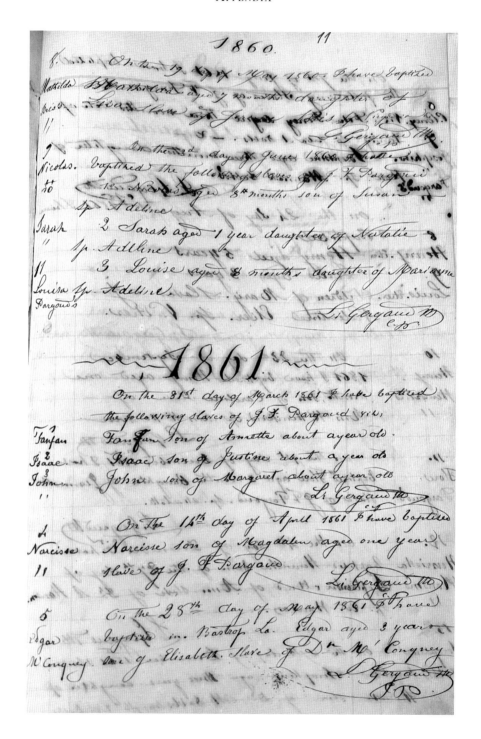

On the 7th of July 1861 I have baptized
the following Slaves of J. F. Fargoud.

6
P. Perey Viz. Peter Perey aged three months son of
7 Fanny. Sp. Julia A Dabbs. — & —
Josephine. Josephine aged three months daughter of
Fargoud's Row. Sp. Hannah Dabbs.

L. Gergaud M.

On the 24 Day of August 1861 I have
6 Baptized:
Henry. Etr. Henry aged 5 years
9 Louis aged 3 years
Louis. Etr. Children of Mary. Slaves of
Valentine Etier. Sp. V. Etier.

L. Gergaud M.

10 On the 22d day of September
Henry. 1861 I have baptized Henry aged one
Henskens. month, son of Caroline Slave of —
11 Miss H. Henskens. Sp. Miss H. Henskens

L. Gergaud M.

11. On the 1st day of December 1861 I have
Flore. baptized Flore aged 5 months daughter of Jeannette
Fargoud's Slave of J. F. Fargoud. Sp. Charlotte.

L. Gergaud M.

12. On the 4th day of December & have
Henrietta baptized Henrietta born of the 27th day of
Hanson's September ultimo of Ann. Slave of Dr A Hanson.
11 Sp. Ed. Hanson.

L. Gergaud M.

13th
Seraphina On the 27th day of December 1861 I have
Dabbs's baptized Seraphina aged three years, daughter of
Henrietta Slave of Dr A. Dabbs. Sp. Al J. W. Dabbs.

L. Gergaud M.

13

1862.

On the fourth day of April 1862
I have baptized the following Slaves of
Jerome Bres.

1. Patrick born in July 1861. of Betsey.
2. Amanda, aged one year, born of Mary.
3. Eve aged 4 months born of Lila.
   Sponsor Mrs F. A. Bres.

L: Gergaud m.
C. P.

On the 27th day of April 1862 I have baptized the
following Slaves of J. F. Fazoud.

4. Antoinet aged 3 months, son of Susan.
5. Nicolas aged 1 year son of Elisabeth
6. Henry aged 2 months son of Corinne
7. Basil aged 3 month son of Madeleine.
8. Harriet aged 3 months daughter of Rose.

L: Gergaud m.
C. P.

9.
Anna
Felicity
Ludwig's
On the 25th day of July 1862 I have baptized
Anna Felicity daughter of Felicity, aged one year
Slave of Mrs C. Ludwig. Sp: Mrs J. N. Dubbs.
Emmanuel orphan ... 1862. L: Gergaud m.
see among white C. P.

On the 6th day of November 1862
I have baptized:

.10.   Paul George aged 2 years & 6 months
son of Louisa. Sp. Rodolph Dossat & Ellen M'Geary.

.11.   Sarah Elisabeth aged 14 months daughter
of Louisa. Sp. A. Gilly & Mrs Dossat. —
Slaves of R. Dossat.

L: Gergaud m.
C. P.

12
Mary Jane
Johnson's
On the 23d day of November 1862 I have
baptized Mary Jane daughter of Ann, aged 9 years
" Slave of Thomas Johnson
L: Gergaud m.
C. P.

13th
Henry
M'Conqueys

On the 28th day of November 1862 I have
baptised Henry born February 11th illtimo of
Elisabeth Slave of Mrs M'Conquey
L. Gergaud
cap.

1863.

On the 19th day of January 1863
I have baptised the following slaves
of W. H Dinkgrave's

1 Serena aged 30.
2 Jane aged 25.
3 Isiah aged 16, son of Rachel
4 Harriet aged 12, daughter of Rachel
5 Alexander aged 15 months son of
6 Lavinia aged one year Daughter of Serena.
L. Gergaud

On the 10th day of February 1863 I have
baptised the following slaves of Dr. C.H Dabbs.

7 John Louis aged about 15 months son of
Martha Sp. Mrs. G. W Dabbs.
8 George Spencer aged 6 months son of Martha
Sp. J. Ad. Dabbs.
L. Gergaud
cap.

On the 12 day of April 1863 I have
baptised
9. David aged 2 years son of.
10 Emmanuel aged 4 months son of.
Slaves of Mrs N Bry.
L. Gergaud
cap.

15

On the 26th day of April 1863 I have baptized
the following Slaves of J. F. Pargoud:

11. George & Washington son of Augustine aged 8 months
12. Julia daughter of Natalie aged 1 year
13. Angelina daughter of Mary Jane aged 8 months
14. Adeline daughter of Fanny aged 5 months

L. Gergaud Pr.

On the 3rd day of May 1863 I have baptized
daughter of Mary
15. Mary Eliza aged 4 months Slave of Mrs Hawkins

L. Gergaud Pr.
C.P.

On the 21st day of October 1863 I have
baptized the following Slaves of Mr Maher

16. Abram aged 6 years son of Bodey
17. Aleck aged 1 week son of Percilla   Sponsor
18. Spencer aged 5 months son of Jane.   Mr
19. Margaret aged 5 years daughter of Jane. W. Maher
20. Eliza aged 7 years daughter of Coelia.   11.

L. Gergaud. Pr
C.P.

On the 21st day of November 1863 I have
baptized

21. Melinda aged 2 months daughter of
Marie. Sponsor Mrs Etier.

22. Rosette aged 2 years, daughter of Marie
Sp. Mrs Etier. both Slaves of Valentine
Etier.
L. Gergaud Pr
C.P.

1864.

On the 19th day of Feb. 1864 I have baptized
the following Slaves of Mrs C. More

1. — John aged three years son of Mathilda Sp. J. O'Neil
Dumoulin & Mrs C. More
— Placide aged 5 years son of Teresie. Sp. Julie Mourin.
— Henriette aged 1 year daughter of Mathilda Sp. Julie Mourin.
L. Gergaud.

16

On the 23d day of February 1864 I have baptized
the following slaves of G. Fithiol.

4   Baptiste son of Louise.
5   George   "   Louise.
6   Germain   "   Liza.
7   Etienne Douglas   "   Finary
8   John Bell   "   Laura.
9   Henry   "   Cecile.
10 Jerome   "   Celeste
11 Jane   daughter of Cecile
12 Agathe   "   Cecile
13 Albine   "   Mary.
14 Theresa   "   Mary.

               L. Gergaud th

On the 23 day of February 1864 I have baptized
15. Martha daughter of Nancy. Slave of Jerome Bra
16.   L. Gergaud th

On the 22 day of May 1864 I have baptized Frances
Frances aged 14 years daughter of   Slave of John Ray.
Sponsor Mrs C. Ray
               L. Gergaud th

17.   On the 28 day of May 1864 I have baptized Eliza aged
Eliza   one year daughter of Louisa slave of Mrs Dabbs for Mrs J. W Dabbs.
               L. Gergaud th

On the 8th day of June 1864 I have baptized the
following slaves of J. F. Pargaud.
18   John aged 2 months son of Kitty.
19   Christine aged 1 year daughter of Rose.
20   Ada aged 4 months daughter of Anette.
21. Rebecca aged 6 months daughter of Rachel
22   Hannah, aged 3 months daughter of Mary.
23   Liza aged 4 months daughter of Ann.
               L. Gergaud th

127

17

On the 27th day of August 1864 I have baptized the following slaves of Mrs More. Viz.

24 Vincent born April 5th ult° Son of Felicie

25 Maria born July 6th ult° daughter of Matilda.

L. Gergaud
c. P.

On the 1st day of October 1864 I have baptized the following slaves of Pellips Maher. Viz.

26 Albert aged 4 months son of Lucy.

27 John Douglass aged 5 month son of Betty.

28 Sallie aged 3 months daughter of Emiline

29 Lila aged 4 months daughter of Teeney

30 Eucharis aged 1 months daughter of Esther

31 Henrietta aged 2 weeks daughter of Melinda

L. Gergaud
c. P.

32 On the 16th day of Octob 1864 I have
Rob. Kes baptized William Keston aged 3 months son
ton of Jennie Slave of Mrs D. Dumesgrave

L. Gergaud
c. P.

On the 17th day of Octob 1864 I have baptized the following slaves of Jerome Bres &c.

33 Louis aged 4 months son of Cherry.

34 Abraham Linsey aged 6 months son of Rose

35 Mary aged 3 months daughter of Nancy.

J. B. fontille

On the 17th day of October 1864 I have baptized the following slaves of G. Filhiol Viz.

36 Pauline aged 4 months daughter of Mary

37 Charles aged 6 months son of Rosine.

J. B. fontille

On the 15th day of November 1864, I have baptized the following slaves of F. Pargoud. viz.

38 Louis son of aged one year, son of Jane.

18

39. John Lovett aged 4 months, son of Cathérine

40. Maria Cathérine aged 10 months daughter of Mahely.

41. Isabelle aged 10 months, daughter of Virginie

42. Ella Anne, aged 5 years, daughter of Virginie

43. Egla aged 5 years daughter of Maria

44. Arthémise aged 5 years, daughter of Annette.

45.   On the 28th day of November 1863 I have
Adèle   baptized Adèle Vennie Elisabeth born on November
        28th 1863 daughter of Mary Ella, slave of Miss A Roch
        Sp. Mrs E.J. Pulley.

                                        L. Gergaud tt.

1865.

1. On the 16th day of April 1865 I have baptized
    Mathildas aged 17 years slave of N. Bry.
                                        L. Gergaud tt

2. On the 19th day of April 1865 I have baptized
    Mary aged 5 months daughter of Mary
    slave of D. Sanford
                                        L. Gergaud tt

        On the 5th day of May 1865 I have
        baptized

3. Annas aged 11 years daughter of Frankey
4. Tabitha aged 2 years daughter of Sarah
    slaves of Hippolyte Pollick
                                        L. Gergaud tt.

        Slavery ended

NOTES

1. Introduction

1. "Report of the Committee."
2. Louis Marie Gergaud birth record, Vital Records of Héric, France, copy of original in possession of the authors.
3. Louis Marie Gergaud was born on March 22, 1832, to parents Sébastian and Anne Father Gergaud, baptism recorded in the Sacramental Register of St. Nicholas Church, Héric, France.
4. Grand Seminary of Nantes Records.
5. Ibid.
6. Correspondence of Bishop Auguste Martin to Archbishop Anthony Blanc of the Archdiocese of New Orleans, Diocese of Natchitoches Collection, University of Notre Dame Archives.
7. Ordination record of Louis Gergaud, Records of the Grand Seminary of Nantes, Archives of the Diocese of Nantes, France.
8. Grand Seminary of Nantes Records.
9. Annals of the Propagation of the Faith, 1855, reprinted in the *American Catholic Historical Researches* 2, no. (April 1906): 78–192.
10. Baudier Historical Collection, Archdiocese of New Orleans.
11. Ibid.
12. Correspondence of Mother Mary Hyacinth Le Conniat.
13. Bishop Auguste Martin Annual Reports; correspondence of Bishop Auguste Martin, Diocese of Natchitoches Collection, University of Notre Dame.

14. Ouachita Parish History, unpublished manuscript, Archives of St. Matthew's Church.

15. Ibid.

16. Bishop Auguste Martin, Notice on Very Rev. Father Gergaud from the Right Reverend Auguste Marie, Bishop of Natchitoches, Archives of St. Matthew's Church.

17. Correspondence of Mother Mary Hyacinth Le Conniat.

2. Servant of God Father Louis Gergaud: In His Own Words

18. Correspondence of Bishop Auguste Martin, Diocese of Natchitoches Collection, University of Notre Dame Archives.

19. Correspondence of Bishop Auguste Martin to Archbishop Anthony Blanc of New Orleans, Diocese of Natchitoches Collection, University of Notre Dame Archives.

20. Correspondence of Bishop Auguste Martin to the Society for the Propagation of the Faith in Paris, Diocese of Natchitoches Collection, University of Notre Dame Archives.

21. *Richmond Dispatch*, July 8, 1863.

22. Records of the Young Catholic Friends' Society, Archives of St. Matthew's Church, Monroe, Louisiana.

23. Archives of St. Matthew's Church, Monroe, Louisiana; Father Louis Gergaud files, Archives of the University of Louisiana at Monroe.

24. Father Louis Gergaud files, Archives of the University of Louisiana at Monroe.

25. Ibid.

26. Ibid.

3. Shreveport 1873 and Beyond: Father Louis Gergaud Remembered

27. Correspondence of Mother Mary Hyacinth Le Conniat.

28. Ibid.

29. *Daily Shreveport Times*, September 23, 1873

30. Correspondence of James Muse Dabbs; *New York Times*, September 23, 1873; Baudier Historical Collection, Archdiocese of New Orleans.

31. Correspondence of Bishop Auguste Martin, Diocese of Natchitoches Collection; Baudier Historical Collection, Archdiocese of New Orleans.

32. Correspondence of James Muse Dabbs.

33. Correspondence of Mother Mary Hyacinth Le Conniat.

34. Ibid.

35. Ibid.; perhaps this statement indicates he was also confirming deathbed Christians.

36. Ibid.

37. His final resting place would ultimately become the same cemetery he established in Monroe.

38. Daughters of the Cross Collection, Noel Archives and Special Collection, Louisiana State University at Shreveport.

39. Reverend F.T. Rawson, Memorial of Father Louis Gergaud, *Ouachita Telegraph*, October 21, 1873.

40. *Shreveport Times*, October 14, 1873.

41. Grave marker inscription of Father Louis Gergaud, St. Matthew's Church cemetery, Monroe, Louisiana.

42. *Daily Shreveport Times*, December 3, 1873.

43. *Ouachita Telegraph*, February 6, 1874.

44. "The Roman Catholic Church in Monroe," Archives of St. Matthew's Church, Monroe, Louisiana.

45. Correspondence, Father Louis Enaut to Bishop Auguste Martin, Archives of the Archdiocese of New Orleans.

46. Correspondence, Father Louis Enaut to Bishop Auguste Martin, Diocese of Natchitoches Collection, University of Notre Dame Archives.

BIBLIOGRAPHY

American Catholic Historical Society. "Southern Historical Notes." *American Catholic Historical Researches* 2, no. 2 (1906).

Archdiocese of New Orleans, Louisiana, Archives.

Baudier Historical Collection, Volume 23 (Heroes of '73). Archives of the Archdiocese of New Orleans.

Blanc, Archbishop Antoine. Correspondence. Archives of the University of Notre Dame, South Bend, Indiana.

Booth, Augustine R. "An Inaugural Dissertation on History of the Epidemic of Shreveport, Louisiana." University of Kentucky Medical School, 1873.

Carrigan, JoAnn. *The Saffron Scourge: A History of Yellow Fever in Louisiana, 1796–1905*. Lafayette: University of Southwestern Louisiana Press, 1994.

Dabbs, James Muse. Letters. Ouachita Parish, Louisiana. www.usgwarchives.net.

Daily Shreveport (LA) Times.

Daughters of the Cross, Register. Archives of the Diocese of Shreveport, Louisiana.

"Daughters of the Cross Victims of 1873 Yellow Fever Epidemic." Unpublished manuscript. Archives of the Diocese of Shreveport, Louisiana.

Diocese of Alexandria, Louisiana, Archives.

Diocese of Nantes, France, Archives.

Diocese of Shreveport, Louisiana, Archives.

Enaut, Father Ludovic. Letters. Archives of the Archdiocese of New Orleans.

————. Letters. Archives of the University of Notre Dame, South Bend, Indiana.

Gentille, Father Joseph. Personal Diary. Archives of the Diocese of Shreveport, Louisiana.

Gergaud, Father Louis. "The Catholic Church in Monroe, Louisiana." Archives of St. Matthew's Church, Monroe, Louisiana.

————. Letters. Archives of the Diocese of Alexandria, Louisiana.

————. Letters. Archives of the Diocese of Nantes, France.

————. Records of The Young Catholics Friends Society, Archives of St. Matthew's Church, Monroe, Louisiana.

Grand Seminary of Nantes. Records. Archives of the Diocese of Nantes, France.

Hennessey, James. "The First Vatican Council." *Archivium Historiae Pontificiae* 7, 1969.

Howard Association, *Report of the Committee on the Yellow Fever Epidemic of 1873 at Shreveport, Louisiana.* Shreveport, Louisiana, 1874.

Joiner, Gary D., and Cheryl H. White. *Shreveport's Oakland Cemetery: Spirits of Pioneers and Heroes.* Charleston, SC: The History Press, 2015.

Le Conniat, Mother Mary Hyacinth. Correspondence. Noel Archives and Special Collections, Louisiana State University at Shreveport.

Mahe, Rev. C. "History of the Missions of the Ouachita." Unpublished manuscript, 1929. Archives of the Archdiocese of New Orleans, Louisiana.

Martin, Bishop Auguste Marie. Annual Reports to the Society for the Propagation of the Faith, Paris, France. MPFP-096, Archives of The University of Notre Dame, South Bend, Indiana.

————. Correspondence to the Society for the Propagation of the Faith, Paris, France. MPFP-096, Archives of The University of Notre Dame, South Bend, Indiana.

————. Letters. Daughters of the Cross Collection, Noel Archives and Special Collections, Louisiana State University at Shreveport, Shreveport, Louisiana.

————. Letters. Register of the Daughters of the Cross, Archives of the Diocese of Shreveport, Louisiana.

————. "Notice on Very Rev. Father Gergaud from the Right Rev. Aug. Marie Martin, Bishop of Natchitoches." *Catholic Propagator*, November 12, 1873.

McCants, Sr. Dorothea Olga. *They Came to Louisiana: Letters of a Catholic Mission, 1854–1882.* Daughters of the Cross, 1983.

O'Pry, Maude Hearn. *Chronicles of Shreveport.* Shreveport, Louisiana, 1928.

Ouachita Citizen (Monroe, LA).

Ouachita Telegraph (Monroe, LA).

Partain, Fr. Chad A. *A Tool Pushed by Providence: Bishop Auguste Martin and the Catholic Church in North Louisiana.* Austin, TX: Persidia Publishing: 2010.

"Priests Who Have Died at Shreveport." *The Scholastic* (South Bend, IN), 1873.

Rawson, Rev. F.T. "Memorial of Father Louis Gergaud." *Ouachita Telegraph*, October 24, 1873.

"Report of the Committee on the Yellow Fever Epidemic of 1873 of Shreveport, Louisiana." *American Journal of the Medical Sciences* 66, no. 134 (1874).

St. Matthew's Church Archives, Monroe, Louisiana.

St. Nicholas Church, Héric, France, Sacramental Registers.

Vital Records Registry, Héric, France.

ABOUT THE AUTHORS

VERY REVEREND PETER B. MANGUM was raised in Shreveport, the oldest of five sons, parishioner of St. Jude Church in Bossier City and graduate of Christ the King School in Bossier City and Jesuit High School (now Loyola) in Shreveport. He attended Holy Trinity Seminary at the University of Dallas and then the Pontifical Gregorian University in Rome, where he remained for five years, receiving degrees in sacred theology and canon law and making numerous pilgrimages to the shrines and tombs of saints in Rome and throughout Europe. Ordained a priest in 1990, Father Peter served in various parishes before becoming rector of the parish and school of the Cathedral of St. John Berchmans in 2005. He served as chaplain of Loyola College Prep and is now also the director of vocations for the diocese. He has researched and actively promoted the causes of the five priests who died in Shreveport's yellow fever outbreak of 1873. In his capacity as diocesan administrator of Shreveport he led a Shreveport delegation to Brittany, France, to the native dioceses and villages of the Shreveport Five as well as visited twice the Congregation for the Causes of the Saints at the Vatican to learn more of the process of canonization as it applies to those who freely offered their lives and heroically accepted, out of Christian charity, a certain and untimely death. He also led a second delegation to Brittany in 2022 to further collaboration and foster ongoing research into the lives of the five Shreveport martyrs. He coauthored *Shreveport Martyrs of 1873: The Surest Path to Heaven*, published by The History Press in 2021, and features prominently in *The Five Priests*, a full-length feature documentary that was produced by Strategery Films.

W. RYAN SMITH is a native of Shreveport. A husband and father of three, he serves as the director of hospital operations at Ochsner LSU Health Shreveport, the contemporary descendant of the city's first charity hospital, which was established as a direct result of the 1873 yellow fever epidemic. He worked with his staff throughout the COVID-19 pandemic, coordinating higher level of care hospital transfers, inpatient capacity management operations and outpatient COVID-19 vaccine scheduling for the region. He holds both a master of arts and a bachelor of business degree from Northwestern State University of Louisiana in Natchitoches and has completed postgraduate work with both the Pennsylvania State University and Villanova University. He makes his home in Shreveport and became alerted to the story of the five priests while researching the medical history of the city of Shreveport. He has served on the board of Catholic Charities of North Louisiana, is a Knight of the Equestrian Order of the Holy Sepulchre of Jerusalem (a nearly one-thousand-year-old chivalric order) and was named one of the Greater Shreveport Chamber's Young Professional Initiative's "40 under 40" in 2018. He is a parishioner of the Cathedral of St. John Berchmans in Shreveport. Smith is the author of *Sang pour Sang*, a novel published by the University of Louisiana at Lafayette Press (2018), and coauthor of *A Haunted History of Louisiana Plantations* (2017, The History Press), a work completed along with friend and fellow researcher, Dr. Cheryl H. White. With Father Mangum and Dr. White, he also coauthored *Shreveport Martyrs of 1873: The Surest Path to Heaven*, published by The History Press in 2021, and features prominently in *The Five Priests*, a full-length feature documentary that was produced by Strategery Films.

CHERYL H. WHITE, PhD, is a professor of history at Louisiana State University at Shreveport, where she has taught medieval European and Christian Church history for twenty-five years. Dr. White currently holds the distinguished Hubert Humphreys Endowed Professorship, which has provided many research opportunities involving the field of Christian history, resulting in numerous peer-reviewed articles and professional academic conference presentations. A passionate preservationist, she is actively engaged in historic preservation advocacy and policy-making at both the local and state levels. As a native of northwest Louisiana, Dr. White's deep love of history was first nurtured in the rich narratives of her own home state, meaning that her research has been equally focused on stories much closer to home, many of which have been published in books and articles on regional history and folklore. It was the nexus of local history and Christian history that shaped her interest and collaboration in the extensive research on the five Shreveport martyr priests of 1873, shared with colleagues Father Peter Mangum and W. Ryan Smith. She also coauthored the 2021 book *Shreveport Martyrs of 1873: The Surest Path to Heaven*, and features in *The Five Priests*, a full-length feature documentary that was produced by Strategery Films. This is her seventh book to be published with The History Press.

Visit us at
www.historypress.com

The

FLORIDA CRACKER
COOKBOOK

Recipes & Stories from Cabin to Condo

JOY SHEFFIELD HARRIS

AMERICAN PALATE

Published by American Palate
A Division of The History Press
Charleston, SC
www.historypress.com

Front cover, top left: Crowley Museum and Nature Center in Sarasota; *top right*: Patrick Owens
Sheffield; *center*: author's collection.
All photos courtesy Florida Memory Archives (FMA) unless otherwise noted.

First published 2019

Manufactured in the United States

ISBN 9781467143196

Library of Congress Control Number: 2019945076

"Guava Glazed Cinnamon Sausage Gems," "Collard Greens Florida Style," "Deeper than
Deep South Hoppin' John," "Sunlight Fluff" and "Oatmeal Bars Florida-Style" from
Easy Breezy Florida Cooking by Joy and Jack Harris (Gainesville: University Press of Florida,
Seaside Publishing, 2008).
Reprinted with permission.

"Bucky's Banana Pudding" and "Delicious Deviled Eggs" from *Harris & Co. Cookbook: I
Can't Believe I 8 the Whole Thing* by Charles Knight (Tampa, FL: Health Craft Inc., Depot
Press, 1994).
Reprinted with permission.

Notice: The information in this book is true and complete to the best of our knowledge. It is
offered without guarantee on the part of the author or The History Press. The author and
The History Press disclaim all liability in connection with the use of this book.

To Jack, my husband, and Jackson, our son.
They are my inspiration and at-home editors.
And to all the Cracker cooks who have fed generations of hungry children.

CONTENTS

PREFACE

A side from the final chapter, most of the recipes in this book have previously been published, either by myself—in *Harris & Co. Cookbook: I Can't Believe I 8 the Whole Thing, Jack Harris Unwrapped, Easy Breezy Florida Cooking, A Culinary History of Florida* or *Florida Sweets*—or in cookbooks found in the public domain. Many cookbooks published before 1924 are considered part of the public domain, and those recipes help illustrate the cooking styles of previous generations. For example, the 1878 cookbook *Housekeeping in Old Virginia* by Marion Cabell Tyree offers insight into methods used for early cooking. Although these are not classic Cracker recipes from Florida, they represent a style of cooking. Since early written recipes from Cracker kitchens are scarce, these older cookbooks from other southern states help answer questions about cooking methods used at the time Florida was being settled. These books also show the progression of recipe writing, which evolved with a clearer understanding of methods and measurements, and how cookbooks were eventually streamlined. From open-hearth cooking with tin roasters and spiders to the modern age of ferromagnetic pans and induction cooktops, the flavor and quality of our foods have grown with fits and starts to reach an age of easy, economical dishes served every day. Project Gutenberg's *Housekeeping in Old Virginia* can be found as an eBook "for the use of anyone anywhere at no cost and with almost no restrictions whatsoever. You may copy it, give it away or re-use it under the terms of the Project Gutenberg."

In 1796, Amelia Simmons wrote *American Cookery*, the first cookbook to introduce American ingredients in the recipes. Many women of the previous century were not only great cooks but were also prolific writers. S.R. Dull explains in *Southern Cooking*, "The interest taken in my weekly page, in the magazine section of the *Atlanta Journal*, which I edited for twenty years, convinced me of the need for an authoritative source of information on the preparation of foodstuffs 'the Southern way,' and as a consequence *Southern Cooking* was born in 1928."

ACKNOWLEDGEMENTS

T hank you to Amanda Irle, formerly with Arcadia Publishing and The History Press, for getting this project started and to Joe Gartrell for following through. Thank you to Kelly Smith for her diligent work and delightful comments while editing *The Florida Cracker Cookbook*.

Thank you to all my friends and family who contributed to this book, with special thanks to:

Mary Owens Sheffield

Lisa Tamargo

Ellen Nafe

LeAnn and Charles Knight

Patrick Owens and Carolyn Sheffield

Dennis Floyd and Laurelyn Sheffield

Marlene Forand

Peter Borg

Thank you to all my Flora-Bama aunts, uncles and cousins who are baked into my culinary Cracker memories.

Thank you to Lisa Kalmbach and her mother, Betty Cook, for providing me with beautiful family photos, including those of Granny Mattie and Lisa's grandfather David Jackson Cook, whom my father admired and Granny Mattie adored. We are proud that our son, Jackson Arthur Harris, shares his name.

OUR HERITAGE

The desire to know our heritage passes mysteriously from generation to generation, skipping over some members and possessing others powerfully. To understand what a man has endured is to know the man.
—Merewyn Stollings McEldowney

The stories of our food and how we eat are deeply rooted in our family tree. When you shake that tree, with its gnarly branches and loose leaves, it's surprising what you may find. As a seventh-generation Florida Cracker, our son, Jackson, can add "hillbilly" and "redneck" to his lineage, as well as British and Scotch-Irish roots that go back to the founding of America. With a little bit of Seminole Indian mixed in, from both Florida State and our Native American culture, he has a heritage to be proud of.

My father, Floyd Sheffield, was born at home on June 4, 1925. As a fifth-generation Floridian growing up in the piney woods of North Florida, he was a true Cracker. I need an asterisk beside my claim as a Cracker.* My birth on a military base in Libya makes me a naturalized American citizen, but we moved back to Florida when my father was transferred to Tyndall Air Force Base for my formative years from kindergarten on. My Cracker father, GrandFloyd Sheffield, and redneck mother, GrandMary Owens, brought together the best of both when they met at a Florida rodeo and married in Alabama less than a year later. State lines are only imaginary boundaries between Florida Crackers and Alabama rednecks living in LA (Lower Alabama) and the Florida Redneck Riviera.

Above: Margie Yates and James Elwood Cook family, circa 1915, with Margie's brother Cornelius Yates on the far right and Mattie Lenora Cook in the middle of the back row. *Courtesy of Lisa Kalmbach and Betty Cook.*

Left: Mary Frances Owens (GrandMary) and Floyd Sheffield (GrandFloyd) on their wedding day, October 27, 1951. *Author's collection.*

Katherine Elaine Stollings Harris (McIntosh) on her honeymoon on Panama City Beach, 1940. *Author's collection.*

When I met my husband, Jack, on a TV show he was hosting while I was promoting Florida seafood, I did not know he referred to himself on the radio as Jocular Cracker Jack Crack Jock Jack. He hails from West Virginia and calls himself a high-altitude Cracker. After more than thirty years of marriage, we discovered his strong Scotch-Irish heritage of almost 50 percent when his DNA results arrived in the mail last year. Knowing that much of the Florida Cracker way of life started with Scotch-Irish immigrants, our son and I decided to give him the honorary title of Cracker-in-Waiting. Jack has strong British ties as well, making him even more compatible with my side of the family.

While visiting the Museum in the Park at Chief Logan State Park in West Virginia, I discovered that seashells from the Gulf Coast Panhandle area were used for trade in that region hundreds of years ago. But it wasn't until I began research for *A Culinary History of Florida*, a book I wrote for The History Press, that I saw the strong Scotch-Irish influence on Crackers and hillbillies, both hardworking, God-loving people. While going through some old photographs after Jack's mother, Katherine Elaine Stollings Harris McIntosh, passed away, I discovered her honeymoon photos on Panama City Beach. The branches of the Stollings, Harris and McIntosh clans are a little more gnarly than my side of the family.

Elaine's first husband, William Harrison Harris, Jack's father, turned out to be someone they could not count on when needed. She packed up and left him one day in Virginia and moved back to West Virginia. She then married Robert McIntosh, called Grandpa Bob, from Grafton, West Virginia, and he is the one Jack credits with creating a happy, stable life for him and his mother. Some of the postcards Grandpa Bob's family sent to one another around the turn of the century are featured in this book. They show a love and devotion between Waitman T. McIntosh and Bessie Mae Statler, Grandpa Bob's father and mother. Waitman was born at Pleasant Creek, West Virginia, and worked for the B&O Railroad as a conductor.

West Virginia train wreckage photo from Robert McIntosh, 1925. *Author's collection.*

One day before returning home from work at Paynes Crossing, about eight miles from Grafton, a truck hit the caboose, and Waitman jumped between two rail cars to stop the train. Waitman McIntosh perished while saving the lives of those on the train.

Aside from my mother, two women who had a profound impact on my desire to study the foundation of our food preferences were my mother-in-law, Elaine, and my paternal grandmother, Mattie Sheffield. Granny Mattie passed away when I was ten years old, and Elaine influenced my life for about eight years before she died. Both of these sweet ladies were out of my life too soon. In my quest to know more about them, I started researching their lives and what it must have been like for them growing up near the turn of the twentieth century. The research uncovered family ties to Seminole Indians on the Sheffield side and Anderson (Devil Anse) Hatfield on the Stollings side.

When I inherited Elaine's *The Boston Cooking School Cook Book*, published in 1948, I proudly put it on a shelf with my mother GrandMary's first cookbook, *The American Woman's Cook Book, New and Revised*, published in 1953. Growing up with that book, I studied the pictures and recipes produced by the Culinary Arts Institute of Chicago. At the time, I had no way of knowing that I would one day attend the very same Culinary Arts Institute as part of my training as a merchandising specialist for the Florida Department of Natural Resources. Following trips to Paris, Toronto, Indianapolis, Los Angeles and back to Chicago to promote Florida seafood, I returned to my field office in St. Petersburg, Florida. That is where I met Jack. We were later married in my hometown of Panama City but had a little competition that weekend with the Possum Festival in Wausau, just up the road a piece. Years later, we opened a restaurant in Tampa with friends, Harris and Company, and now I spend my time researching our culinary heritage and creating menus and recipes to pass along to our son, Jackson.

After publishing some of our favorite recipes in a book of essays called *Jack Harris Unwrapped* in 2010, Jack and I wrote *Easy Breezy Florida Cooking*. I developed and tested new recipes while he supplied the commentary. *A Culinary History of Florida* and *Florida Sweets* are the results of traveling throughout the state looking for the roots of our dishes and what we find in sweet shops today. My brother Patrick Owens Sheffield added to the commentary in *Florida Sweets* with some of his sweet childhood memories. At the end of each chapter is a "PS from Pat," with his personal musings of life growing up in the Florida Panhandle.

Our Harris family culinary roots run deep with dishes like ramps and poke salad, leather britches and swamp cabbage. They are foods you don't commonly see on menus today, yet these were survival foods for both hillbillies and Crackers. Ramps are a sweet and strong-flavored wild onion, native to the United States and found growing wild in West Virginia every spring. Ramp festivals celebrate this once lowly food. Poke salad has been immortalized in the 1968 song "Poke Salad Annie." Also known as pokeweed, pokeberry, poke, poke salat or sullet, this springtime leafy green weed is now considered toxic and must be prepared properly before it is eaten. Leather britches, also known as shuck beans or greasy beans, are smooth and green. To preserve them for winter use, they are strung together like popcorn and hung to dry in the summer. Soaked overnight and cooked with ham, pork or other seasoning, they are a welcome winter treat. Swamp cabbage can be found in the wilds of Florida year-round and is occasionally served in Florida restaurants. The canned version is called hearts of palm, but authentic swamp cabbage is best served freshly cooked with pork and a little salt and pepper. You can enjoy a taste at the Swamp Cabbage Festival in LaBelle and possibly see how the sabal or cabbage palm, the state tree of Florida, is processed into this tempting dish by removing the tender shoot from the core of the tree. This, in turn, kills the tree, so today a state law protects the sabal palm. An excerpt from *A Culinary History of Florida* describes the process:

Cook brothers with ox and cart, circa 1925. David Jackson Cook is seated on the left. *Courtesy of Lisa Kalmbach and Betty Cook.*

Swamp Cabbage

Talking with Seminoles living in the Fort Myers area, they told me how they procure and prepare swamp cabbage: First find a tree on private property and get permission to cut it down, since state law prohibits cutting unless on private property. Once the tree is cut, strip the outer boots (each frond makes layers or boots) from the trunk and fronds from the head, and then peel away the outer layers to reveal the tender heart. They even gave me some swamp cabbage tips: The longer the palm fronds, the more cabbage inside and the smaller trees with long fronds are best. Cut one or two feet below where palm fronds emerge. For cooking, just add salt, pepper, pork and sugar to a pot of boiling water and put in the chopped cabbage, simmer for thirty minutes, or up to a few hours.

A sweet spot of our heritage is Florida's state fruit, the orange, widely grown and enjoyed throughout the state. European explorers introduced the orange, and soon St. Augustine was blossoming with citrus groves. Orange trees still cover the hills of central Florida, and many homeowners and institutions nurture those growing on their property. The beauty and fragrance of orange blossoms also made it an easy selection for the state flower.

Growing up in Tampa, Jackson played in the grapefruit, tangerine and orange trees in our backyard. The small community of Parker, where I grew up in northwest Florida, was at one time covered with orange groves. As children, we would roll an orange between our hands to soften and warm it, then cut a hole in the top and suck. You don't see too many people enjoying a delicacy like that anymore, but here are a couple of recipes from *Easy Breezy Florida Cooking* that capture the essence of the orange.

Sunlight Fluff (revised)

According to Jack: Joy got this recipe while she was training to cook for the Florida Department of Natural Resources. It was from the recipe collection of an elderly woman in Pascagoula, Mississippi, who had cooked for a wealthy family. I imagine that family had a higher cholesterol count than two or three branches of the armed services. I have it only once in a blue moon, but if I were a condemned prisoner, I would request it to top off my last meal.

Servings: 6

1 cup sugar
2 tablespoons flour
⅛ teaspoon salt
3 eggs, separated
1 ½ cups warm milk
½ cup orange juice
1 teaspoon orange zest
2 tablespoons butter, melted
6 scoops vanilla ice cream (optional)

Preheat oven to 350 degrees.

Whisk together sugar, flour and salt. Stir in well-beaten egg yolks and milk. Add orange juice, zest and butter.

Beat egg whites until they form very soft peaks. Fold into sugar mixture.

Spoon the batter into 6 buttered custard cups. Place cups in a larger pan that has been filled with enough hot water to reach 1 inch up the side of the pan. Bake for 45 minutes or until set.
Serve hot or cold with ice cream, if desired.

⌒

Oatmeal Bars Florida Style (revised)

According to Jack: Great taste doesn't mean a food isn't healthful. This combination of nutritious oatmeal and orange is proof. The oatmeal cookie is tempting on it its own, but topped with delicious orange glaze, it is unforgettable. Joy's orange glaze makes just about anything taste better. Even oranges taste better with orange glaze.
Servings: 16

1 teaspoon orange zest
1 cup butter, softened
1 cup light brown sugar, packed
¾ cup granulated sugar
2 eggs
1 teaspoon vanilla
1 ½ cups flour
1 teaspoon salt
1 teaspoon baking soda
½ teaspoon ground ginger
3 cups old-fashioned oatmeal
½ cup raisins, optional
Orange Glaze

Preheat oven to 350 degrees.
Combine zest, butter and sugars in a medium-size mixing bowl; add eggs and vanilla and beat well until light and fluffy.
In another mixing bowl, combine flour, salt, baking soda and ginger; add to butter and sugar mixture. Stir in oats and raisins, if using, and mix well.
Bake in an ungreased 13-by-9-inch pan for 30 to 35 minutes.
While still warm, drizzle with Orange Glaze. Cut into 16 bars.

Orange Glaze
Yield: about ½ cup

2 tablespoons orange juice
1 cup powdered sugar

Whisk ingredients together until sugar dissolves.

The landscape of our surroundings has so much to do with our food choices today, just as it did when our ancestors lived off the land. The Golden Delicious apple is the state fruit of West Virginia, and Jonathan Chapman, a planter and preacher, is credited with its beginnings. In the early 1800s, he roamed the area and planted so many orchards and apple seeds that he earned the nickname Johnny Appleseed. Apple trees soon replaced the peach trees introduced by Spanish explorers. Peach Creek, near Jack's hometown, was at one time most likely a peach orchard, but now it's a rail yard. Jack's second cousin Phyllis Marshall, whom the Marshall Center at the University of South Florida is named for (but that's another story), gave me a copy of a cookbook she made in honor of her mother called *Myrtle's Favorites*. The daughter of Jack's great-aunt Eliza Beagles Stevens, Myrtle left behind a legacy of home-cooked specialties that Phyllis fondly remembered.

From the mountains of West Virginia to the piney woods of Cracker country, a homemade layer cake is more than simply two sheets of moist cake held together and topped with a sweet buttercream frosting. West Virginia has the Six-Layer Apple Stack Cake, with layers of spicy cake filled with thick applesauce or a reconstituted dried apple mixture. The wiregrass region of North Florida and South Alabama is known for something a little sweeter: the many-layered—anywhere from five to fifteen—chocolate or caramel cake. For me, family reunions were not only a time to reconnect with relatives but also a smorgasbord of sweets. The food was homegrown and fabulous, but the dessert table was my highlight, and pies were my favorite—unless there was one of Granny's Seven-Layer Chocolate Frosted Cakes. The amount of batter Granny made determined the number of thin layers, each made in a flat cast-iron skillet. GrandMary told me Granny Trixie usually stopped long before she made it to fifteen, unlike many of her church friends and neighbors. But each layer was covered with a warm, boiled chocolate frosting. The thickness of the cake layers was almost equal to that of the sweet chocolate icing, which to me made it the perfect cake. My version of both cakes can be found in chapter 9.

Leaving their homelands and making the voyage across the Atlantic Ocean to a British North America, many people were looking for new opportunity and a better life for themselves and their families. On Jack's side of the family, it all started with Richard Stallings of Stallings Busk in the English midlands. As an indentured servant, he eventually paid his debt and bought property that he left to his children. His son Jacob, in turn, left more land to his son of the same name. Cast-iron cookware was considered valuable and passed from one generation to the next. The 1819 will of Jack's fifth great-grandfather, Jacob Stallings, included a variety of household implements: tea kettle, flat irons, shovel, candle mold, loom chest, milk pan, pepper caster, candle snuffer, crockery, teaspoon, six cups and saucers, six pewter plates, three pewter dishes, wire sifter, skillet, kettles and hooks. Log cabin living was harsh, but they managed to survive and prosper. This Jacob Stallings was the last of the clan to spell his surname with an "a" instead of an "o." Jack's cousin Merewyn Stollings McEldowney wrote a paper explaining possible reasons for the spelling change and what life was like at the time. The change might have been an oversight when transcribing documents, as he and his brother moved to different parts of the United States. That explains the West Virginia relationship to one notable Carolina ancestor: George Tweedy Stallings, who in 1914 led the Boston Braves from last place to World Series champions. Later came Floyd Dryden Stollings, founder of the town of Stollings, West Virginia. In 1873, Floyd married Louella Stone, a descendant of Devil Anse Hatfield. One of his youngest children was Lonnie Floyd, Jack's grandfather. The gnarly mess becomes untangled at this point, but it would take another book to explain that family.

After European explorations, the Spanish, French and British settlers began to make homes for themselves, and the colonial period was established. The Sheffield clan was part of the migration of settlers from the Carolinas to North Florida. My great-grandfather Zachery Taylor Sheffield and his brother, George Washington Sheffield, were born of true Patriots, even though they had a hard life in the wilds of the Florida Panhandle. Running moonshine was an easy way to make a living, and meanness ran in the family. My father told me this about his grandfather: "He had a long white beard, he was scary and I would hide in the woods every time he came by." Daddy's father followed that path as well, but Granny Mattie was one of the gentlest souls I ever knew. Her grandparents

Cook family children as adults with father James Elwood Cook. *From left to right*: Roy, Goldie, Eula B., Ruby, Annie, Hattie, David Jackson, Carlton, Arthur, Mattie and James Elwood. *Courtesy of Lisa Kalmbach and Betty Cook.*

were James C. Cook and Harriett Emily Harris Cook. Their son, James Elwood Cook, married Margie Yates. Yates's father was Jackson Yates, a Civil War veteran who was nursed back to good health by a Union nurse, Nancy Elvira Gibson, whom he married. Granny Mattie's brothers were James Arthur, David Jackson, Roy Coy and Carlton. She had five sisters: Hattie, Annie, Ruby, Eula B. and Goldie. They doted on Daddy and left him with many sweet memories. David Jackson Cook was a remarkable man in Granny Mattie's life, and Daddy told stories of how he always looked out for her. He became a Florida state trooper, and the old Moss Hill Road in North Florida is named in his honor. We have one other relative we're pretty proud of: our second cousin once removed is Clay Cook, a member of the country music group Zac Brown Band. He doesn't know us, but we're big fans of his music.

Living in an era of no electricity or indoor plumbing, Granny Mattie had a smokehouse and an outhouse. She was slow to accept a modern way of life, so it was always a treat to visit her in the sand hills of North Florida. My father inherited her strong jawline and her strong will, so he later wired her house for electricity, and light bulbs were installed. At first, she didn't want electricity or a telephone. She never got the telephone, but she never complained about the electricity. Growing up, they dined on fish from nearby lakes or rivers. The fish were cleaned and coated with cornmeal before they were pan fried in lard. Nothing fancy but awfully

Floyd Sheffield along a
dirt road in North Florida.
Author's collection.

tasty, according to GrandFloyd. Granny Mattie was known for her tender and delicious smothered chicken. This recipe from an old cookbook by Marion Cabell Tyree reminded me of Granny Mattie:

Smothered Chicken

Kill the day before it is smothered. Split open the back, as if to broil. When ready to cook, wipe dry with a clean towel, rub well with butter and sprinkle with pepper and salt. Put in a pan with a slice of bacon or pork and a pint of water. Simmer an hour or more, basting frequently. When thoroughly done, place on a hot dish.

Stir into the gravy remaining on the fire a beaten egg, mixing it carefully. Pour this into the dish, but not on the chicken. Sift over it cracker, first browned and then pounded. Garnish with parsley, and serve.—*Mrs. S.T.*

Although my father had to drop out of Liberty School at Miller's Ferry early during the Depression to help take care of his mother and siblings, after his father deserted them, he excelled in class and loved reading. Upon entering second grade, his teacher asked him to read a poem to himself and recite it back. This earned him a promotion from second to third grade in one day. I can still hear my dad's voice reciting the childhood poem he never forgot:

Whisky, frisky, hippity, hop.
Up he goes to the treetop.
Whirly, twirly, round and round,
Down he scampers to the ground.
Where's his supper?
In the shell.
Snap it, crack it,
Out it fell.

Chapter 1

THE CRACKER, THE CABIN, THE CULTURE

Happiness is a way of life.
—*Aristotle*

L ike patches of a crazy quilt, the eclectic enclaves of Crackers are intermeshed with the wiregrass region of Florida, Georgia and Alabama. Homesteads were settled from the sand hills of the Panhandle and the grassy knolls to the east, then south through the heartland of Florida— the horse farms, orange groves and cattle ranches—and eventually to the Everglades and Lake Okeechobee. Grocery stores were scarce, and it was usually the men who hunted and trapped wild game in the backwoods and scrub or fished from the creeks and rivers. The women slopped the hogs, churned the butter, milked the cows, shucked the corn, plucked the poultry, canned the crops, preserved the produce, shelled the pecans, snapped the peas, baked the bread and cooked three meals a day. This was all in addition to the other household chores. Tending to the fire for cooking in the tropical heat, they also were fighting off swarms of mosquitoes and hostile Indians, as well as wild animals and outlaws. The family had to make just about everything they needed to survive, even their living quarters.

The Cracker culture, a southern subculture with Scotch-Irish ancestry, is as unique as its architecture. Crackers embraced the modern architecture mantra "form follows function" to bring design alive in their dwellings, both inside and out. Once they settled on a location, a barn usually was put up first, before the settlers quickly built their crude one-room cabins,

The S.P. Howard family, with friend Verdie standing to the left, 1905.

A drawing of a pioneer log cabin when Florida was under British rule.

called single-pens. Other rooms were later added, creating different home styles with terms such as double-pen and saddlebag. A dogtrot, for example, is a house divided into two equal sides with a space down the middle to channel the breeze. Pine lumber was plentiful, and the sap it contained helped harden the soft wood. Doors and windows were strategically placed to catch slow-moving Florida breezes, and the houses were built high off the ground on pilings made of brick or wooden piers so cool air could circulate underneath. High ceilings aided in keeping the temperature down inside, as the hot air slowly wafted upward. Sweltering kitchens were at times in the back of the house, detached or in separate buildings.

Florida vernacular architecture brought together local resources, knowledge and skills to protect new settlers from the Sunshine State's hot, humid and hurricane-riddled environment. Wraparound porches provided shade for outside work and living spaces, with maybe a hand pump and water basin for washing up before dinner, ideal for hanging out and cooling down during the steamy days. The yard was swept clean of debris to keep brush fires at bay. Homes were furnished sparsely with beds, a table, chairs, perhaps a trunk or fancy dresser and a pie safe in the kitchen. A garden or sweet potato patch near the kitchen provided variety and much-needed nutrients to their diets. The first capitol building in Tallahassee was a Cracker

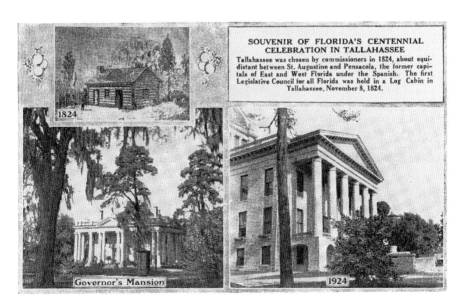

Photo collage of the two old capitols and the Governor's Mansion in Tallahassee, 1824.

cabin, possibly two stories, first built for the Florida Territory. Today, the state's double-high-rise capitol building is indicative of the lifestyle changes over generations.

Most Crackers were self-reliant when it came to feeding their families. Many were hardworking settlers trying to make a better life for themselves. Subsistence farming was a way of life, and they planted corn, sweet potatoes and sugar cane. At times, a sweet potato patch was all they had, but corn eventually became a staple of the Cracker diet. Depending on location, a grape arbor, figs or citrus, peach and pear trees might be found growing on their property. A kitchen garden also might include collard, turnip or mustard greens, along with white potatoes, onions, lettuce and tomatoes.

Settlers constructed livestock pens and hog-tight fences to keep farm animals in and the wild hogs, known as piney woods rooters, out. Chickens roamed the yard or roosted in a chicken coop, protected from weather and predators. After being dug up in the early fall, sweet potatoes were put in a potato house, which provided dark and relatively cool storage. For some, the potatoes were stored near the house, covered in layers of pine straw for protection. A hardwood fire burning in the smokehouse was home to hanging pork for curing and smoking, to preserve it for future use. Another common sight on a Cracker homestead might be a corncrib used for livestock fodder.

Just as first-generation Floridians and their descendants are often called Crackers, stretching from the piney woods of the Florida Panhandle to the central heartland and south to the tropical frontier, those who helped tame the Keys are called Conchs. Conchs have their own history and are known for epicurean delights such as conch chowder, conch fritters, conch salads and the state pie of Florida, Key lime pie.

THE CRACKER.

The Cracker, 1871.

Historic northeast Florida is known for Minorcan datil peppers used in stews and seafood dishes, while the Seminole Indians of the Everglades developed their fry bread, perfecting it once self-rising flour was introduced to the area.

Seminole Fry Bread

Heat enough oil to cover the fry bread in a large, deep, flat-bottomed pan until very hot. Take about two cups self-rising flour and mix with about two-thirds of a cup of water, using one hand to mix the flour, while slowly adding water with the other hand. Then carefully place golf ball–sized balls of dough in the hot oil and cook about five seconds per side. Use a fork or slotted spoon to turn and brown the bread on both sides. When done, place on a paper towel to drain. Serve hot, sprinkled with powdered sugar.—*A Culinary History of Florida*

Tampa has always had a rich Latino heritage. At one time, home delivery of Cuban bread from La Segunda Bakery in Ybor City was a daily occurrence. Casitas had a nail next to the front door, and the delivery man would impale the three-foot-long bread on the nail. The Greek enclave in Tarpon Springs adds a sweetness to the area, as nice as baklava, and the area is famous for a popular Greek salad. Louis M. Pappamichalopoulos, who shortened his name to Pappas after arriving in America, created his version of the Greek salad by adding a scoop of potato salad to the bottom of the bowl. His salad is dressed with distilled white vinegar, olive oil and oregano. Today, the humble café that started in 1925 in Tarpon Springs has developed into a chain of restaurants called Louis Pappas Fresh Greek, serving the popular salad with other Greek specialties. Here is my version from *A Culinary History of Florida*.

Little Greek Salad

Potato salad
Romaine, chopped
Tomatoes, seeded and chopped
Cucumber, seeded, peeled and chopped
Radish, grated
Kalamata olives
Beets, chopped
Feta cheese, crumbled
Anchovies (optional)
Shrimp, cooked (optional)

Put a scoop of your favorite potato salad in the bottom of a salad bowl before topping it with romaine, chopped tomatoes, cucumber, radish, Kalamata olives, beets and feta cheese. Top with anchovies and cooked shrimp, if desired.

Easy Greek Dressing
¾ cup white vinegar
2 tablespoons olive oil
2 tablespoons vegetable oil
1 teaspoon dried oregano

Combine all ingredients in a jar with a tight-fitting lid and shake well.

What began with the weathering of the Appalachian Mountains resulted in perfectly shaped oval quartz grains of sugar-white sand, which drifted down waterways to the shores of the Florida Gulf Coast. This contributed to another Florida specialty: the Donax, or coquina clam, broth. Exported north at one time, it was made from those little bivalve mollusks that burrow into the shoreline as the waves along the Gulf Coast beaches recede. Thousands of years ago, the submerged land mass evolved into the shape of Florida that we recognize today. As the ice ages came and went, the shoreline of the state receded and expanded accordingly, at times more than fifty miles out into the Gulf of Mexico. The Florida Ridge became fertile ground for the citrus seeds brought by early European explorers in the 1500s. It became the backbone of our state and our economy as it blossomed into an enchanted land of orange groves.

Spanish cattle and pigs came to Florida with early European explorers. Pumpkin and squash were already a staple of the indigenous people. By the time Spain ceded Florida to the British, the 1696 story of Jonathan Dickinson and his shipwreck, survival and walk to St. Augustine was old news. *Jonathan Dickinson's Journal* was one of the first written records of this wilderness trek and described how the group aboard the ship *Reformation* washed ashore along the southeast coast of the state. In a territory mostly populated with indigenous people, they survived on the kindness of those showing them how to live off the land, eating unpleasant-tasting berries, fire-roasted pumpkin and freshly caught fish before reaching St. Augustine and civilization as they knew it.

Colton's Florida, circa 1855, Florida's early statehood period. *FMA/J.H. Colton & Co., New York.*

The population continued to evolve. Decades later, indigenous tribes were replaced as Creek Indians from Georgia and Alabama pushed farther south. Many were later known as Seminole Indians. They tended to the citrus groves abandoned by the earlier Spanish and British settlers, but three wars later, many were driven north out of the state or south to the Everglades. A few remained in the Panhandle. Early migration to the state during the plantation period brought wealthy owners who sought cheap or free labor, turning to indentured servants and slaves to keep the Florida plantations working. One of the first plantations was dubbed "Crackertown," a nickname given to Denys Rolle's plantation on the St. Johns River near Palatka. According to Bernard Bailyn in *Voyagers to the West*, Englishman Rolle started his soon-to-be-failed plantation with "no more than a scattering of log cabins thrown up in a riverside clearing hacked out of a forest of scrub oaks and pine trees." More plantations were established, but pioneer families led a very different lifestyle.

Grady McWhiney explained how the term *Cracker* was used to describe these immigrants in his book *Cracker Culture: Celtic Ways in the Old South*. At one time, the term *Cracker* was considered an ethnic slur. When you trace the origins, you begin to realize these mostly poor whites came from a heritage of hardworking Scotch-Irish immigrants from the Celtic region of the British Isles and English Uplands. Northern Ireland was settled by Scots, bringing about the term Scot-Irish or Scotch-Irish. When they came to America, they brought many of their homeland traditions with them, including the equipment and knowledge to set up distilleries for "moonshine making." Known as far back as the 1500s, the term *Cracker* was used in the often-cited William Shakespeare play *The Life and Death of King John*: "What cracker is this same that deafs our ears with this abundance of superfluous breath?" Here the term refers to someone who is full of hot air. The Scotch-Irish called the loud-mouthed braggarts who tended to herds of cattle Crackers, which helps explain the meaning of the word *wisecrack*.

The Industrial Revolution after the Revolutionary War helped establish American towns and cities, while the Second Industrial Revolution following the Civil War benefited those same towns and cities but did little to improve the lives of Florida Crackers in the wilderness. It wasn't until after the end of Reconstruction that Cracker families began to prosper. Florida became a territory in 1822, and by 1830, according to census data, the population was more than 34,000, swelling to more than 180,000 by 1870. This increase was due in part to the Armed Occupation Act passed in 1842, followed by statehood in 1845 and later the 1862 Homestead Act. Both encouraged pioneers to set up homesteads with the promise, in part, of a 160-acre claim if they lived on the land for at least five years. Families became even more self-sufficient in remote areas throughout North Florida, and the Cracker population grew. Florida is America's oldest cattle-raising state and started out as an open range state, with unfenced cows freely roaming central Florida's scrubland. Cracker cattle, as they were called, were offspring of Spanish breeds and launched Florida's new settlers into the cattle industry. That is when cowboys became Florida cowmen as they branded and claimed what roamed free. They came to the area in search of a better life for themselves and their families, as they eked out a bare living in the tropical Sunshine State.

Cracker cowmen—not cowboys in Florida—introduced a whole new way of life. They rode Cracker ponies, and Jacob Summerlin, an early Florida cowman, was known as "King of the Crackers" because of his cattle-driving empire. They snapped their long leather whips, which made a cracking

Florida cowman on a marshtackie (Florida Cracker horse) near Fort McCoy, circa 1910.

sound due to the grass tip, to round up cattle from the scrub and swamps of Florida and get them back on the trail for roundup. These people were poor for the most part, except for Summerlin and a few others who shipped cattle to Cuba for a profit. Cracker cowmen camped out for months, branding and rounding up cattle as they sheltered their horses inside wooden pens scattered over the range, often spaced about one day's ride apart. Cows were scrawny and thin with tough, stringy meat. Raising cattle gave Crackers the leisure time and independence they prized. Unlike growing citrus or vegetables, cattle herding required little money and labor. Today, the reference to Cracker has a different meaning to different people. Some think they were a group of poor white people who migrated from Georgia to Florida—so poor that they had to crack and cook their own corn as a mainstay of their diet rather than take their dried corn to a mill.

Statehood and steamboats slowly brought change to the Florida Cracker lifestyle, with steamboats delivering groceries up and down the St. Johns River and carrying tourists who cruised through the interior of the state. The cuisine on these cruises reflected some of the dining choices most Crackers enjoyed. A dinner menu on the *Okeehumkee* offered soup, broiled shad, turkey and roast beef, with dessert including pumpkin pie and pudding. For breakfast, they were served thin-sliced broiled ham, fresh eggs, tender beefsteak, coffee, cornbread and biscuits. Soon to follow were railroads with refrigerated rail cars, bringing factory-made goods and tourists for the first time to wilderness areas of the state. Wealthy northern families of the Gilded Age came to spend the winter in luxury hotels along the railroad lines of Henry Flagler and Henry Plant. From Flagler's Breakers Hotel in Palm Beach to Plant's Tampa Bay Hotel, and northeast to St. Augustine, the dichotomy of lifestyles was stark, but the railroad and steamships made it easier for Cracker families to get supplies, food gadgets and even what seemed like exotic foods at the time. Open-hearth cooking was being replaced by coal- or wood-burning stoves for the middle class, but this was not as common in the rural areas.

By the late 1800s, iconic writers started to bring attention to the Florida lifestyle. In her book *Palmetto Leaves*, Harriet Beecher Stowe described the orange trees as stately and intoxicating, among the Indian raids and alligators. Her descriptions of dining show how she struggled to find a cook who knew how to make something other than hoecakes and fried salt pork, ham or chicken. Fishing outings ended with a dinner cooked clambake style. They even set up a portable kerosene stove for making French coffee and served ham sandwiches, cakes, crackers and cheese. Her descriptions of the tropical paradise of Florida, as she cruised along the St. Johns River on a steamboat, gave the economy a boost as she encouraged her readers to travel south to Florida.

Stowe wrote of growing cabbage, cucumbers, tomatoes, sweet potatoes, sugar cane, Irish potatoes and peas. In May when the oranges were gone, the nursery-grown strawberries, early peaches, blackberries, huckleberries and two species of wild plums filled the void. She discussed stock breeding and dairy farming, describing Florida butter as "pure and sweet, like solidified cream, and as different as can be from the hard, salty mass which most generally passes for butter among us." She praised the buttermilk as well, as sweet and rich. Stowe eventually hired a cook who made beautiful bread, biscuits and rolls but "was worth more than we could give and went from us to enjoy forty dollars per month as cook in a hotel."

Pulitzer Prize–winning author Marjorie Kinnan Rawlings arrived in Cross Creek, Florida, in the 1930s and documented life among Florida Crackers in her fact-based fictional book *The Yearling* and her memoir *Cross Creek*. Her Cracker homestead is now a part of the Florida State Parks system. She

Vernon street scene with the James Monroe Jones store to the left and the courthouse at the end of the street, circa 1900.

penned *Cross Creek Cookery* about her time there and the recipes she created while living at "the Creek."

Another iconic writer, Laura Ingalls Wilder, along with her husband, Almanzo, and their daughter, Rose Wilder, boarded a train and came to live in the hot and sandy Panhandle wilderness of Westville. They realized it wasn't what they had hoped for, so the future author of *The Little House on the Prairie* series moved back north. This was just a few years before my paternal grandmother, Mattie Lenora Cook, was born east of Westville on Christmas Eve 1896. In the early 1900s, these frontier communities were beginning to tame the wilderness and swamps and embrace the woodlands as home. During my father's childhood, women were still doing most of the household chores, and Granny Mattie was no exception. She lived in a time when artesian wells, hand pumps and shared gourds or tin dippers were common along the side of the wood-frame Cracker house. Her yard was swept clean, and the ashes from the coal- or wood-burning stove were emptied out each day. Electricity would soon change the way of life and cooking styles for those living in cities, but it would take longer to set up power grids in the rural areas. That meant many were still toting in wood if they didn't have a gas stove, drawing water from a well or pump, reading by gas lamps, traveling by horse and buggy, sleeping with windows and doors open since there was not yet air conditioning and living without a telephone or phonograph until after the Great Depression and World War II. Granny Mattie was a true Florida Cracker and embraced her religion and her rural life. She read her Bible endlessly and would do without in order to give to the church. Mistreated by her husband, she found peace with the Lord when she died in 1967.

READING LIST

Cracker: The Cracker Culture in Florida, Dana Sainte Claire
Cracker Culture: Celtic Ways in the Old South, Grady McWhiney
Cross Creek, Marjorie Kinnan Rawlings
A Land Remembered, Patrick D. Smith
Palmetto Leaves, Harriet Beecher Stowe
Strawberry Girl, Lois Lenski
Yesteryear I Lived in Paradise, Myrtle Scharrer Betz

Chapter 2

CRACKER COMMUNITY

Monday: Wash
Tuesday: Iron
Wednesday: Sew
Thursday: Market
Friday: Bake
Saturday: Clean
Sunday: Rest

Dish towels of the past were embroidered with chores for each day of the week. Fortunately, today they are more cute than meaningful. Sunday, the day of rest, was often filled with all-day church, along with preparing for and attending dinner on the grounds. For some, the rules were strict; if you missed three Sundays in a row, repenting was strongly urged. The same was true for dancing, swearing, drinking and fishing on Sunday. Meanwhile, others had fun dancing at Florida backwoods frolics. Churches and schools, often housed in the same building, also were used for local gatherings. Hog killings and sugar cane grindings in the fall were community affairs and good reasons to throw a party, even though celebratory foods were limited to mostly chicken, sweet potatoes, corn and sweet treats made with cane syrup and nuts. Eggs, bacon and sausage were usually plentiful for a hearty breakfast, as were grits if a gristmill was nearby. Marjorie Kinnan Rawlings proclaimed that adding cheese grits to the breakfast menu constituted a feast. Homemade sausage was a simple combination of fresh, fat and lean pork, chopped fine with added spices such as salt, pepper and sage. Small game and fish, preserved in barrels of salt, added variety to their diets. Seasonal cooking played a large part in the daily diet.

When Florida cowmen got ready for the roundup, they packed dozens of biscuits and sweet potatoes and would bring along a slab of salt bacon, perhaps an onion and coffee. Joe G. Warner described what it was like on the trail in *Biscuits and Taters: A History of Cattle Raising in Manatee County.* When water was in short supply, they would make coffee by reusing the same water that had boiled the bacon. "Greasy salty coffee was good…ate taters first, scraped mold off the hardened biscuits and toasted them." Taking care of the home was left to the wife, the children and the neighbors.

Before ice was common, fishermen would clean their fish and then pack them in salt for a few days, creating a brine, and if done properly, the fish would keep for up to a year. My father and his sister, Ila Jean, went from Vernon to St. Andrews in what is now Bay County to walk along the beach looking for salted fish for sale to take home for dinner. Today, we might have a community fish fry of mullet, grouper or catfish along with coleslaw, cheese grits, hush puppies and sweet tea. Cracker community celebrations of the past would often include a big pot or two of chicken

Family in front of home, Monticello, circa 1930.

Etching of a Cracker family going to church, circa 1875.

perlou, also spelled perloo, purloo, pilau, pillau or perlow. Chicken dishes were reserved for company or Sunday dinner until the price of chicken fell. The perlou chicken was one too old to lay eggs, so the dish allowed for a long cooking time to tenderize the old hen. The servings were extended by adding enough rice to feed the community. Cooked in large pots outside over a hot fire, the combination is now popular at family reunions and dinner on the grounds. The Spanish version of chicken and yellow rice, or *arroz con pollo*, is similar. A popular recipe in the 1970s was chicken and wild rice, baked in the oven.

Many cooking techniques were passed down from early American settlers. Cookbooks published by those in colonial towns represent the methods used in many Florida households as well. Marion Cabell Tyree's 1878 cookbook *Housekeeping in Old Virginia* offers insight into some of those methods with her descriptions of preparations and cooking, using her own experience as well as those of her "sister housekeepers." The following is a recipe from her book for stewed chicken with dumplings:

Stewed Chicken

Cut up and lay in salt and water. Put them in water enough to cover them, with some slices of middling. Let them boil till nearly done. Then put in the dumplings, made like biscuit but rolled thin, and let them boil till done. Roll a piece of butter in flour, with pepper, salt, chopped parsley and celery, or a little celery-seed. When the gravy is thick enough, pour in a teacup of cream or milk, and let it boil up once. Take off the fire and serve hot.—*Mrs. Col. W.*

Some recipes from Tyree noted that you should never cook a chicken the same day it is killed, unless it is fried, and there lies a controversy if you follow her recipes closely. The following recipe for fried chicken states the chicken should be killed the night before:

Fried Chicken

Kill the chicken the night before, if you can, and lay on ice, or else kill early in the morning. When ready, wipe dry, flour it, add pepper and salt, and fry in a little lard. When nearly done, pour off the lard, add one-half teacup water, large spoonful butter, and some chopped parsley. Brown nicely and serve. Meal mush fried is nice with the chicken.—*Mrs. Col. W.*

Fried chicken, along with chicken and dumplings, was usually reserved for Sunday dinner. Up until the 1950s, chicken was considered a delicacy and served mostly at luxury restaurants and first-class dining cars on trains. It became much more affordable once industrialization changed farming and transportation. No longer did you have to wring its neck yourself and pluck its feathers; you could pick up whole or cut-up chicken at the market.

Reading recipes written more than one hundred years ago can be insightful and entertaining. The following is another Tyree recipe for chicken pie, followed by one I developed for *A Culinary History of Florida.*

Mrs. Bilinski in her chicken yard, Monticello, circa 1929.

Chicken Pie

Make into a paste one quart of flour with the weight of four eggs in butter and a large spoonful of lard. Put the paste in a deep dish, lining the bottom and side with chicken interspersed with layers of very thin bacon. Add some large crumbs, some pepper, and a quarter-pound butter. Fill the dish with cold water, and yolks of four or six hard-boiled eggs, then dredge with flour and put on the top crust. Let it bake gradually. It will take two hours to bake.—*Mrs. Col. W.*

Cast-Iron Skillet Chicken Pie

½ cup chopped Florida sweet onion
½ cup chopped celery
½ cup chopped carrot
¼ cup (4 tablespoons) butter
⅓ cup flour
1½ teaspoons salt

½ teaspoon white pepper
2½ cups chicken stock (see page 45)
½ cup heavy cream
2 cups chicken, cooked and chopped
1 cup fresh or frozen peas
9-inch pastry (see page 132)

Preheat oven to 450 degrees.

In a cast-iron skillet, sauté onion, celery and carrot in butter over medium heat. Stir in flour, salt and pepper; cook 2 to 3 minutes while stirring.

Gradually stir in chicken stock and cream; continue cooking and stirring occasionally until thick, 20 to 25 minutes.

Add chicken and peas; heat to bubbling.

Place pastry over chicken mixture and bake in oven for 15 minutes, or until the pastry is golden brown.

Following is a recipe for chicken salad from Tyree:

Chicken Salad

One large chicken boiled; when cold remove the skin and chop into a dish, over which throw a towel slightly dipped in cold water to keep the meat moist. When the celery is cut, put between clean cloths to dry.

Take one tablespoonful best mustard, the yolk of one raw egg, which drop into a dish large enough to hold all the dressing; beat well for ten minutes and slowly add to the mustard one tablespoonful vinegar.

When well mixed add three-eighths bottle of oil, a drop at a time, always stirring the same way.

Rub the yolks of six hard-boiled eggs very smooth and stir in half a teacup of vinegar. Pour this mixture to the mustard, oil, etc., stirring together as lightly as possible.

Add to the chicken one pint chopped celery, a little yellow pickle, and half a loaf of stale bread crumbs, and the oil taken from the water in which the chicken has boiled. Salt and pepper to taste.

Pour on the dressing just before serving. If the salad is kept too cool the dressing will curdle.—*Mrs. E.*

I make this simplified version of chicken salad with a recipe my mother gave me. Jack, my husband, liked it so much it made it into his book of essays, *Jack Harris Unwrapped*. His book also includes my recipe for a quick chicken stock, which is more like a hearty broth. When I am trying to save up chicken stock for holiday cooking, I use the chicken for this salad and freeze the stock for chicken and dumplings, dressing and gravy. My recipe for chicken and dumplings can be found on page 138.

Mother-in-Law's Chicken Salad

8 ounces cream cheese, softened
¼ cup mayonnaise
2 tablespoons lemon juice
½ teaspoon salt
¼ teaspoon ground ginger
4 drops red pepper sauce
2 cups finely chopped cooked chicken
1 hard-cooked egg, chopped

Mix cream cheese, mayonnaise, lemon juice, salt, ginger and pepper sauce. Stir in chicken and chopped egg.
Cover and refrigerate several hours.
Serve with crackers or toast.

⌒

Quick Chicken Stock

1 tablespoon olive oil
1 ½ pounds chicken breast and thighs
3 medium onions, chopped
2 carrots, chopped
3 stalks celery with leaves, cut into 2-inch pieces
1 quart water
2 teaspoons salt
2 bay leaves

Heat oil in large stock pot. Sauté the chicken about 5 to 10 minutes on each side.

Add onion, carrots and celery to pot and sauté about 5 to 10 minutes.

Increase heat to high and add water, salt and bay leaves.

Simmer, covered, about 45 minutes.

Remove chicken and strain stock for use in soups and stews.

High in protein, vitamins and minerals, eggs were also a staple of Cracker diets. If you had a laying hen, eggs were plentiful and could be enjoyed for breakfast, dinner or supper, as a dessert or snack. If you didn't have a hen, eggs were not quite "a dime a dozen," but close, at twenty to thirty cents a dozen in the 1880s. Boiled and chopped, they were added to many main dishes and soups. Fried, scrambled, baked, pickled or deviled, the egg is still popular on Cracker tables today.

Many Cracker homesteads had sweet potato and sugar cane patches in their fields or gardens. Sweet potatoes became a staple food for Florida Crackers, and sugar cane could be processed into syrup for personal use or sold for extra income. Hoecakes and cane syrup were often the only dessert at simple Cracker tables. Sweet potatoes were served in a variety of ways, including baked or fried with butter, added to cornbread and used in waffles or substituted for pumpkin in recipes such as pies and cakes. Tyree had this suggestion:

> *Nearly everybody likes sweet potatoes, and this way of preparing them will be a revelation to those who have only known them in their plain form. To make the waffles, take left-over sweet potatoes and mash; to each two rounding tablespoonsful, add one each level tablespoon butter and sugar, one pint of milk and four tablespoons of flour, one-half teaspoonful salt. Beat together and add two eggs well beaten; pass through a sieve and bake in a hot waffle iron. Serve with whipped cream flavored with four tablespoonsful of strained honey added before whipping, or omit the honey and sweeten with maple syrup. Mashed cooked carrots can be used in place of the potatoes. In this case, omit the sugar and cream and serve the waffles with dusted sugar over the top.*

Cracker families had sweet potatoes baked for dinner and leftover for breakfast without the luxury of putting them into waffles with maple syrup; however, sweet potato pie is still a Cracker favorite. My father showed me

Sweet potato storage bank, December 12, 1908.

the best way to cook sweet potatoes in order to bring out their naturally sweet flavor. So, I slow bake the potatoes in a 275- to 300-degree oven for about ninety minutes, depending on size, then top them fresh from the oven with butter.

Sugar cane syrup was a staple in Florida households, and community cane-grinding celebrations were part of these homesteaders' highlights. The Cracker community came together in the fall to pool their time, energy and resources and produce enough Florida cane syrup for all who volunteered to help. Working in the fields required men to cut, load and haul the cane to the animal-drawn cane grinder or press. Stalks were fed by hand, as the animal walked in a circle, hitched to a pole that turned the press. (By 1910, mules, oxen and horses were replaced with gasoline engines.) The extracted juice went into a huge broad-brimmed iron kettle, where it was then ready for boiling over a steady fire as it slowly thickened into syrup. When the color changed from amber to dark brown, the sweet syrup was nearly finished. But it took the knowledge of a syrup master to know just when to remove the kettle. Removed too early, it would sour; removed too late, it turned to sugar. It took about ten gallons of juice to make one gallon of syrup. The syrup was

Making syrup from cane juice, Eustis, 1892. The man in the bowler hat to the right is
E.N. Spinney.

then stored in mason jars or cans for later use. But some was poured onto a
buttered plate to cool for making taffy. Chewing on a cut of sugar cane was a
treat, but the taffy pull was the highlight of the community event. After days
or weeks of hard work, the celebration would begin, at times culminating
with a taffy-pulling contest. Cane grindings were also social gatherings,
called frolics. Fiddles, dancing, courting and taffy pulling were part of this
community event.

Taffy wasn't the only candy made using Florida cane syrup. Granny
used cane syrup and peanuts to make a simple candy. From the first time
my mother made it for us using her mother's recipe, I was hooked. A
youngster at the time, I didn't write down the recipe, so I experimented a
bit, and a recipe for Trixie's Cane Syrup Peanut Candy can be found on
page 161. Today, we have the luxury of visiting living history museums
where demonstrations show how syrup was made during the early
pioneer days. Dade City's Pioneer Florida Museum and Village features
a cane syrup mill, and Dudley Farm holds an annual Cane Day. The

A Cracker family on their way to a frolic, 1887. *From* Frank Leslie's Illustrated Newspaper, *April 30, 1887.*

first Saturday in December, there is a Robert E. Long Cane Syrup Day in the community of Two Egg. A few years ago, Jack and I were driving through the area on the eve of Cane Syrup Day and saw a soft, warm light glowing under a shed in the distance as preparations were being made for the next day.

Hog-killing time was another fall community event, due to the number of men necessary to take on the task of killing, cleaning, cutting and storing the meat. As explained in *A Culinary History of Florida*:

The cool fall weather was a perfect time for social gatherings and a good old-fashioned hog killing. The meat was shared, due to lack of refrigeration, and the process took a few strong men. After the hog was shot, it was put into a huge vat of scalding hot water to loosen and help remove the bristles on its skin. The skin was saved for cracklings and pork rinds. The meat was then cut into sections, salted and hung to dry in the chimney or smokehouse. Nothing went to waste, the fat was used to flavor vegetables when cooking, the tail was skinned and chopped for stew, the bones for soups, the brains were fried, the hooves were boiled for jelly and the feet were pickled.

Old-fashioned bacon and ham were made by packing in salt or soaking in a strong salt brine, turning, re-salting and draining frequently, for several weeks to a month, until the salt is soaked through and the meat is cured. Then, it is slowly smoked, until darker in color, with the taste of smoke throughout the meat. Salt is a preservative that stops the growth of molds and bacteria, and smoke, also a preservative, was necessary without refrigeration.

Vernon Grammar School, 1935.

Salt pork, similar to bacon, was often fried and called "poor man's chicken." It was first soaked in milk or water for a couple of hours to help leach out the salt, then rolled or dipped in cornmeal and fried in hot fat. The use of liquid smoke is not entirely new, as Martha McCulloch-Williams mentioned in her 1913 book *Dishes and Beverages of the Old South.* She noted that three dips into liquid smoke (crude pyroligneous acid) would reduce the smoking time from six weeks to two weeks. She went on to say a smokehouse needed to be kept dark, dry, cool and well-ventilated to prevent the meat from spoiling. To discourage pests, some meats were coated with molasses and black pepper. "Ham perfectly cured and canvassed keeps indefinitely in the right sort of smokehouse—but there is not much gain in flavor after they are three years old."

Tyree gives suggestions for curing bacon and making sausage:

To Cure Bacon

Pack the meat in salt and allow it to remain five weeks. Then take the hams up, wash off, and wipe dry. Have some sacks made of about seven-eighths shirting, large enough to hold the hams and tie above the hock. Make a pot of sizing of equal portions of flour and corn meal, boil until thick, and dip each sack until the outside is well coated with sizing. Put the hams in bags, and tie tight with a strong twine and hang by the same in the smoke-house.

Seasoning for Sausage
18 pounds meat
9 pounds back fat
2 ounces sage
4 ounces black pepper
12 ounces salt—Mrs. J.P.

Two of Daddy's favorite foods were leftover cold fried fish and boiled peanuts. Ground nuts, or pinders, are a southern legume. When boiled, they have been called "Cracker caviar" or "redneck edamame," better known as boiled peanuts. My father loved his peanuts roasted or boiled. Here is his recipe for boiled peanuts from *A Culinary History of Florida.*

GrandFloyd's Boiled Peanuts

3 pounds young green peanuts, in the shell
3 tablespoons salt

Wash the peanuts in the shell under cool running water. Place peanuts in a large pot and add enough water to cover. Add approximately 1 tablespoon salt for each quart of water.

Bring to a boil; reduce heat to medium and continue to simmer rapidly. Cook 2½ to 3 hours, adding water as needed. Allow peanuts to sit in the pot to absorb desired amount of salt.

Remove the shell before eating.

PLACES TO VISIT

Big Bend Farm, Tallahassee Museum
Bradley's Country Store, Tallahassee
Cow Camp, Lake Kissimmee State Park
Cracker Country Living History Museum, Tampa
Cracker Homestead, Forest Capital Museum State Park, Perry
Crowley Museum and Nature Center, Sarasota
Dudley Farm Historic State Park, Newberry
Fort Christmas Historical Park, Christmas
Heritage Village, Largo
Hogan's Cabin, Morningside Living History Farm, Gainesville
Manatee Village Historical Park, Bradenton
Marjorie Kinnan Rawlings Historic State Park, Cross Creek
Pioneer Cabin, Orange County Regional History Center
Pioneer Florida Museum, Dade City
Pioneer Settlement, Barberville
Pioneer Village at Shingle Creek, Kissimmee
Robert E. Long Cane Syrup Day, Two Egg

Chapter 3

CRACKER KITCHEN

Man may work from sun to sun, but woman's work is never done.
—old proverb

ince the turn of the twentieth century, the evolution of food preparation
has taken a substantial shift. From open-hearth cooking in detached
kitchens to wood-burning stoves and eventually gas and electricity, the
kitchen has moved from the back of the house to the heart of the home.
Before air conditioners, refrigeration, indoor plumbing, electric lights and
window screens, the Cracker cook spent most of her day planning and
preparing meals in a hot and humid environment. Cookware and cooking
methods slowly changed and improved, and recipes evolved to match.
Wooden lug poles suspended across the fire to hang cooking pots and pans
were replaced with adjustable trammels and swinging cranes, but cooking
was still dangerous. Cookware hanging from these devices was heavy and
hot, often burning or scalding the cook. Controlling the heat was perfected
by using a cast-iron three-legged spider set among the coals or a Dutch
oven covered with ash or coals. Later, the roasting kitchen or tin roaster
was developed. This roaster was open on one side and placed in the hearth,
which allowed the contents to cook.

When baking in wood-burning ovens, the temperature was difficult to
regulate. Wood was added as needed to control the heat, and vents had to
be controlled manually. When baking bread, the fire was allowed to burn
down, and then ashes were swept away and the bread was put in. To check

Clifford Mathis kitchen, Tampa, 1942.

Mrs. W.D. Sawyer's electrified kitchen, Jefferson County, 1940.

the temperature, cooks would throw in some flour, and if the flour burned quickly, then the oven was too hot. Experienced cooks could judge the oven temperature simply by sticking their hand inside, estimating degrees by how long it took for their hand to become unbearably hot. A quick or hot oven of 400 to 450 degrees would take a matter of seconds, while a moderate oven of 350 degrees and a slow oven of 200 to 300 degrees would each take progressively longer.

While the Gilded Age of the Victorian period brought railroads and wealth to Florida seaside resorts, it did little to improve the Cracker kitchen. The post-Victorian period marked the beginning of a kitchen revolution as the population became more aware of the importance of nutrition and the harmful effects of germs. Kitchens would become convenient, economical and sanitary. As big cities lit up, electric appliances, ranges and refrigerators were common in towns long before they reached Cracker country. The day might start with toting water from the well to the kitchen, where the fire had already been tended. Collecting eggs from the henhouse and cured meat from the smokehouse was only a part of meal preparation. Other chores included milking the cow and churning butter a couple of times a week, as well as skimming cream off the top after the fresh milk had been strained through a sieve.

Author and cook Marion Cabell Tyree offers suggestions in *Housekeeping in Old Virginia*:

> In warm weather, sweet milk should be set on ice, if practicable, or if not, in a spring-house. Never put ice in sweet milk, as this dilutes it. One pan of milk should always be set aside to raise cream for coffee. A bucket with a close-fitting lid should be filled with milk and set aside for dinner, one for supper, one for breakfast, and a fourth for cooking purposes.
>
> For making butter, strain unskimmed milk into a scalded churn, where the churning is done daily. This will give sweeter butter and nicer buttermilk than when cream is skimmed and kept for churning, as this sometimes gives a cheesy taste to the butter. Do not let the milk in the churn exceed blood heat. If overheated, the butter will be white and frothy, and the milk thin and sour. Churn as soon as the milk is turned. In summer try to churn early in the morning, as fewer flies are swarming then, and the butter can be made much firmer.
>
> Butter should be printed early in the morning, while it is cool. A plateful for each of the three meals should be placed in the refrigerator ready for use. Do not set butter in a refrigerator with anything else in it but milk, or in a

safe with anything but milk. It readily imbibes the flavor of everything near it. After churning, butter should be taken up in what is called "a piggin," first scalded and then filled with cold water. With an old-fashioned butter-stick (scalded) wash and press the butter till no water is left. Then add a little salt, finely beaten. Beat again in a few hours, and make up in half-pound prints. I would advise all housekeepers (even those who do not make their own butter) to keep a piggin, a butter-stick, and a pretty butter-print.

Cottage Cheese

When the teakettle boils, pour the water into a pan of "loppered" milk. It will curd at once. Stir it and turn it into a colander, pour a little cold water over it, salt it and break it up. A better way is to put equal parts of buttermilk and thick milk in a kettle over the fire, heat it almost boiling hot, pour into a linen bag and let it drain until the next day. Then take it out, salt it, put in a little cream or butter, as it may be thick or not, and make it up into balls the size of an orange.

Other common routines in a Cracker kitchen included scraping sugar from the bottom of a syrup can—for some that was the only sugar they had—while others collected honey. A pie safe, used to store fresh baked goods, was covered with a screen that allowed air to circulate throughout the cupboard. Before indoor plumbing or hand pumps in the kitchen, a dry sink held a pitcher or bowl of water brought in from the well. Water drawn up with a bucket and shared with a gourd or tin dipper was welcome in the subtropical wilderness scrub. There was also tending to the horses, slopping the hogs, feeding the chickens, shelling peas and pecans, shucking corn and the handwashing of laundry and hanging it on a line to dry. The washing, sewing, ironing, baking and cleaning often were done on a schedule.

Meat roasting over the fire with a cauldron of water simmering at the large fireplace, pie safes and dry sinks have been replaced with all-electric kitchens. No need to milk your cow or wait for the milkman. Now, you drive to the market in your air-conditioned car and pick up a quart or gallon of skim, whole, buttermilk, chocolate, 2 percent, almond, soy and so on. Today, you take your pick of an ever-growing mix of time-saving food preparation items. No more waiting for the ice man to deliver ice blocks—at least eight inches thick—to put in the icebox, if you were lucky enough to have one.

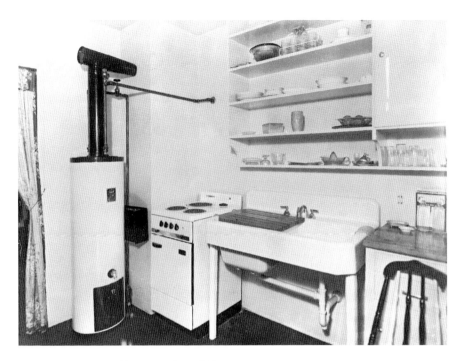

Kitchen in a Jacksonville home, circa 1940.

Some would wrap the ice in burlap and enjoy the cooling refreshment on the front porch while it lasted. Kettles, saucepans, colanders, cake pans, pie dishes, funnels, scoops and dippers were starting to fill the Cracker kitchen shelves. An oblong wooden bowl for mixing flour, lard and milk was used daily for biscuit making. A meat grinder and sausage stuffer would be welcome additions to the kitchen, along with measuring spoons and cups, graters, coffee bean grinders and roasters. One of the most common and popular gadgets was the eggbeater. Linoleum floors were considered modern, along with electric appliances and labor-saving devices such as electric irons, toasters, waffle irons, coffee percolators, pressure cookers and mixers.

No longer do you have to walk to the chicken yard to select a chicken, wring its neck and pluck the feathers before cooking. Now you make a trip to the market to select the cut you want, already cleaned and packaged for cooking that evening or placing in the freezer. Better yet, you can pick up an oven-roasted chicken, cooked while you shop. Some things couldn't be replaced. Cast-iron skillets, with a smooth black surface from years of use, were often passed from one generation to the next and are still an essential part of Cracker cooking. Cast-iron cookware distributes heat evenly, quick-

Mamie Bryan outside the chicken house, Woodville, circa 1910.

Live alligator and ox team, Orlando, circa 1882–87. *FMA/Stanley J. Morrow.*

seals meat, slow-cooks stews, adds iron to the diet and can be used for cooking a large variety of foods.

To supplement the Cracker diet, "varmints" and other unusual Florida foods were part of the dinner table. Some we wouldn't think of eating today, while others are on restaurant menus across the state. For example, I ordered a *soupe a la queue de boeuf* from a fancy French restaurant in central Florida. I thought I was getting beef stew. When I inquired, "What is that delicious bite I've never tasted before?" the waiter informed me, "*Oh oui, Madame*, that would be oxtail." Oxen were the preferred mode of travel for pulling the family wagon. Not only were they strong and able to withstand swarms of horseflies, but they could be eaten at the end of their service. Once an ox had served its purpose as a work animal, it could be slaughtered and made into a stew and the brains fried with eggs, while the hooves were boiled into jelly.

Tyree offers a recipe for oxtail:

Ox-Tail Soup

Wash and soak three tails; pour on them one gallon cold water; let them be brought gradually to boil, throw in one and a half ounce salt, and clear off the scum carefully as soon as it forms on the surface. When it ceases to rise, add:

4 moderate sized carrots.
2 or 3 onions.
1 large bunch savory herbs.
1 head celery.
2 turnips.
6 or 8 cloves, and ½ teaspoonful peppercorns.

Stew these gently from three hours to three and a half hours. If the tails be very large, lift them out, strain the liquor and strain off all the fat. Cut the meat from the tails and put it in two quarts or more of the stock. Stir in, when this begins to boil, a thickening of arrow-root or of rice flour, mixed with as much cayenne and salt as may be required to flavor the soup, and serve very hot.—*Mrs. P.*

Turtles caught on a trotline, Clermont, 1905.

Venison is no longer a common sight at the dinner table and might be considered a luxury for those who don't have the skill or desire to go hunting. A crude method for preparing venison was to cut the meat in thick slices and roast with a little water and lard. While alligator and frog legs still grace menus and dinner tables across the state, they are not commonly found in the market. The Florida Department of Agriculture and Consumer Services suggests using one of your favorite recipes for veal, chicken or seafood to prepare alligator after it's been cleaned and prepped: "Alligator has its own unique flavor that is easily enhanced with seasonings and sauces." As for frog legs, considered a delicacy to some and Cracker food to others, they are usually served sautéed in oil, butter or old-fashioned lard. Alternatively, they can be brined, dredged in flour and fried as you would chicken.

Then there are the varmint entrees of squirrel, opossum and rabbit. While Jack and I were jogging in historic St. Augustine one morning, a fellow passing by on a bike asked if we wanted to buy some squirrels, freshly caught, I presume, by the look of the bag on his back. We declined, but I discovered they could be broiled over hot coals with melted butter, pepper, salt and a little vinegar. Other cooking methods are stewed, barbecued or fried like chicken. Rabbit also can be barbecued, as well as stuffed, roasted, stewed, baked or fried. The preparation of opossum alone is time consuming, which is one of the reasons you won't see opossum on our dinner table. Turtle and terrapin are also time consuming to prepare, but at one time they were offered canned, as well as fresh turtle steaks, at the market. Now many types are on the endangered species list.

Sea turtles are from the ocean, terrapin (also known as cooter) from swampy waters and gopher tortoise from the land. Minorcans used the gopher tortoise in a stew. Author Marjorie Kinnan Rawlings shared her recipe in *Cross Creek Cookery* for Minorcan Gopher Stew using the turtle eggs as well. She lost me with, "Wash the decapitated gopher," although it sounds like a delicacy. Some recipes suggest frying the tortoise meat first, or boiling the meat and simmering the vegetables separately, before adding hard-cooked egg yolks and other spices. "Hoover Chicken" was another name for gopher tortoise after Herbert Hoover's presidential campaign slogan was, in part, "A chicken in every pot." During the Great Depression, the gopher tortoise was all some Floridians could afford. These ancient reptiles have

Illustration from *Strawberry Girl*, written by Lois Lenski, of Cracker children playing with turtles.

lived for millions of years and can be found in all sixty-seven counties of Florida. Turtle soup wasn't just survival food for the poor; recipes for mock turtle and terrapin soup were commonly found in cookbooks. The Federal Writers' Project of 1940 described land turtles in *Florida Seafood Cookery* and referred to terrapin as a species of land tortoise used for Florida gopher stew or steaks. Recipes for turtle soup were common in early cookbooks, including this one from Tyree:

Turtle Soup

Kill the turtle at daylight in summer, the night before in winter, and hang it up to bleed. After breakfast, scald it well and scrape the outer skin off the shell; open it carefully, so as not to break the gall. Break both shells to pieces and put them into the pot. Lay the fins, the eggs and some of the more delicate parts by—put the rest into the pot with a quantity of water to suit the size of your family.

Add two onions, parsley, thyme, salt, pepper, cloves and allspice to suit your taste.

Mrs. Oscar Odulund frying fish in the kitchen, November 1959, Odulund Island. *FMA/Karl E. Holland.*

About half an hour before dinner thicken the soup with brown flour and butter rubbed together. An hour before dinner, take the parts laid by, roll them in brown flour, fry them in butter, put them and the eggs in the soup; just before dinner add a glass of claret or Madeira wine.—*Mrs. N.*

The modernization of the kitchen (1919–40) would introduce measuring cups and spoons, mixing bowls and knives. The rolling pin, flour sifter, food grinder, lemon reamer, biscuit cutter, can opener, grater, teapot, teakettle, pot holder, ice cream freezer, frying pan, griddle, waffle iron, roaster, soup pot, casserole dishes, cake and bread pans, baking sheet, muffin pans, pie pans, potato masher, strainers and appliances became more reliable, affordable and easier to use. If you were lucky, you might have had an all-in-one Hoosier or freestanding cupboard. By 1927, electricity ushered in refrigerators, stoves, mixers, frying pans or skillets, coffee percolators and, by the 1940s, freezers, which became a necessity as the frozen foods of Clarence Birdseye were commonplace. With electricity and appliances slow to reach the poorer Cracker kitchens, home canning was still essential for a year-round supply of fruits and vegetables and even meats. The pantry was full of pickled, potted or canned foods that graced the tables of many Cracker families. Home canning was a way of life, yet these days most opt for canned goods at the store, and for good reason; canning is also part chemistry, and following guidelines can seem daunting. So daunting, in fact, that the U.S. Department of Agriculture makes available a *Complete Guide to Home Canning.*

Before John L. Mason introduced glass jars with the screw band and self-sealing lids in 1858, fruit canning generally followed the rule of one pound sugar to one pound fruit. One suggestion of old was to add enough sugar until the mixture would float an egg. Jellies and jams were topped off with a thick layer of paraffin to seal in the fruit. I recall my mother making jelly only one time, using melted wax to seal the jars. It was exciting for me to watch the process, but GrandMary felt it was so old-fashioned and a waste of time. Granny Mattie was true to her roots and had kitchen shelves full of foods she "put up" (aka canning, preserving, cooking for later use), and her fig preserves were my favorite. Here is her recipe from my *Florida Sweets* book:

Mattie's Fig Preserves

1 quart fresh figs
3 cups sugar
2 cups water
1 teaspoon lemon juice

Layer figs and sugar in a Dutch oven. Add water and bring to a boil, stirring occasionally. Reduce heat, stir in lemon juice and cook over medium heat 2 hours, stirring occasionally, until syrup thickens and figs are clear. Serve with hot buttered biscuits.

My brother Pat has that magic touch when it comes to making jellies and jams, and a few weeks before Hurricane Michael came ripping through the Florida Panhandle, he picked strawberry guavas from his tree to make a tasty jam. Like a true Florida Cracker, he took his guava jam with him when

Patrick Owens Sheffield (aka the tree whisperer) holding strawberry guavas from his yard in Panama City shortly before Hurricane Michael. Fortunately, the tree survived after the hurricane hit. *Courtesy of Patrick Sheffield.*

he evacuated and distributed it to family and friends as Christmas gifts. He promised to share the recipe with me for this book, but recovering from the storm took priority, so we'll have to wait. Through all the devastation of the hurricane, Pat kept his sense of humor. After losing two oak trees in his yard, he simply slashed through his "Made at 13 Oaks" jam labels and penned in "11." The oaks did not fall on his house—but unfortunately, neighboring pine trees did, tearing through the roof and into his house.

Other classic Cracker condiments include fruit preserves, jams and marmalade, along with pepper vinegar and watermelon rind pickles, as described by Tyree:

Strawberry Preserves

Cap the berries. Put one and a half pounds sugar to each pound fruit. Let them stand two or three hours, and then boil thirty minutes.

Strawberry Jam

Cap and wash the berries, and put them on to stew with a very small quantity of water. Stir constantly. When thoroughly done and mashed to a soft pulp, add one pound sugar to each pound fruit. The advantage of adding sugar last is that it preserves the color and flavor of the fruit. Stew till sufficiently thick, scraping constantly from the bottom with a batter-cake turner.—*Mrs. S.T.*

Orange Preserves

Peel a thin rind off the oranges and make a hole in each end, getting out all the seed. Pour boiling water over them and let them stand till next morning. If the water tastes bitter, search for seed. Pour boiling water over them every day, as long as the bitterness remains. Boil till soft enough to run a straw through them. Add a pound and a half sugar to each pound fruit. Make a thin syrup of half the sugar, and boil the oranges in it a short time. Let them stand in the syrup three days, then pour the syrup from the fruit, put the rest of the sugar to it, and boil it down thick. Then pour it over the fruit. A few lemons added is a great improvement.—*Mrs. J.H.*

⌒

Orange Marmalade

Peel the oranges, taking all the seed and tough skin out of them. Cut the peel in small pieces, put in cold water and boil till tender. Make a syrup, one pound sugar to one pint water. Put a pound of the oranges (mixed with the peel) to a pint of the syrup, and boil all for two hours.—*Mrs. C.C. McP.*

⌒

Pickle of Watermelon Rind

Cut in pieces and soak the rind in weak salt and water for twenty-four hours—of course having first peeled off the outside. To seven pounds rind put three pounds sugar; scald well in ginger tea, and make a syrup of the sugar and vinegar, enough to cover the rind. Season the syrup with mace and ginger, and boil the rind in it till tender. A delicious pickle.—*Mrs. Dr. P.C.*

⌒

Pepper Vinegar

One dozen pods red pepper, fully ripe. Take out stems and cut them in two. Add three pints vinegar. Boil down to one quart; strain through a sieve, and bottle for use.—*Mrs. Dr. J.*

By mid-century, we were back outside grilling over an open fire and cooking pizza in stone or brick ovens, just for the fun of it. Microwaves, convection ovens and conduction cooking came on the scene with detailed directions and cooking classes. In this era, it seemed people were eating out more than ever before. Theme parks and hurricanes may have changed the look of old Florida, but the Florida Main Street program was established so we could still walk the streets of the once burgeoning small-town communities. The shopping cycle went from country peddler to country store, from mail-order catalogues to the future of computer drones' delivery service.

Just thinking about my Granny Mattie Sheffield's cozy Cracker cabin brings back happy memories of not only her cooking but also her warmth as a special person. Sweeping her front yard with a homemade broom, she would wear a long dress with an apron and her handmade sunbonnet. It was almost like stepping back in time when we drove down that lonely dirt road to her house. She left me with so many memories of feather pillows and piles of quilts, fig preserves and buttered biscuits, but mostly I remember her devotion as a Christian woman. GrandFloyd once described her faith as out-of-this-world. I like to think of that as heavenly. This prayer was hanging in her kitchen when she passed away in 1967:

Bless this house,
Oh Lord we pray
Make it safe
By night & day.

Chapter 4

CRACKER COOKBOOK

Chronology of Community Cookbook Credits
1940s and '50s: Mrs. (Jack) Harris
1960s: Mrs. Jack Harris (Joy)
1970s: Joy Harris (Jack)
1980s: Joy Sheffield Harris
1990s: Joy Harris

Long before cookbooks were a common part of kitchens, cooks kept journals reflecting culinary techniques and regional food ways, often describing a hunting trip, an outing for fishing and picnicking or a day of baking. Recording recipes goes back to ancient times with the creation of hieroglyphics and the Great Pyramids of Egypt. A few thousand years later, the Old Testament gave mention of some of the common foods and their sources. Between the writings of the Old and New Testaments, Jesus Christ was born and the first bakery opened in Rome. Recipes have been written and passed along to the next generation since at least the days of the ancient Roman Empire.

Cookbooks reflect a moment in time and are one way to keep a record of changes—not only in our culinary ways but in our lifestyles and mores. For example, Christopher Columbus reached America and brought about the Columbian Exchange. Oranges and citrus were then introduced to Florida, while others brought pigs and cows to the area, determining what was on the dining table. Following the path of a recipe shows the gradual changes

Crowley Museum and Nature Center Cracker cabin, Sarasota. *Author's collection.*

from homemade to commercially produced products. Condiments are a good example; homemade walnut catsup was replaced by Lea & Perrins Worcestershire sauce in recipes. By 1961, *Food from Famous Kitchens: The Brand Names Cookbook*, sponsored by Saran Wrap, featured tested recipes using brand-name products. Recipes found on commercially packaged products were popular and usually easy to prepare, as well as tasty. The companies and home economists producing those recipes wanted the homemaker to be successful using their product. Today, we have more cookbooks available to us than ever before, along with television cooking shows and the seemingly endless information from the Internet.

Cookbooks are a lifeline and roadmap to the past. They have long been treasured resources and welcome additions to the home kitchen; most importantly, they give guidance to cooks. Handwritten cookbooks sometimes recorded methods, but many only listed ingredients, assuming any cook would instinctively know how to finish the dish. Temperatures and cooking times were missing, which is understandable since early ovens were without temperature controls or timers. Measuring was not exact, yet accurate measuring, baking times and temperatures helped to ensure the same quality every time a dish was prepared. Just as important is the quality of food used in the dish. Seasonality has always played a role in food choices, but today, we have more variety than ever with rapid shipping methods from all parts of the world.

Once the home cook found more time on her hands, self-published cookbooks became popular, and many went on to be bestsellers with numerous reprints. Cookbooks of the past help us understand the methods used today and provide historical significance to certain dishes. The chronology of colonial American cookbooks began with trailblazers such as Susannah Carter, who wrote *The Frugal Housewife, or Complete Woman Cook*, based on English recipes that included only an American recipe appendix. In the 1796 Amelia Simmons cookbook *American Cookery*, the recipes were adapted to the region by substituting American ingredients for British ones, as stated on the cover: "Adapted to this country, and all grades of life." Hannah Glasse wrote *The Art of Cookery Made Plain and Easy* and used the same appendix as Carter with similar recipes.

In 1824, Mary Randolph wrote *The Virginia Housewife*. A direct descendant of Pocahontas, Randolph was born in Virginia in 1762. She left her plantation home and moved to Richmond after marrying David Meade Randolph. With relatives such as Thomas Jefferson, Robert E. Lee and descendants of George Washington, they were a well-known and well-respected couple, for a time. Their large brick house was called Moldavia, combining the names Molly, as she was called, and her husband, David, and stood in downtown Richmond on a street bearing her mother's maiden name, Cary. It was the place to be for lavish dinner parties and lively conversations. Some of those conversations led to a series of political differences. Subsequently, David lost his job, and they had to sell Moldavia. Molly had earned a reputation as the finest hostess in the area, and her experience overseeing her kitchen help and servants gave her the skills she needed to open a boardinghouse to support her family. The loss of income and property forced them to move to tenant housing in the Shockoe area of Richmond. She earned a reputation for serving fine meals at her boardinghouse from 1808 to 1820. Interestingly, Randolph was the first person to be buried in what is now Arlington National Cemetery.

Randolph showed attention to detail and the importance of using precise measurements, not yet seen in cookbooks. She not only saw a need to list ingredients with general instructions but also recorded the steps necessary to run an orderly household, including cooking and cleaning. Her background running a plantation home gave her a wealth of information and helped with the difficulties she encountered when she no longer had many servants and a large budget. She wanted to share with other homemakers clear and concise instructions so as not to waste time or money. She stated, "The government of a family bears a Lilliputian resemblance to the government of a nation." She backed up that philosophy with three rules of management: "Let everything be done at a proper time, keep everything in its proper place, and put everything to its proper use." Most notably, she is considered the first American cookbook author, having published the first regional cookbook printed in this country. Until then, reprints of English classics, along with plagiarism, were common.

Lydia Maria Francis Child, author of *The American Frugal Housewife*, was another remarkable American woman. She dedicated her book to those who were not ashamed of economy. Originally called the *Frugal Housewife*, the book title had to change to the *American Frugal Housewife* "because there is an English work of the same name, not adapted to the wants of this country," Child said. She gave practical information for the home cook, who did not have extra help in the kitchen, and for those on a budget. A section on herbs and their uses for teas and medicinal purposes was included, along with instructions on how to cure a ham the "old-fashioned way," taking ten weeks for the process. Although her cookbook was popular, her other writings revealed an impressive part of her life, promoting human rights. An abolitionist and a women's rights and Native American rights activist, her compassion for all classes of people showed in her other works as well. She wrote historical fiction, Native American history and romantic novels, including a love story called *Hobomok*, about a colonial woman and Native American man. She also wrote an instruction manual for mothers, *The Mothers*

Book. Child also was credited with publishing the first American children's magazine, *Juvenile Miscellany*. Childless herself, she fondly remembers her grandparents' house near the Mystic River on South Street in Medford, Massachusetts. This is the home that was the inspiration for the beloved Thanksgiving poem turned song she wrote in 1844. "Over the River and Through the Wood" was published years before Thanksgiving became an official federal holiday.

Marion Cabell Tyree, the granddaughter of Patrick Henry, wrote *Housekeeping in Old Virginia*, published in 1879. She compiled this post–Civil War guide to food preparation and household management with the help of "two hundred and fifty of Virginia's noted housewives," whose names and hometowns are listed under most recipes. For generations, domestic art and domestic economy went hand in hand as new settlers had to cope with survival as well as cooking, cleaning and organizing the kitchen and home for an efficient, healthy and happy life. But times have changed, and we find the following quote from *Housekeeping in Old Virginia* humorous today, though taken seriously in the 1800s: "If she, above all, shall succeed in making American homes more attractive to American husbands, and spare them a resort to hotels and saloons for those simple luxuries which their wives know not how to provide…she will have proved in some measure a public benefactor, and will feel amply repaid for all the labor her work has cost." In a mostly male-dominated workforce, using quotes from the Bible to reinforce the role of "woman in the kitchen" might have boosted the morale of women who did not feel they had the option or inclination to strike out on their own.

Established in 1879, the Boston Cooking School, of Fannie Farmer fame, was probably the most influential cooking school in American society. Farmer went on to publish her own cookbook in 1896, *The Fannie Farmer Original Cookbook*. She was dubbed "the mother of level measurements," which led to successful recipes in general, along with the advent of temperature controls and standardized dials. When Fannie Farmer created *The Boston Cooking-School Cook Book*, she laid the foundation for proper recipe writing. Influenced by Ellen Richards, Farmer's cookbook became a model for new American cookbooks, introducing standardization of written recipes. Her step-by-step instructions along with recommended cooking temperatures and times took the guesswork out of cooking. It was renamed *The New Fannie Farmer Cookbook* in 1959, and her influence was felt across the nation.

The colonial influence on southern cooking can be attributed to the use of English cookbooks during the birth of the nation. By the late

Mr. and Mrs. Maxon plucking chicken, St. Andrews, circa 1898–1904.

1800s, George M. Barbour in his book *Florida for Tourists, Invalids, and Settlers* mentions "grub boxes," which included supplies Crackers set up for outdoor cooking before the use of cookbooks in Florida was common. Fried fish or tortoise was eaten along with fatback, hoecakes, grits with molasses and coffee. Sweet potatoes were served baked, mashed in a casserole or fried, without the use of a recipe. Mostly, Crackers learned cooking by watching. Being illiterate, for the most part, was only part of the struggle; cookbooks were expensive to a struggling family, and keeping a recipe journal was time consuming. Following a recipe was often a more reliable way to cook with confidence, but it was the oral recipe tradition that continued in the Cracker kitchen.

Just after the turn of the previous century, Martha McCulloch-Williams (1913) wrote *Dishes and Beverages of the Old South*, describing many dishes as old-fashioned by then. The same year the Overseas Railroad was completed, connecting mainland Florida to Key West, a Florida cookbook was published by the First Presbyterian Church of Miami, *The Florida Tropical Cook Book*. With recipes using canned goods and a fireless cooker, it might have been the first regional cookbook in Florida. Published in 1912, it was written for those new to the burgeoning tropical south Florida paradise and not necessarily for the Crackers of the frontier and wilderness. The recipes were original, old family favorites, perfected through trial and error during their early years in Florida. All were tested by the pioneer women of Florida, "to whom we desire to express our appreciation of their kind contributions." The book has recipes using commercially canned products such as crab, shrimp and salmon, along with a recipe for canning scuppernongs. *A Culinary History of Florida* comments:

> *The thick-skinned, bronze-colored scuppernong, a type of muscadine grape, has long been a Florida Cracker favorite. The sweet and musky-tasting muscadine is used for juice, wine, pie and jelly. But the late summer scuppernong was easily plucked from climbing vines at Granny Mattie's and eaten on the spot. Harper Lee wrote in* To Kill A Mockingbird, *"helping ourselves to someone's scuppernongs was part of our ethical culture, but money was different." Scuppernongs are the larger green variety of the muscadine. The South's muscadine grape ripens as individual grapes on the cluster, like the sea grape.*

Canned Scuppernong

One peck of scuppernongs, one quart of water, one quart of sugar. Press the seeds and pulps from the skin and put to cook in a granite vessel. Have the skins and water cooking in a larger vessel. When pulp is soft, strain from seeds and add to the sugar and skins. Boil all together twenty minutes and put in well sterilized jars, and seal at once.—*The Florida Tropical Cook Book*

Also included are recipes for many classic Florida foods such as arrowroot, roselle, avocado, pineapple, grapefruit, guava and papaya, along with recipes using peaches, figs and tomatoes. Recipes for Waldorf salad, johnnycake and graham gems were included, along with a section from Fannie Farmer called "Soups Without Stock" for each day of the week, ending the section with a recipe for Fireless Cooker Vegetable Soup and baked Florida pumpkin.

Baked Florida Pumpkin

Do not peel it. Cut in pieces as large as one's hand. Put a slice of breakfast bacon on top of each piece, salt, pepper and a lump of butter. Bake four hours in fireless cooker or two in an oven. Very good. This pumpkin makes excellent pies when used as any other pumpkin.—*Miss Nan Merritt*

In 1914, Frances Barber Harris of Jacksonville wrote *Florida Salads*, which she called a collection of practical and palatable recipes, all tested by the author, for young housekeepers to make their meals attractive and dainty. Salads were beginning to appear on the menus of elegant restaurants in the big cities to the north, so this book was most likely a welcome read in the larger towns, though acquiring the cookbook and ingredients might be a challenge for rural Cracker families. Harris added her own advice to the pages of her book: "We all know that celery and onions are soothing to the nerves" and "With few exceptions, the materials used in these salads are produced in Florida." She added, "When canned meats are used for salads, the can should be opened at least half hour before using, meat placed in a porcelain, glass or china bowl and thoroughly aerated." For measuring: "An ordinary tea cup, level full, rounded table spoon and tea spoon are used for measuring these recipes." She included general kitchen tips such as, "Onions should be sliced and soaked at least one hour in ice water before using for salads. They are milder and not so apt to disagree with one." Also, "A tiny pinch of sugar improves most salads." She recognized that tuna fish is often called the "chicken of the sea." Here are a few of her recipes:

Celery Stick Salad No. I

Wash celery well with a brush, crisp in ice water and dry. Select well grooved stalks, remove strings or threads, cut in uniform lengths and fill grooves with cold tomato jelly, just before it hardens. Serve two stalks on two romaine lettuce leaves with a teaspoonful of mayonnaise on side of plate. Eat with fingers, dipping celery ends in dressing.

Celery Stick Salad No. 2

Prepare celery as in recipe for Celery Stick Salad No. 1. Fill grooves with cream cheese mashed with pimento. Serve in same way.

After the freezes of the late 1800s wiped out many citrus groves, some farmers turned to celery. Celery was popular, and by the 1900s, railroads were picking up carloads to transport north from Sanford. Later, there was even a celery drink created in Bradenton called Celo Soda.

Florida Salad

Peel grapefruit, oranges, and tangerines; divide into lobes, remove white skin and seed, and put on lettuce leaves. Cut a pineapple into small square blocks and pile a little on top of each plate of salad. Around the salad put slices of banana with a little lemon juice squeezed over. Serve with mayonnaise.

Cabbage Palm Salad

Get tender, white buds from tops of cabbage palmettoes, cut in inch pieces and soak in ice water one hour. Drain, sprinkle with cayenne and mix with equal quantity of diced celery. Served with Cooked Dressing and a few pearl onions.

There is no recipe included for "Cooked Dressing" in the book, since many cookbook authors at the time assumed the reader had a basic understanding of how to prepare common dishes.

Paw Paw Salad

Cut ripe paw paw and measure, to this add one-sixth as much grated onion, salt and vinegar to taste, mash and let stand until it forms a jelly, then cut in slices and serve.—*Mrs. Chas. Montgomery*

Pawpaws are being rediscovered in Florida and other places around the country. The large, green, fragrant fruit from the pawpaw tree has been featured in a Michelin-starred restaurant in Washington, D.C., along with apple pandowdy. Mind you, they were as far from a Cracker dish as possible, but the ingredients were still a reminder of the early days.

Orange Salad

Cut six oranges in halves, take out the pulp, and remove veins and sections. To the pulp add one-fourth cup powdered sugar, one-quarter cup chopped mint, and two tablespoons each of wine, lemon juice and orange juice. Serve in champagne glasses, and garnish with one red cherry and a bit of angelica (herb).—*Mrs. Geo. F. Cook*

Along with the advent of emerging technology came the need to understand how to safely use unfamiliar appliances and, to some extent, ingredients, so cookbooks often were included with purchase. To promote the use of its baking powder, the Calumet Baking Powder cookbook was made available in 1916 for two dollars. A Chautauqua lecturer, Marian Cole Fisher, wrote *Twenty Lessons in Domestic Science* for the company, with an introduction to food and organic chemistry, followed by a lesson on leavening agents. Many of the lessons cover basic recipes followed by advice on selecting kitchen equipment.

Lily Haxworth Wallace, a lecturer and writer on home economics, wrote *The Revised Rumford Complete Cook Book*, originally published in 1908. The tenth revised edition came out in 1939 with a new preface from the Rumford Company stating that after the original work "was promptly accepted as a standard in American homes," with more than five million copies printed, the population of the United States was around ninety million at the time. "Retaining all the best features of the original edition the revised Rumford

Cook Book covers many developments undreamed of when the first book was compiled." Emphasizing the use of level measurements as standard, it pointed out that Rumford Baking Powder had uniform, scientifically controlled double-action. "This new use of an all-phosphate baking powder is worth consideration by all interested in home cooking."

In the 1930s, the booklet *A Handy Guide for Busy Cooks* was published by the Crystal and Dial brands of baking soda, which were produced by the Detroit Soda Products Company. The introduction read, in part:

> *To get a clear and rapidly moving picture of this progress it is only necessary for us to recall the fact that, as the old time buggy has been replaced by the motor car, the washtub by power washers, and the old oaken bucket by running water, the kerosene lantern by electric lights and the silence and lack of entertainment in the home by radio—so the research staff of the Detroit Soda Products Company together with other scientific agencies have helped replace the old wasteful, and often unhealthy method of "living to eat" with the newer method of "eating to live."*

This tiny booklet was packed with information for those wanting to understand the science behind the product and new cooking methods.

"For the benefit of housewives who follow the newer method of cooking-by-temperature, and for those who wish to learn this method," the booklet included a temperature table. "The temperatures on this table are for gas ranges. If a coal range is used deduct 85 degrees F in each case from the temperatures given above." Although most new appliances came with instruction manuals that included recipes, many rural cooks may have ignored the new ways by adapting recipes to the more familiar and traditional methods. The time and skill it took to learn how to use new products might have seemed unnecessary when the old ways worked just fine. Over time, simplicity was stressed, and even the electric can opener came with a recipe book.

After the success of *The Yearling* and *Cross Creek*, in 1942 Marjorie Kinnan Rawlings wrote her best-selling cookbook, *Cross Creek Cookery*. She recalled the time her mother used the Farmer cookbook, and Rawlings studied it in hopes of creating delicious Florida dishes in her newfound rural home at Cross Creek. For Rawlings, who lived among the Crackers, "Some of my best dishes are entirely native and local." As we follow the path laid out by these early Cracker cooks, we can see a pattern emerging that parallels our history and society in general. Looking even closer at community cookbooks,

Marjorie Kinnan Rawlings and her first husband, Charles, arrived at Cross Creek in 1928.

not only were they packed full of regional recipes, they also reflected the era in which they were written.

In 1973, *Jane Nickerson's Florida Cookbook* was published. She included culinary traditions that reflected the ethnic diversity of the state, with recipes that ranged from Cracker (without calling it that) to Cuban, Conch, Minorcan, Jewish, Seminole, Spanish and soul. We had the pleasure of working together when I first moved to the Tampa Bay area while she was food editor at the *Lakeland Ledger*. Nickerson was the food editor for the *New York Times* before moving to Florida. She was an inspiration and encouraged me to continue my research of Florida foods.

As Cracker communities grew with schools, churches and general stores, these pioneer homesteaders had more time and resources on their hands, and a bound book with handwritten recipes might be collected from newspapers, magazines, neighbors, friends and relatives. Another common example of recipe collecting came from Flora Mae Hunter in her 1979 cookbook *Born in the Kitchen: Plain and Fancy Plantation Fixin's*. Cooking on a plantation in

Above: Joy Harris, *far left*, judging a cooking contest with Jane Nickerson, *far right*, food editor of the *Lakeland Ledger*, 1986.

Left: Peter Hunter and Flora Mae Hunter on their wedding day, Leon County, March 9, 1933.

Georgia and then Florida, Hunter learned to cook from her mother and grandmother. Their original recipes and cooking secrets were passed along from one generation to the next. She seldom used written recipes, "depending on her recollections of her mother's methods," and made up her own as she went along. Her boss said that her food "was the best he had ever had since he had been coming South." Hunter also cooked for the former King of England, who abdicated the throne and married a divorcée; they were the Duke and Duchess of Windsor.

FAVORITE FLORIDA COOKBOOKS

Bay Leaves, Junior Service League of Panama City, 1975
Born in the Kitchen: Plain and Fancy Plantation Fixin's, Flora Mae Hunter, 1979
Caladesi Cookbook: Recipes from a Florida Lifetime, 1895–1922, compiled by Terry Fortner and Suzanne Thorp, 2012
The Cracker Kitchen, Janis Owens, 2009
Cross Creek Cookery, Marjorie Kinnan Rawlings, 1942
Famous Florida Recipes: 300 Years of Good Eating, Lowis Carlton, 1972
The Gasparilla Cookbook, Junior League of Tampa, 1961
Jane Nickerson's Florida Cookbook, Jane Nickerson (1973), reprint 1984
Seasonal Florida: A Taste of Life in North Florida, Jo McDonald Manning, 1994

Chapter 5

CRACKER COFFEE AND HOT COCOA

When you follow the path of a recipe sometimes it leads to places familiar yet miles and miles from where you started.
—Joy Harris

The savory aroma of coffee drifting through the rafters of a Cracker cabin, with a cool morning breeze blowing through the open windows, is something of a dream. Looking back in time to some of the first methods of preparing this morning beverage in rural Florida, up to today with all of our time-saving devices, it's a story of ingenuity and perseverance. After the Civil War, supplies were limited, and Florida frontier communities were some of the last to receive help in rebuilding and restocking their food supply. (When it came to coffee beans, substitutions were made or the product was adulterated so unscrupulous sellers could make a higher profit ratio.) Advice on selecting coffee beans proliferated in post-colonial cookbooks, and post–Civil War shortages were remedied by substituting or augmenting the coffee supply with more commonly found ingredients. According to an article in *Cracker Times and Pioneer Lives*, Sarah Pamela Williams recalled people were using "parched rye, peas, beans and okra, even corn meal and sweet potatoes.…If we mixed in a portion of real coffee (java, for instance) with a substitute, it made it more palatable. We even tried peanuts." Other substitutes included parched and ground acorns, chicory, corn, cotton seed and even potatoes and rice—all a part of the coffee charade. A substitute for cream was suggested by whipping

John Wiley Hill family in front of double-pen log house. *From left to right*: Horace, James, Ned, Dorothy, Holly (Bowen) holding Roxie, in Homeland, Polk County, 1800s.

together an egg and boiling water. Another account noted that when milk is scalded, the taste is richer and can be used in place of cream, as we find in the lattes of today.

Today, with coffee shops and a varied selection of coffeepots and machines available, it might be hard to imagine how much time and effort went into preparing something as simple as a cup of morning coffee. For a Cracker, it meant rising in the predawn hours and tending to the fire, or setting one in the stove, after fetching water from the spring or well and putting it on to boil. The beans had to be roasted before they were ground with a hand-turned coffee mill. Cream, which came from a cow that was milked the day before, was skimmed from the top of the milk jug. Sugar, cane syrup or honey might be added for sweetness. My morning coffee today, with sugar and steamed milk, takes minutes to prepare, and I can practically make it in my sleep. Now I can better appreciate why coffee was mostly served black in the early pioneer days.

Turner and Wilson coffee roaster wagon, Tampa, circa 1890.

Cookbooks dating back to the nineteenth century were full of advice for selecting and roasting green coffee beans and making the perfect cup of coffee, even on a budget, noting that it was more economical to buy a higher-grade coffee bean because the flavor was stronger. Roasting brings out the flavor and aroma of raw green coffee beans, and cookbooks included suggestions such as stirring in butter or egg whites immediately after the beans were parched. Here is a suggestion from author and cook Marion Cabell Tyree:

To Toast Coffee

Wash and pick the coffee, put it in a very large stove-pan in a hot oven. Stir often, giving constant attention. It must be toasted the darkest brown, yet not one grain must be burned. It should never be glazed, as this destroys the aroma. Two pints of coffee become three pints after toasting.—*Mrs. S.T.*

The proper grind was considered as important then as today. It was stressed that using steel-cut beans produced a fine and even ground, and this process was preferred over crushed beans, which produced a container of particles and dust. Because it was easy to mess up a good cup of coffee, it was important to use the proper brewing techniques, the right amount of coffee grounds, the proper grind for the coffeepot and a clean coffeepot. Suggestions for more flavorful coffee included buying coffee beans freshly roasted in a small quantity and grinding only as much as you needed for the day. Freshly drawn, high-quality water and a higher-grade coffee resulted in better fragrance and flavor.

By the start of the twentieth century, instant and decaffeinated coffee along with powdered milk, or Klim, were available. (Klim, milk spelled backward, was the brand name.) Roasted beans became available in grocery stores and specialty shops. At one time, a twelve-foot coffeepot in a Franklin Street storefront in Tampa released the aroma of freshly roasted beans from a roaster inside the store through a pipe attached to

Workers with loaded truck in front of the Wilson Coffee Co. Store, Tampa, 1919. *FMA/ Burgert Brothers.*

the spout outside. This intriguing publicity stunt came to an end when the hurricane of 1921 came roaring through downtown and the pot went head-over-heels, rolling down the street, as described in a 1923 article in the *Tampa Tribune*. Coffeepots evolved just as the roasting and processing of beans improved, and commercially produced ground coffee flooded the market.

Boiling coffee in a pot on the stove or over a fire—where the grounds would settle to the bottom of the pot, trapped by egg or fish skin—was replaced with a stove-top drip pot or French biggin, which had a removable midsection that filtered water as it percolated down through the grounds. Pressed and filtered coffee were popular until the electric percolator came along. By the mid-twentieth century, new developments brought the vacuum brewer and later the Chemex glass drip pot, followed by the Melitta drip pot. Easy to use, Mr. Coffee changed the beverage for the better as it dripped and filtered to precision. Today, we have espresso machines in our kitchens for instant high-quality coffee at home.

Java and mocha are synonymous with coffee today, but at one time, the terms referred to the area from which the beans came. According to Corby Kummer in *The Joy of Coffee*, the port of Mocha was on the Arabian Peninsula, in what today is known as Yemen, and java beans are still cultivated on the Indonesian island of the same name. The mixing of the two distinctly different-flavored beans complemented each other for an exceptional taste. Java is still a slang term used for coffee, but mocha now refers to a chocolate-flavored coffee beverage. The cut, dried and ground root of the chicory plant is a widely appreciated addition to coffee for many. From camp coffee made over an open fire to after-dinner coffee lit up by a spoonful of cognac-laced sugar, we are blessed with such variety today. It is hard to imagine that tying grounds in a muslin cloth and placing it in boiling water to create a beverage could be as satisfying to our ancestors as a drive-through to-go cup is to us today.

The aroma and freshness along with strength and richness were as important at the start of the previous century as they are now. However, the turn of the century was just the beginning of many changes in coffee brewing. The *1902 Cook Book*, published in New York City, featured economical recipes for only ten cents, emphasizing that choosing a "good coffee, java, or some other expensive quality, is as economical as the cheaper kinds, for it requires a smaller quantity." It offered another pearl of wisdom: "Housewives who wish to excel in making this beverage, if for breakfast, should never make it until the family is nearly ready for

Coffee can display at a general store in Two Egg, circa 1969–72. *FMA/Toby Massey.*

the table, so that it may not be spoiled by standing." The book explained in detail how to set up a slow-drip coffeepot with a homemade filter, for leaching the flavor from the grounds, with the coffee ready in ten minutes or less. Marian Cole Fisher, in her 1916 book *Twenty Lessons in Domestic Science*, suggested this preparation for after-dinner coffee: "When cognac is served with the black coffee, the loaf or domino sugar is placed in the spoon over the coffee, and the cognac is poured over the sugar and lighted match touched to it. When burned away, the spoon and contents are dipped into the cup. This caramelizes the sugar and when added to the coffee imparts to it a special flavor, that is very appropriate after a heavy dinner." Grandma Elaine's 1948 copy of *Fannie Farmer's Cook Book* included an egg in her boiled coffee recipe, preceding her electric percolated coffee recipe with these words of advice: "If electric unit does not provide change of heat, remove connections 3 times to slow up the process." By 1980, Farmer's coffee section had moved from the front of the book to the appendices in the back.

While I do not remember the method Granny Trixie used to make coffee for Granddaddy, I do recall the way he sipped his coffee from a saucer. He wanted his coffee "scalding hot," as my mother would say, and Granny would take the pot from the stovetop burner and fill his cup. He then would pour a small amount into a saucer, allow it to cool and sip, filling the saucer as necessary. Still a child, I felt so special when he let me have a sip of his strong, black, cold coffee, but that ended my coffee drinking for a while. At home growing up, the coffee was brewed each morning, first on the stovetop, then with an electric percolator. Cleaning the insides of those pots and disposing of the grounds lodged in the tiny holes of the metal filters was a thing of the past as soon as Mr. Coffee was introduced to the world. Not a coffee drinker yet, I still loved the smell and watching the amber-colored liquid bubble up through the glass knob on the top of the stovetop pot and the electric percolator.

Two of my mother's friends helped me find my own taste for coffee. Susie Seyfried and Jane Johnson, neighbors down the street, took me into their kitchens like one of their own, introducing me to their special style of entertaining. While I was still attending Everitt Junior High School, I stood in Susie's contemporary kitchen with the coffee brewing, and she asked me if I'd like a cup. I so wanted to "like a cup," but I recounted Granddaddy's

A fisherman pouring a cup of coffee below deck on a fishing boat, Naples, 1949. *FMA/ Joseph Janney Steinmetz.*

saucer story, and she proceeded to tell me how to enjoy a cup of coffee. First you take in the aroma, then slowly take a sip of nice, hot coffee from a cup. What a difference that made! The atmosphere around her house was always exotic. As you approached the front door down a brick pathway, the fishpond flowed around, under and into an open fishpond in their home in one flawless design. This dream home was in sharp contrast to Jane's brick house, which looked as if it were lifted right out of the pages of *Southern Living* magazine, both inside and out. While a student at Rutherford High School, I helped Jane with one of her parties, where she served coffee frappe. This sounded so fancy to me, as I had no idea what it was. It was frothy, thus I assumed it was full of whipped raw egg whites, which I had learned was definitely not for me. Much to my delight, Jane showed me how she made it with freshly brewed, sweetened, cold coffee poured over a quart of vanilla ice cream in a crystal punch bowl. Once again, I experienced one of the most sublime tastes on earth.

For a taste of the past, one summer while camping I got up early to start the fire and make the coffee, eager to try an old recipe for coffee that had an egg in it. After rinsing the enamelware pot with hot water, I added half a cup of ground coffee and stirred in the slightly beaten whole egg, shell and all. I then added a few grains of sea salt and about half a cup of cold water to moisten the grounds and activate the coffee. I stuffed a paper towel into the spout on the pot to prevent the aroma from escaping while the coffee steeped. After adding boiling water, I put the pot back over the campfire to slowly boil for about three minutes. After removing it from the heat, I let it sit for about five minutes so the egg and coffee grounds could settle to the bottom of the pot. It was neither bitter from boiling it too long nor cloudy from not boiling it long enough. To me, it was perfect. I excitedly woke up my fellow campers to taste this delightful morning brew. To my dismay, one commented that it tasted like egg—"Yuck!"—and the other asked, "Did you put salt in the coffee?" They both went back to bed while I enjoyed the peaceful morning with a full pot of eggy-salty coffee.

The first time I ordered a *café au lait* in a little coffee shop, I fell in love. The taste on my lips was luscious, the frothy, creamy foam on top was beautiful and I was in the most romantic place on earth, Paris. My love affair with coffee continues. I was almost as happy when I discovered my first coffee cart on a street corner in Seattle and again on a trip to Chicago. Now it seems that coffee shops, not coffee carts, are on every street corner of every town. Returning home from a family trip to Italy, I decided to try to replicate the flavors we discovered while stopping to shop in Rome. When they offered me an espresso at one of the shops, my husband, Jack, made one of those faces and said, "How much did you spend, if they are giving us these free coffees?" Well, it was worth it, as we all came home wanting a cup of fancy Italian coffee. The pop of a pod, using espresso for a Nespresso machine, makes the task of producing a tasty latte easy. However, Tampa and especially Ybor City are also destinations for a delicious Spanish-Cuban coffee, *café con leche*. Following is a version found in *A Culinary History of Florida*:

Café con Leche

You can make a great-tasting cup of café con leche at home with steamed milk and a bold Cuban coffee such as Café Bustelo, Pilon or Naviera Coffee. Prepare a shot of espresso and stir in at least an equal amount of steamed milk. If you don't have a milk steamer, just heat the amount of whole milk you will need in the microwave until almost boiling. Add sugar to taste. Serve with buttered Cuban toast for a light breakfast.

Café au lait is French for coffee with hot milk, *latte* is Italian for espresso with steamed milk and *café con leche* is Spanish for Cuban coffee with scalded milk. Here are three ways I make steamed milk:

1) Heat the milk in a saucepan over medium-high heat until hot, whisking to create a steamy-frothy milk.
2) Use a milk steamer. It makes perfect steamed milk with a nice froth.
3) Scalded milk can be made by heating the milk in the microwave to just before boiling.

From pots to presses to percolators to pods, a cup of sweet, creamy, hot coffee, or rich and flavorful mocha, reminds me how lucky I am to live in a time when the press of a button or a quick stop at a coffee shop can bring such joy to the start of my day. And a couple of shots of espresso in a cup of my hot cocoa make a great mocha. Hot chocolate is usually made with scraped, shaved or ground chocolate bars. Cocoa powder is used to make hot cocoa. Both are made from ground cocoa beans, but chocolate has more fat. Cocoa scorches, so cooking on a low temperature is recommended.

Hot Cocoa

2 tablespoons Dutch process cocoa
3 tablespoons sugar
Dash salt
½ cup boiling water
1 ½ cups scalded milk
¼ teaspoon vanilla
Whipped cream (optional)

Whisk together cocoa, sugar and salt in a saucepan, add half a cup of boiling water and cook, stirring constantly, for 5 minutes. Whisk in milk and cook 5 minutes longer or until just below boiling point, slowly stirring. Remove from heat, stir in vanilla. Serve with whipped cream, if desired.

Chapter 6

BISCUITS, BREADS AND BREAKFAST

We serve cold baker's bread only to our enemies,
trusting they will never impose on our hospitality again.
—Marjorie Kinnan Rawlings

As the countryside stretched into the distance, with occasional cross roads breaking up the monotony, I knew we soon would be pulling up to Granny Mattie's house. The drive doesn't seem as far today as it did when I was a child, but the memories seem almost ancient when I try to reach out and touch them, or at least re-create them. My granny's and my mother's biscuits are a reminder of water drawn from a well, a red kitchen pump, a treadle sewing machine tucked away in a corner, the smell of her wood-burning stove and freshly churned butter. Today you can drop, roll and cut, pull, pat or beat the dough to create a biscuit. The choices are plentiful: soda, buttermilk, sweet potato, cheese, cathead, ham or sausage, angel biscuits, British scone and Italian biscotti. With each change of ingredient, the texture and taste of the biscuit are altered.

It seemed both of my grannies were always adorned with an apron unless they were going to church. The flour sack aprons and dresses they wore showed how saving money was taken seriously by those struggling to get by. When I look at the flour sack apron from Granny Mattie and the old buttermilk pitcher from Granny Trixie, it brings back memories of "scratch" biscuits baking in an old wood-burning stove. Making biscuits was an everyday event for these hardworking women. The first time I tried to make biscuits for breakfast like Granny Mattie, mine resembled golf balls and

Tampa warehouse workers load goods onto a truck in front of a wholesale grocery warehouse, circa 1920. *FMA/Burgert Brothers*.

Rolling pin and biscuit bowl on display in a Cracker cabin at the Crowley Museum and Nature Center, Sarasota. *FMA/James L. Gaines*.

were about as hard. Through trial and error, the use of measuring utensils and help from GrandMary, my mother, I finally mastered the art of making Granny Sheffield's biscuits, or at least something that comes close. Here is the biscuit and sausage gravy recipe from *A Culinary History of Florida*.

GrandMary's Buttermilk Biscuits with Sausage Gravy

2 cups flour
1 tablespoon baking powder
½ teaspoon baking soda
¼ teaspoon salt
½ cup (8 tablespoons) butter, chilled and cut into 6 pieces
¾ to 1 cup buttermilk, as needed

Preheat oven to 450 degrees. Whisk together flour, baking powder, baking soda and salt. Cut in butter with a pastry blender until mixture resembles coarse crumbs. Stir in ¾ cup buttermilk with a fork, stirring in more if needed to moisten dough; stir, lightly and rapidly, until a soft non-sticky dough forms, being careful not to over mix. Knead on a lightly floured surface three to four times, then roll dough or pat to ½-inch thickness. Cut with a 2- to 3-inch biscuit cutter. Place in a cast-iron skillet and bake for 14 minutes, or until tops are lightly golden.

Sausage Gravy
6 ounces ground pork sausage
2 tablespoons butter
¼ cup flour
1 ½ cups whole milk
½ teaspoon salt
½ teaspoon pepper
Sage, to taste

Crumble and cook sausage in a large skillet over medium heat until it is no longer pink. Remove sausage with a slotted spoon, drain on a paper towel. Melt butter in skillet with sausage drippings over low heat. Whisk in flour and stir for 3 minutes, until light brown, like a roux. Whisk in milk, salt, pepper and sage. Cook over medium heat until thickened and bubbly, about 1 minute more. Stir in crumbled sausage. Serve over biscuits.

A housewife making jelly and filling jars, 1970.

These biscuits are also delicious served with homemade butter and jelly or simply with honey butter.

Orange Blossom Honey Butter

½ cup (8 tablespoons) butter, softened
¼ cup honey
½ teaspoon orange zest
Pinch of salt

Mix all ingredients together until thoroughly blended, or whip until light and fluffy. Chill before use.

Biscuits are well suited to hold luscious strawberries for a shortcake using this recipe from *Florida Sweets*.

Strawberry Shortcake

Strawberry shortcake was often made using biscuits. Preserves could be used to top the biscuit if fresh strawberries were out of season. This simple recipe makes a quick, old-fashioned strawberry shortcake.

¼ cup shortening
1 cup self-rising flour
⅓ cup milk
2 cups sliced strawberries, divided
½ cup sugar
1 tablespoon cornstarch
¼ cup water
1 cup sweetened whipped cream

Cut shortening into flour until it looks like coarse crumbs; stir in milk with a fork. Dust hands with flour and pull off pieces of dough and hand-roll, making 12 tiny biscuits. Place in cast-iron skillet and tap tops of each biscuit to flatten slightly. Bake at 425 degrees for 12 minutes or until golden.

Mash 1 cup strawberries and mix with sugar; heat slowly.

Combine cornstarch and water and pour over heated berries, cooking and stirring until thick.

Stir in remaining sliced berries.

Slice open biscuit and top with strawberries and whipped cream.

Leavening, the lightening or raising of biscuit dough, can be accomplished in a variety of ways. Naturally occurring yeast has been around for thousands of years, yet commercially packaged yeast was not produced until the Industrial Revolution. Fermentation with yeast is time consuming, so other, quicker methods were devised. Here is some background on biscuits from *A Culinary History of Florida*:

> *Before baking powder was widely used, beaten biscuits on the plantation were considered an upper-class status symbol due to the excessive labor and*

time necessary to incorporate enough air and lightness into the dough. Using a rolling pin, mallet or the side of an ax, the dough was beaten hundreds of times on a biscuit block, taking fifteen minutes to hours until it was glossy and "blistered" with air bubbles. These flat, round, firm, dry biscuits had a texture like a crisp but chewy soda cracker. By the 1900s, wheat flour was common, but soft, low-gluten Southern flour is needed to make great Southern biscuits. At first, baking powder was considered dangerous, for fear it could explode, but once it was accepted, the Southern biscuit was on the rise. In 1930, General Mills introduced Bisquick and refrigerated unbaked stacks of biscuits in pop-open cardboard tubes. Self-rising flour made the process one step easier and, by the 1960s, crescent rolls and the Pillsbury Doughboy were popular. Most of the work was already done, and mixing bowls, measuring cups, and flour-covered pastry boards were no longer needed. The chemical reaction of buttermilk and soda is the magic that makes these biscuits rise. A substitute for buttermilk is to add a little vinegar to whole milk, but the buttermilk is so much better.

The beaten biscuit was labor intensive and time consuming, even with a machine to take the place of the manual labor. The introduction of baking soda and baking powder during the Industrial Revolution contributed to the demise of the beaten biscuit, and pearl ash became a bygone product

Mrs. Breen slicing bread, Pensacola, circa 1930.

for leavening as well. By 1913, these biscuits were considered old-fashioned, according to Martha McCulloch-Williams in her cookbook *Dishes and Beverages of the Old South*. With so many advancements, from baking soda to self-rising flour, Cracker cooks also were beginning to place light, southern biscuits alongside cornbread on the dining table.

Of course, homemade biscuits are best eaten hot from the oven, but did you know Crisco gives the biscuits longevity? If they are to be eaten right away, using butter is fine. However, if you plan to serve them later you might want to use Crisco or a combination of Crisco and butter in your biscuit dough. Here are a few more biscuit tips: Soft, low-gluten southern flour like White Lily makes the best biscuits because it's blended more for biscuits than bread. Vinegar and milk can be used as a substitute for buttermilk, but the real thing is always best. Using cream instead of buttermilk may make the biscuits too crumbly. If you want a biscuit with a taste of sausage and cheese, try this recipe from *Easy Breezy Florida Cooking*.

Guava-Glazed Cinnamon Sausage Gems

According to Jack: My wife says this recipe will make 30 appetizers, which would be good for 30 tiny people, but if you love these things as I do, you'll get about 4 or 5 servings, maybe fewer. They're great with beer or other beverage of choice.

Yield: 30 appetizers

4 ounces medium cheddar cheese (see note)
½ pound hot sausage
1 cup all-purpose flour
1 teaspoon cinnamon
2 tablespoons guava jelly

Preheat oven to 400 degrees.

Grate the cheese and bring it and sausage to room temperature. Mix sausage with flour and cinnamon. Mix in cheese. Form sausage mixture into 1-inch balls and place in a single layer on a 15-by-10-inch baking sheet. Place in the oven and bake for 12 minutes.

Meanwhile, in a small saucepan, melt the jelly over medium heat. Keep warm. Remove sausage balls from oven. Drizzle with melted jelly. Serve with wooden picks.

NOTE: Do not be tempted to substitute sharp or extra sharp cheddar, as they tend to be drier than medium cheddar. And do not use pre-shredded cheese. Pre-shredded cheese has an ingredient that keeps it from sticking together. If you want to make a large batch but only bake a few at a time, you can place the unbaked sausage balls on a lined baking sheet and freeze them. When firm, transfer them to a large baggie and store in freezer for a few weeks. When ready to bake, remove from freezer and let come to room temperature. Then bake according to recipe directions and drizzle with melted jelly if desired.

Jack Harris Unwrapped features my mother's recipe, from her friend Mary Clark, for biscotti. After forming the logs of dough on a baking sheet, I put them in the freezer to chill for a bit before baking.

Cranberry Biscotti

2½ cups flour
1 teaspoon baking powder
½ teaspoon salt
1½ cups sugar
½ cup unsalted butter, softened
2 eggs
1 teaspoon vanilla
1½ cups dried cranberries

Preheat oven to 350 degrees. Line a large baking sheet with parchment paper. Whisk to blend flour, baking powder and salt. Set aside. In a large mixing bowl, beat sugar, butter, eggs and vanilla until well blended. Mix in flour mixture and dried cranberries. Using floured hands, divide dough in half and shape each piece into 2½-inch-wide, 9½-inch-long and 1-inch-high loaf. Place on parchment-lined baking sheet, spacing evenly. Bake about 35 minutes. Cool completely on sheet on wire rack. When cool, transfer loaves to cutting board. Use a serrated knife and cut crosswise into ½-inch-wide slices. Arrange slices, cut side down, on freshly lined baking sheet. Bake for 10 to 15 minutes. Transfer to rack to cool.

Although flour, canned milk, coffee, sugar and dried beans could be purchased from a general store, not everyone had access, so corn continued to be the staff of life for most Crackers. Along with grits and cornmeal from a nearby gristmill, it was more plentiful and easier to cook with minimal ingredients. Independently owned gristmills served nearby farmers with power supplied by water or steam and, later, electricity. Farmers brought in their dried corn, and the miller poured it down the hopper for grinding by a huge granite stone. From the pop! pop! popping of the dried kernels to the corn syrup found in many southern and Cracker recipes, the oldest farm-raised crop in North America can be prepared in a seemingly endless variety of ways: husked and shelled at the time of harvest for chowders, soups and stews or in a side dish such as creamed corn. My Aunt Faye was known for putting up the best creamed corn in the area. Corn is one of the most versatile vegetables to cook with, whether dried and ground; pounded into meal or grits for pone, hoecakes and cornbread; or used as breading for fish. It also can be scraped or cut and milked. On the cob, it can be roasted, boiled, fried, grilled or steamed. It can also be used to create delights such as popcorn balls, caramel corn, corn pudding and chess pie, along with fritters, corn chips and cornbread. Much can be credited to the Native Americans and the Spanish for introducing corn and pork, respectively, but it is corn that influenced everything from a simple snack to a delicious dessert.

When buying fresh corn from the market, a quick test for ripeness is easy. Open the husks and pierce a kernel; it should have a milky white substance inside. Fresh corn sliced from the cob and fried in butter in a cast-iron skillet until brown is another simple yet delicious way to prepare it. Whether for breakfast, lunch, dinner, snack or dessert, corn was essential for settlers, as well as feed for their farm animals. Cookbook author Marion Cabell Tyree has a simple plain cornbread recipe similar to one of my favorite corn dishes, homemade corn chips, from *A Culinary History of Florida*.

Plain Corn Bread

1 pint sifted meal
1 teaspoonful salt
Cold water sufficient to make a stiff dough

Work well with the hands, pat out in long, narrow pones, six or seven inches long and as wide as the wrist. Bake quickly in a hot pan.—*Mrs. P.W.*

〜

Homemade Corn Chips (revised)

1 cup boiling water
1 cup fine (white, stone-ground) cornmeal
3 tablespoons butter, melted
½ teaspoon salt
Corn oil

Preheat oven to 350 degrees. Stir boiling water into cornmeal until smooth, using only enough water for a thick batter. Stir in butter and salt. Pour into greased cast-iron skillet and bake for 45 minutes. Remove from oven and cut into 1-inch by 1-inch strips. Heat skillet with ½ inch of corn oil on the stovetop. Add strips a few at a time to hot skillet and cook until crisp. Drain on paper towels.

Cornmeal hoecakes were replaced by hush puppies and served at fish fries with cheese grits. But fried cornbread is still my favorite. Someone explained to Marjorie Kinnan Rawlings that if you poke a hole in the round corn cake, like a doughnut, it will fry up crispier. My Aunt Jo of Hartford, Alabama, would squeeze the batter and let it ooze between her fingers just before dropping it into the hot grease, which would accomplish the same result— tender on the inside and crispness all over the outside. Hartford is also home to a family favorite, J.T. Pollard extra-fine white cornmeal. But here is how my brother Pat makes his hush puppies: "I use regular old Martha White yellow type cornmeal, with a tincy wincy pinch of sweetness, by stickin' my finger in the mixin' bowl (most normal folks have to use a teaspoon of table sugar), then some onion that is cubed up."

On a sweeter note, quick breads and gingerbread were welcome additions to the Cracker table. Gingerbread dates back at least to the Middle Ages, made with stale bread, spices and honey. Later, during the Restoration period, molasses replaced the honey to make a thick, dense cookie that was often cut out and decorated. Florida Crackers used cane syrup as a sweetener, but molasses lends a richer flavor to this dark, moist, spicy cake or cookie. One heirloom recipe suggests adding the amount of flour necessary to create a cake using a thin batter or, for a cookie, a stiff batter. In the sixteenth century, the family recipe collection *Martha Washington's Booke of Cookery and Booke of Sweetmeats* includes one for "pepper cakes." It's a gingerbread recipe without pepper, but it does contain the peppery-tasting ginger root.

Although cookbooks from this time did not include cooking times or temperatures, Amelia Simmons gave detailed instructions in her book *American Cookery*. Plant ashes were used to create potash (potassium carbonate); when heated again to remove the ashy residue, this purer form turned pearly white, hence the name change from potash to pearl ash. Simmons used pearl ash in her recipe for gingerbread and introduced this new leavening agent to North America in her cookbook. Saleratus, a precursor to baking soda and more powerful than pearl ash, is a term found in cookbooks before baking soda became a common household ingredient. Other early leavening agents were eggs and yeast. Simmons's recipe for "Gingerbread Cakes, or butter and sugar Gingerbread" called for three pounds of flour, grated nutmeg, two ounces of ginger, one pound of sugar, three small spoons of pearl ash dissolved in milk, one pound of butter and four eggs. After the ingredients were combined, it was to be kneaded stiff and shaped before baking for fifteen minutes.

Mary Randolph, in *The Virginia Housewife: Or, Methodical Cook*, provided three gingerbread recipes: one without leavening, one with pearl ash and one with frothy eggs. Her recipe for Plebeian Ginger Bread called for three large spoonsful of pounded ginger, three quarts of flour, three teaspoons of pearl ash dissolved in a cup of water, half a pound of melted butter and a quart of molasses. The instructions were to mix, knead well, cut in shapes and bake. *Mrs. Hill's New Cook Book*, by A.P. Hill, included more than one thousand numbered recipes with a dozen variations of gingerbread for cakes and cookies. For her Soft Ginger Cake, she suggested "a teaspoonful of soda stirred well into the molasses, or two teaspoonfuls of yeast powders sprinkled into the batter." Another recipe, Fruit Ginger Cake, called for currants, raisins and citron, along with the common spices of ginger, cinnamon and allspice. Cooking directions were brief or nonexistent, with quips such as "bake in a pan" and "bake in a moderate or quick oven." Her recipe for Soft Ginger Cake was simple: one cup of sugar, three cups of molasses, one cup of butter, one cup of sweet milk, three eggs, seven cups of flour, one teaspoon of soda beaten well into the molasses, ginger and spice to taste.

What Mrs. Fisher Knows about Old Southern Cooking, by Abby Fisher, included 160 recipes and was the first African American cookbook written by a former slave. She included two gingerbread recipes: Old-Time Ginger Cake, leavened with soda and eggs, and her recipe for Ginger Cookies, which required yeast powder. Teacups were used as measuring utensils, and baking instructions were brief: "bake in oblong pans" and "bake as you would a biscuit." She also used a combination of butter and lard for her cookies.

Then came Fannie Merritt Farmer, who wrote *The Boston Cooking-School Cook Book* and laid the foundation for proper recipe writing. I inherited a copy of the eighth edition, which includes a chapter on gingerbreads and doughnuts. Farmer was the first to publish a cookbook with detailed cooking instructions for each recipe. She wrote: "Gingerbreads vary from the simplest eggless mixture made with hot water to a rich and buttery sour cream recipe, which makes no pretense of being inexpensive." Those recipes were included in her book along with a recipe for Soft Molasses Gingerbread. Rather than including butter or shortening in that recipe, she let the baker make that decision. She explained the versatility of gingerbread: "Gingerbreads fit into the menu in many places. They may be served hot, with butter, as a breakfast or luncheon bread or with afternoon tea or coffee." As a dessert, she suggested cutting it into squares and serving with sweetened whipped cream, a mixture of whipped cream and cream cheese, or applesauce.

Cracker recipes for quick breads are still favorites today. One recipe for pumpkin bread from *Dishes and Beverages of the Old South* suggested substituting persimmons or sweet potatoes:

Pumpkin Bread (Pioneer.)

Sift a pint of meal, add salt to season fully, then rub through a large cupful of stewed pumpkin, made very smooth. Add half a cup melted lard, then mix with sweet milk to a fairly stiff dough, make pones, and bake crisp. Mashed sweet potato can be used instead of pumpkin, and cracklings, rubbed very fine in place of lard. Folks curious as to older cookery, can even make persimmon bread, using the pulp of ripe persimmons to mix with the meal—but they will need the patience of Job to free the pulp properly from skin and seed.

Buttermilk and butter are essential to successful Cracker cooking. Buttermilk comes in two forms. One is traditional buttermilk, which is the liquid left when butter is churned out of cream, and the other is artificially fermented or cultured buttermilk. Sweet milk is the old-fashioned term for whole milk as opposed to sour milk, or milk that is starting to go bad. Once fresh milk has settled and separated into low-fat milk and cream, the cream can be skimmed off the top and churned with a cross-bottomed dasher. The dasher is a long pole inserted in the churn and moved up and down to agitate the cream and start turning it into a rich, creamy butter. Butter was scooped out of the churn, pressed together and then washed to remove leftover milk. It was then salted or left sweet before kneading and pressing into molds. When I was visiting Granny Mattie, homemade butter was mixed with wild honey and put on a cracker for a treat.

Chapter 7

SUNSHINE AND SUGAR

If God had meant cornbread to have sugar in it, he would have called it cake.
—author unknown

A long with the new art of cookery and electric appliances came an explosion of new recipes. These helped lay the foundation for the sweet tooth of the South, and Cracker families were no exception. At the same time, the Florida population landscape was changing drastically. Following World War II, soldiers returned to Florida, after initially training here, and suburbanites started to fill the roadways. By then, Cracker cooking had adapted to reflect changing patterns in grocery shopping. Never one to shy away from homegrown and homemade, Cracker cooks nonetheless found the convenience of canned, boxed and frozen foods hard to resist.

Desserts, especially in the South, often have overwhelmed the pages of many new cookbooks. From a simple ambrosia to layer cakes, and all sweets in between, Crackers have always had their go-to desserts. Candies, cakes, cookies, ice cream, puddings and pies filled their sideboards and even their sidewalks, with bake sales and other fundraisers. Traditional colonial desserts with charming names such as jumble, buckle and pandowdy gave way to a new era of Florida sweets. A delightful mix of oranges peeled and sliced, mixed with freshly grated coconut and a little sugar sprinkled on top, served in a cut glass or crystal bowl, delivers a Cracker classic known as ambrosia. Served as a side dish, and often as a holiday dessert, ambrosia's simplicity is part of its appeal. Some liked to tinker with the

Florida Highway Patrol car parked in front of the Sweet Shop in Tallahassee, 1940.

recipe by adding marshmallows, grapes, bananas, grapefruit, pecans, pineapple, wine or orange liqueur.

Here are two ambrosia recipes from cookbook author Marion Cabell Tyree:

Ambrosia No. 1

Pare and slice as many oranges as you choose, in a glass bowl. Sprinkle sugar and grated cocoanut over each layer.—*Mrs. W.C.R.*

Ambrosia No. 2

Cut pineapple and orange in slices, sprinkle with sugar, and put in a deep dish alternately to form a pyramid. Put grated cocoanut between each layer. If you like, pour good Madeira or sherry wine over the dish.—*Mrs. T.*

Recipes evolved with changing tastes and times. For example, the macaroon morphed from an almond cookie to a flaky coconut confection. (Unlike the simple and elegant meringue-based French macaron, the macaroon is quite different.) The following recipe is an example of how the change began, with the suggestion of using coconut instead of almonds at the end.

Almond Macaroons

One-half pound almonds, blanched and pounded, with a teaspoonful essence of lemon, till a smooth paste. Add an equal quantity of sifted white sugar and the whites of two eggs. Work well together with a spoon. Dip your hand into water and work them into balls the size of a nutmeg. Lay them on white paper an inch apart, then dip your hand in water and smooth them. Put them in a slow oven for three-quarters of an hour. Cocoanut may be used instead of almonds.—*Mrs. M.G.H.*

Here is my recipe from *A Culinary History of Florida.*

Coconut Macaroons

1 ½ cups flaked coconut
⅓ cup sugar
2 egg whites
2 tablespoons flour
½ teaspoon almond or vanilla extract
⅛ teaspoon salt

Preheat oven to 325 degrees.
Combine all ingredients, mixing well.
Drop by spoonful onto buttered parchment paper.
Bake 25 minutes or until golden brown on the edges. Cool.
These do not store well and should be eaten right away.

Making peanut brittle with cane syrup, White Springs, 1984. *FMA/Andrea Graham.*

Experimentation in refrigeration began in Florida with Dr. John Gorrie in the 1840s, and eventually home freezers and air conditioning were the norm. Ice cream making, however, goes back to a time when blocks of ice were chipped away from frozen lakes and shipped south wrapped in burlap or packed in sawdust. In the 1780s, Thomas Jefferson was one of the first to introduce ice cream to this country, and recipes began to appear in cookbooks as the process became simplified. Nancy Johnson's patented hand-crank churn of the mid-1800s was followed by an electric one, though the hand-crank model is still popular in Cracker homes today. Ice cream is an extraordinary treat made from simple ingredients: cream, eggs, sugar and vanilla, along with salt and ice. Here are two recipes from the past.

To Make Ice-Cream

Pare and stone twelve ripe apricots, and scald them, beat them fine in a mortar, add to them six ounces of double-refined sugar, and a pint of scalding cream, and work it through a sieve; put it in a tin with a close cover, and set it in a tub of ice broke small, with four handfuls of salt mixed among the ice. When you see your cream grows thick round the edges of your tin, stir it well, and put it in again till it is quite thick; when the cream is all froze up, take it out of the tin, and put it into the mould you intend to turn it out of; put on the lid and have another tub of salt and ice ready as before; put the mould in the middle, and lay the ice under and over it; let it stand four hours, and never turn it out till the moment you want it, then dip the mold in cold spring water, and turn it into a plate. You may do any sort of fruit the same way.—Hannah Glasse, *The Art of Cooking Made Plain and Easy*

Mary Randolph wrote in *The Virginia Housewife* her "Observations on Ice Cream," noting the importance of scraping down the sides and the constant motion of the ice cream container. Randolph included a recipe for vanilla cream using a vanilla bean, rich milk, eggs and sugar, with the

Chattahoochee patients making pies, circa 1940.

comment, "make it very sweet, for much of the sugar is lost in the operation of freezing." Here is an excerpt from her observations:

> It is the practice with some indolent cooks, to set the freezer containing the cream, in a tub with ice and salt, and put it in the ice house; it will certainly freeze there; but not until the watery particle have subsided, and by the separation destroyed the cream. A freezer should be twelve or fourteen inches deep, and eight or ten wide. This facilitates the operation very much, by giving a larger surface for the ice to form, which it always does on the sides of the vessel; a silver spoon with a long handle should be provided for scraping the ice from the sides as soon as formed: and when the whole is congealed, pack it in moulds (which must be placed with care, lest they should not be upright,) in ice and salt, till sufficiently hard to retain the shape—they should not be turned out till the moment they are to be served. The freezing tub must be wide enough to leave a margin of four or five inches all around the freezer, when placed in the middle—which must be filled up with small lumps of ice mixed with salt—a larger tub would waste the ice. The freezer must be kept constantly in motion during the process, and ought to be made of pewter, which is less liable than tin to be worn in holes, and spoil the cream by admitting the salt water.

With access to ice limited, there was another simple dessert: pudding or custard. At one time, pudding was a simple dish, boiled in an intestine, stomach or pudding bag made of cloth. The Americanized version in the eighteenth century became sweet and dairy based. Pudding, custard and Spanish flan are made with the same ingredients. Following the path of a recipe to see how cooking styles adapted to the environment, methods and available ingredients helps uncover the foundation of great Cracker cooking.

For the Florida Cracker, a soft and sweet pudding was created with ingredients already a part of their local diet: henhouse eggs, fresh milk or cream, sugar, maybe flour or cornstarch for thickening and salt. In *The Frugal Housewife*, Susannah Carter devoted an entire chapter to puddings. The first two recipes describe how to make a plain boiled pudding in a cloth or bag served with melted butter and Light Pudding, with added spices such as cinnamon and mace, served with a white wine sauce. Additional recipes include a fine Biscuit Pudding, Boiled Plum Pudding with beef suet, Custard Pudding boiled in a cloth, Boiled Custards in china cups and Almond Custards.

Florida Orange Chiffon Pie, made by combining orange juice concentrate with pudding, water and rind and then pouring into a pre-baked shell before topping. *FMA/National Post Card Service.*

In her book, Randolph included "Observations on Pudding and Cakes" and suggested, "The salt should always be washed from butter, when it is to be used in any thing that has sugar for an ingredient, and also from that which is melted to grease any kind of mould for baking—otherwise, there will be a disagreeable salt taste on the outer side of the article baked." Using fresh eggs and raisins dusted with flour before baking are among the significant cooking observations. Baked Indian Pudding was made using cornmeal and is served as a classic recipe in some restaurants today. In South Florida, the Seminole Indians taught poor Cracker families how to process arrowroot, and Randolph included a baked pudding recipe of milk, arrowroot, six eggs, butter, sugar, nutmeg and a little grated lemon peel, topped with sifted sugar and garnished with citron.

Tyree included the following pudding recipes in her book, *Housekeeping in Old Virginia*.

Sweet Potato Pudding

Boil one and a half pounds potatoes very tender. Add half a pound butter, and rub both together through a sieve. Then add a small cupful milk, six eggs, one and a half cupful sugar. Beat all together and add a little salt, the juice and rind of a lemon. Then beat again, and prepare pastry. Bake twenty minutes. It may be baked without pastry. Irish potato pudding may be made by the same recipe.—*Mrs. A.C.*

Arrow-Root Pudding

Boil a quart of milk and make it into a thick batter with arrow-root. Add the yolks of six eggs, half a pound of sugar, one-quarter of a pound of butter, half a nutmeg, and a little grated lemon peel. Bake it nicely in a pastry. When done, stick slips of citron all over the top, and pour over it the whites of the six eggs, beaten stiff, sweetened with three or four tablespoonfuls of sugar, and flavored to the taste.—*Mrs. S.T.*

Orange Pudding

Peel and cut five good oranges into thin slices, taking out the seed. Pour over them a coffee-cup of white sugar. Let a pint of milk get boiling hot by setting it in some boiling water. Add yolks of three eggs well beaten, one tablespoonful corn starch, made smooth with a little milk. Stir all the time, and as soon as thickened pour over the fruit. Beat the whites to a stiff froth, adding a tablespoonful of sugar, spread over the top. Set it in the oven a few minutes to harden. Serve either hot or cold.—*Mrs. E.P.G.*

Rice Pudding

Boil one cup of rice in one quart of milk. Add six eggs and a small tablespoonful of butter. Sweeten and flavor to the taste, and bake.—*Mrs. B.*

A Bay County birthday celebration, 1927.

The adapted recipe below for Bucky's Banana Pudding is included in the *Harris & Co. Cookbook, I Can't Believe I 8 the Whole Thing,* created by Chef Charles Knight for the television show *Harris and Company.* My husband Jack's nickname growing up was Bucky, and he hosted the show on our local Channel 8 in Tampa.

Bucky's Banana Pudding (revised)

⅓ cup sugar
2 tablespoons flour
2 tablespoons cornstarch
⅛ teaspoon salt
4 large yolks, room temperature
1 ½ cups light cream
1 tablespoon vanilla
2 teaspoons butter
1 cup whipping cream, whipped with 1 tablespoon sugar
1 12-ounce package vanilla wafers
6 medium bananas

Mix sugar, flour, cornstarch and salt in medium bowl. Add egg yolks, mix again, and set aside.
In a medium saucepan, heat cream to simmering; stir in vanilla.
Gradually whisk hot mixture into egg yolks, then pour back into pan and continue cooking over low heat, whisking constantly, until boiling.
Stir in butter until melted.
Pour into a bowl, cover with plastic wrap and chill.
Fold in half of the whipped cream.
Layer one-third vanilla wafers in 3-quart baking dish and cover with two sliced bananas. Pour one-third of pudding over banana and wafers. Repeat two more times.
Top with remaining whipped cream.

Another sweet favorite is a peanut butter candy from my lunchroom days at Parker Elementary, Everitt Junior High and Rutherford High School. I cannot remember the exact name that appeared on the school

Mary Elizabeth Jones and her birthday cake, 1934.

lunch menus, but the ingredients are few: peanut butter, graham cracker crumbs, powdered sugar and vegetable oil. The recipe is so simple.

Cafeteria Peanut Butter Candy

3 cups peanut butter
1 ⅓ boxes graham crackers, crushed finely
3 cups powdered sugar
Oil as needed

Mix all ingredients well, pat into baking pan. Chill.

The following sweet recipe is from *A Culinary History of Florida*. This cupcake recipe is adapted from a cake recipe we used in my Quantity Food Production class at Florida State University in the 1970s.

Orange Chocolate Chip Cupcakes

2½ cups flour
2½ teaspoons baking powder
½ teaspoon salt
⅔ cup butter, at room temperature
1 ¾ cups sugar
2 teaspoons vanilla
2 eggs
1 ¼ cups whole milk
1 cup mini chocolate chips
2 teaspoons orange zest
Orange Chip Frosting

Preheat oven to 350 degrees. Line muffin tin with cupcake papers.
Whisk together flour, baking powder and salt; set aside.
Cream together butter and sugar; stir in vanilla.
Add eggs, one at time, beating well after each addition.
Alternately add flour mixture and milk, beating after each addition until combined. Stir in chips and zest.

Spoon into muffin tin.
Bake 20 to 25 minutes. Cool in pan 10 minutes. Remove from pan and cool completely on rack before frosting.

Orange Chip Frosting
⅓ cup butter at room temperature
3¾ cups powdered sugar, divided
2 tablespoons milk
2 tablespoons orange juice
2 teaspoons vanilla
2 teaspoons orange zest
½ cup mini chocolate chips

Beat butter with 2 cups sugar.
Stir in milk, then beat in orange juice and vanilla.
Beat in remaining sugar. Stir in zest and chips.

Both my mother and father recalled the excitement of coming home from school to find sugar cookies or teacakes waiting for them. Granny Trixie made a simple chocolate sauce for dipping the cookies into, and Granny Mattie made the most delicious sugar cookies Daddy ever had. She may have used Florida cane syrup as her secret ingredient, but my recipe for sugar cookies and chocolate dip can be found on pages 133–34. Brownies were my all-time favorite after-school snack, and here is my recipe.

Brownie Bites

2 eggs
1¼ cups sugar
6 tablespoons butter, melted
⅔ cup flour
½ cup cocoa
½ teaspoon baking powder
¼ teaspoon salt
1 teaspoon vanilla

Preheat oven to 350 degrees.

Beat eggs; add sugar and butter, then beat again.

Whisk together flour, cocoa, baking powder and salt; add to egg mixture. Stir in vanilla.

Pour the batter into a buttered 8-inch square pan.

Bake for 30 minutes.

These are especially nice when topped with a dollop of Peppermint Cream.

Peppermint Cream

2½ cups powdered sugar
¼ cup butter, softened
⅛ teaspoon salt
2 tablespoons milk or cream
½ teaspoon vanilla
½ cup crushed peppermint candy

Cream sugar and butter together.

Stir in salt, milk and vanilla. Beat until smooth.

Stir in peppermint candy.

Chapter 8

HEIRLOOM COOKING

*Remembrance of things past is not necessarily
the remembrance of things as they were.
—Marcel Proust*

The path of a recipe begins with our Founding Fathers, as we follow our heritage and watch the cooking process change as they adapted to the environment. Navigating both the crossroads of our past culinary delights and the back roads crisscrossing our minds delivers a glimpse into the past of small-town charms and country foods. A poor Cracker family, isolated in the backwoods at a time when corn, sweet potatoes and sugar cane were the bulk of their diet, might have a meager breakfast of leftover fish, sweet potatoes and cornbread, along with coffee to wash it down. The children's lunch, tied in a sack or carried in a pail, would include much of the same, with biscuits or cornbread and perhaps a boiled egg. In the days before refrigeration reached the rural population of Florida, preparations for breakfast were more time consuming than the actual cooking. Three balanced meals a day weren't always the tradition, and a big Sunday dinner was something to look forward to. Even that has morphed into fast food on the run; brunch instead of an early breakfast; and noontime lunch, along with dinner out.

Our heritage begins with a look at our ancestors. The diverse cooking styles of Crackers were influenced by many. Spanish and Cuban descendants gave us bolichi, picadillo, ropa vieja and guava tarts; Minorcans of northeast

Family in front of a log cabin, circa 1870.

Florida shared their fromajardis and datil peppers; and the Seminoles taught us how to live off the land with swamp cabbage and wild turkey. But it's the southern and soul pathways that had the most influence on Cracker cooking. From colonial America to the piney Florida backwoods, changes in the kitchen at the turn of the twentieth century help us uncover the foundation of Cracker cooking as it reflected the environment more than personal tastes.

Shortly after the Statue of Liberty was given to the United States and the Eiffel Tower opened, the all-electric kitchen was introduced to the country at the Chicago World's Fair of 1893. Cities were beginning to enjoy this all-electric life, but in the rural South, electricity and running water were still decades away; reading by kerosene lamps would continue, as would priming

Turkey hunters with their camp kill, 1900s Clermont.

the pump and toting water to the house in a bucket. Soon horse-and-buggy days would be replaced with cross-country trains. In the first decade of the twentieth century, Henry Ford would drive a Model T, the Wright brothers would fly and Thomas Edison would continue to light up the world. The two Henrys, Plant and Flagler, would build railroads and grand resort hotels from St. Augustine to Tampa, Palm Beach and Key West. Only the wealthy could afford railroad trips to Florida's posh hotels such as the Casa Monica in St. Augustine, the Breakers in Palm Beach and the Tampa Bay Hotel in Tampa. Many of these hotels later became military housing and hospitals during the two world wars. In the first half of the century, prices were going down for beef, flour, canned goods, poultry, rice, sugar and cheese. Life was still challenging for Crackers, especially in the backwoods of Florida. The Pure Food and Drug Act of 1906 set food standards that helped improve the quality of dining across America.

Electric cooperatives and radio broadcasts were beginning to take hold in the 1920s, about the same time that women attained the right to vote. Prohibition would come and go by 1933. U.S. highways were beginning to spread across the state, and by 1925, the Dixie Highway stretched from the Canadian border to Miami. Like an unwelcomed houseguest, the Great Depression came early and lingered in Florida. But the modernization of the kitchen, with more reliable appliances and a greater variety of foods, soon followed. Crisco, Spam, the frozen foods of Clarence Birdseye with everything from fruit to fish sticks and Karo Syrup were filling up grocery carts as kitchens changed. Cast-iron stoves using coal or wood would later compete with gas appliances and electric cooktops.

The smell of hickory burning brings back a flood of childhood memories for me. Wearing her apron, Granny would sit with a bowl in her lap for snapping peas, stringing beans or shelling pecans. My brother Pat's favorite Cracker meal is a simple glass of iced tea served with hot, salted, flat cornbread made from Hoover's fine ground cornmeal found in Chipley, Florida, and a bowl of field peas with snaps (young pods). Memories of Sunday family dinners at Granny's include a table of savory dishes, with deviled eggs on a special indented crystal plate to neatly hold them in place, along with freshly sliced tomatoes from the garden, fried or pickled okra from the pantry and creamed corn, butter beans and field peas from the freezer. Depending on the season, a side of summer squash seasoned with bacon drippings or sweet potatoes with lumps of butter slowly melting

A dirt road between Jacksonville and St. Augustine later became the Dixie Highway, 1900s.

was served along with a big pot of chicken and dumplings, kept warm on the stove. All of this was accompanied with a pitcher of sweet tea—very sweet tea—since the days of sugar rationing were over. Our tea lost some of its sweetness again in the 1970s when the price of sugar soared, and many families found that cutting sugar consumption in half was possible. Family dining today is often takeout or delivery food. If someone wants dessert, they just order off the menu. The days of the homemade dessert plate waiting on the sideboard are fading—one beautifully created from a family of pies and cakes made by the hands of loving aunts and Granny.

Unlike hand-me-down clothes, recipes passed from one generation to the next seem to improve with each new generation, adapting to the environment in the kitchen and in the community. Dinner at one time meant the midday or biggest meal of the day, served in mostly hardworking rural communities, with a light supper of leftovers served in the evening. As city customs encroached upon the countryside, supper began to seem old-fashioned, while dinner is now the acceptable term for the evening meal. Creating menus from basic heirloom recipes, as simple as a flaky pie crust, a white gravy or a rich chicken stock, provide insight into past generations and their awareness of seasonal foods and magical combinations that made delicious dishes.

From simple one-room cabins in the piney woods of the Panhandle to high-rise condos along the glistening waterways, Florida's kitchens have evolved over the decades just as our country, our state, our tastes and our food supply have. From dinner on the grounds at the community church with covered dishes to spaghetti supper fundraisers sponsored by the local PTA, memories of our favorite meals stay with us throughout our lives. One of my fondest memories is Mother's bacon grease routine. Every weekday morning, and sometimes on weekends, she would fry bacon for Dad's breakfast and drain most of the grease onto a filter that sat atop a canister to collect the drippings for later use, which included frying our eggs and much more. In the tradition of her mother, she used bacon grease to flavor everything from beans to biscuits.

As decades passed, Crackers went from milking cows and churning butter to buying cartons of milk and sticks of butter. After the mid-nineteenth century, homemakers bought more canned and processed foods, ready to trade in their cast-iron skillets and garden vegetables for convenience foods, electric skillets and, later, microwaves. By 1930, only about 10 percent of rural America had electricity, though that would increase over the next decade. The modernization of the kitchen brought new appliances, utensils and gadgets—from new and improved mixing bowls to a variety of rolling pins, to other gadgets such as the flour sifter, lemon reamer, biscuit cutter, can opener, potholder, ice-cream freezer, waffle iron, potato masher and soup pot, along with casserole dishes, strainers and much more.

With the flurry of new electric appliances, it was difficult to know what would make homemaking easier, as some just added to the workload of the (mostly) women in charge of housekeeping. The Good Housekeeping Seal of Approval was given to certain appliances and gave consumers peace of mind; knowing the product had been tested, they trusted it would be reliable. The Kitchen Craft Waterless Cookware proudly displayed the seal on its 1925 recipe book that came with the cooker. The 1930s booklet for Coldspot, dubbed "The Pace Setter for Modern Home Conveniences," also included menus and household hints. In the 1950s, Sunbeam appliances were popular, and the Automatic Frypan became a part of meal planning with the promise, "Everything you cook will be more delicious because you get the correct heat every time." Other electric appliances popular at that time were the electric mixer, deep fryer, toaster, egg cooker, waffle grill and percolator. Most new appliances came with instruction manuals that included recipes.

Years after Piggly Wiggly first introduced the self-service grocery store and shopping cart in 1916, the first Publix Food Store opened in Winter Haven in 1930. Later, in 1940, the first Publix Super Market opened with polished terrazzo floors and air conditioning, providing a truly modern marketplace. The chain expanded, and today the stores continue to live up to their motto, "Where Shopping Is a Pleasure," with sparkling clean stores and modern innovations, all while supporting local communities and charities. As for the Cracker pantry, more commercially canned and boxed foods would sit on the shelves by the 1930s, but home canning was still favored and more economical. The garden might supply tomatoes, collards, beans, lettuce, turnips and okra, with fruit trees and grape arbors a welcome addition.

Recovery from two world wars and the Great Depression took longer in the backwoods of Florida, but once Florida was easier to reach with railroads and automobiles, developers began their push toward the greatest vacation paradise in America. Between World War I and World War II, dirt roads were paved, and people came in Model Ts to explore this tropical state. Camping out along roadways became a new adventure for "tin can tourists," who eventually founded the organization Tin Can Tourists of the World (TCT) in Tampa. Just like Cracker and Piggly Wiggly, the origin of "tin can tourists" isn't known for sure, but it's thought to be based on all the canned

A line of tourist cars, DeSoto County, with the caption "Tourists are going out for a 'swamp cabbage' dinner," circa 1930.

foods they packed. Others consider it to be based on the cars some drove, referred to as "Tin Lizzies" or Model Ts. They later embraced the term as an early emblem of the TCT.

School cafeterias also changed. In 1946, Congress passed the School Lunch Act, along with other government-supported programs. At first, teachers had to pick up ingredients and prepare lunch, record who ate it and collect the lunch money. In the 1970s, trays were prepared for students, but by the 1990s, a buffet line displayed the commodities. During this time, peanut butter was made into candy, cookies and cakes and stirred into brownie batter. Commodity cheese improved the flavor of the already delicious yeast rolls and mashed potatoes. Eating in the school cafeteria was a delight in the Florida Panhandle. We had beets—usually left on the tray, of course—but the lunchroom was packed on fried chicken day, and memories of apple crisp made with apple butter still linger. Roast beef and gravy with those big fluffy yeast rolls was another comfort meal served on the lunchroom tray, but the favorite of mine and many of my childhood friends was the Peanut Butter Candy. The recipe is on page 116.

The innovative cookware Revere Ware of the 1940s held through the 1950s and beyond. Electric refrigeration didn't reach the country folks until after World War II, and many did home canning without electricity

Heritage kitchen at the Lake City Columbia County Historical Museum, 1800s. *FMA/H. Milo Stewart.*

or indoor plumbing. Seasonality wasn't as important, with imported foods filling the grocery store shelves. After the war, home economists and county extension agents working for the government offered their recipes for simple dishes using canned products and convenience foods. Postwar prosperity brightened up the pink, blue and yellow kitchens with Priscilla curtains and Venetian blinds. Glass blocks, wood paneling and linoleum on the floor complemented the copper molds and cuckoo clocks hanging on the walls. Major appliances such as refrigerators and freezers, along with smaller appliances such as pressure cookers, toasters, mixers, skillets, coffeepots and waffle irons, were commonplace. Then telephones, television and, by 1946, Tupperware followed.

Refrigeration meant congealed salads, beautifully molded in a ring or even the shape of a fish to show off skill and creativity in the kitchen. In the 1950s, we saw milk containers transition from caps on top of glass bottles to cartons with tear-and-pour spouts. Ice cream was sold in little paper cups with a wooden paddle that hurt your teeth when eating. On TV and in magazines, ideal housewives planned ahead for a delicious dinner, but in reality, they also enjoyed the convenience of TV dinners and potpies on TV trays that had become part of the household furnishings. The food was good, but the convenience was even better. We began to move away from pilot lights, pressure cookers and Cracker cabins.

The mid-century also gave us Tang and Teflon-coated cookware, along with the growing popularity of Kool-Aid, cake mixes, Cool Whip, Jell-O and candy such as jawbreakers, red hots and fireballs. Suddenly, everything had to be instant, from grits and potatoes to oatmeal and pudding. Easy brown-and-serve rolls replaced a stack of light bread at most evening meals, thanks in part to a Florida firefighter from Avon Park, Joseph Gregor. He had removed his partly baked Parker House dinner rolls from the oven early one evening when he was called away to put out a fire. When he returned, he put the rolls back in the oven and discovered they baked up perfectly. General Mills took up the idea, and brown-and-serve rolls quickly became commonplace on dinner tables throughout the country. The shortcut was quite a breakthrough, because as Marjorie Kinnan Rawlings noted, "The making of Parker House rolls at home was an appallingly messy procedure, for I kept the kitchen littered for the day-and-a-half necessary to complete them." Improvement in transportation and refrigeration provided low-cost produce, and iceberg lettuce appeared on the dinner table most evenings as a small salad with tomatoes and onions. Bottled dressing was the norm, with Thousand Island or French topping the list in our home. Now in our condo I make a special honey mustard dressing just for Jack.

Balsamic Honey Mustard Dressing

½ cup mayonnaise
¼ cup honey
2 tablespoons spicy brown mustard
2 tablespoons balsamic vinegar

Place all ingredients in a bowl and whisk together until thoroughly blended.

Kry Drugstore in Winter Haven with a soda fountain, circa 1940. *FMA/Robert E. Dahlgren.*

By the 1960s, the government had stepped up with nutrition information and agriculture bulletins such as the Home and Garden Bulletin No. 1, put out by the USDA and "vital for family health and happiness," filled with food management tips and recipe shortcuts. It covered nutrition and weight control, food buying, storing, measuring and thriftiness. Picnics were popular, with hot dogs and hamburgers sizzling on outdoor grills. Picnic baskets were supplied with a tablecloth, plates, flatware and cold fried chicken. Our family enjoyed these al fresco dining events at Torreya State Park and Mexico Beach. For me, though, it was the Tyndall Air Force Base Squadron parties by the bay that I remember so fondly. Men tended the grill while women watched the children running past the huge stainless-steel bowls filled with chips of all kinds and relish trays full of ripe and green olives. There was so much more, but those were my favorite snacks, and the bowls were continually replenished. The 1960s were full of lightning bugs, lunchboxes and the excitement of a moon landing.

The 1970s were still a time of home-cooked meals, but convenience was king at our lonely house at the end of the road on Martin Lake in Parker. Times were changing, though, and more homes were being built in the area. Cast-iron skillets continued to linger in the cabinet, even though the bacon-drippings canister disappeared from the stovetop. Chicken went from stewed, to fried, to potpies, to nuggets and back to oven-fried. Sunday dinner consisted of a pot roast in the oven with potatoes and carrots, waiting for us when we returned from church. Meatloaf, macaroni and cheese and our cousin Kathy Sheffield's tuna casserole were common for dinner, with fried chicken and French fries every Friday night. Pork chops and gravy over rice were standard fare. Mother made the gravy from the dregs left in the skillet by adding milk and flour, then cooking to just the right consistency. Controlled breeding has changed the fat content of those animals, thus changing the flavor as well. We had fried salmon patties with ketchup and oven barbecued chicken with scalloped potatoes. For lunch, bologna or a peanut butter and jelly sandwich fit the bill in the summer, but in the fall, canned tomato soup with a grilled cheese sandwich was always a treat. Thanks to the research and development done in Florida, frozen concentrate orange juice was available for breakfast on a daily basis, along with the convenience and variety of sugar-coated cereal. Disney World changed the landscape of central Florida while Hamburger Helper, Mr. Coffee and Cuisinart food processors shaped the kitchen in the early 1970s. Affordable microwave ovens and fondue pots rounded out the kitchen setting, and Krispy Kreme doughnuts of the 1930s became popular in grocery stores.

Feeling sophisticated sipping coffee frappe from punch bowl cups, eating hot hors d'oeuvres fresh from the microwave and nipping at petit fours for wedding showers, we felt the 1980s approaching. We were all busy enjoying the delights of fast-food chains and ready-made meals from the grocer. Gone were the hearty breakfasts of waffles, pancakes, French toast or omelets. All that changed when I married Jack in 1986 and even more so after our son, Jackson, was born in 1991. I wanted to re-create the memorable meals I enjoyed growing up.

Charles and LeAnn Knight of Health Craft Cookware were regular guests on Jack's TV show *Harris and Company* in the 1990s, which aired on local TV in the Tampa Bay area. When Charles created the *Harris & Co. Cookbook, I Can't Believe I 8 the Whole Thing* featuring his cookware, I provided a few of Jack's favorite recipes. Here is one for deviled eggs.

Delicious Deviled Eggs

12 eggs, hard-boiled, peeled, chilled
½ cup sour cream
2 tablespoons chopped green olives
2 tablespoons mustard
1 tablespoon fresh parsley, chopped
4 drops hot pepper sauce
Salt and pepper to taste
Paprika, enough for a light dusting as garnish

Cut eggs lengthwise in half and scoop yolks out into a bowl. Put whites on an egg plate or platter.
Add remaining ingredients, except paprika, to yolks and mix well.
Spoon yolk mixture into egg halves.
Sprinkle with paprika.
Cover and chill.

As the pace has slowed for the home cook, finding restaurants that serve genuine Florida Cracker cuisine, aside from the ever-popular Cracker Barrel, is more difficult than you might think. Just as our habits change over time, so do our tastes in food, but there are a few newcomers making a name for themselves, offering menus with updated Cracker cooking. Backwoods Crossing is a real farm-to-table restaurant in Tallahassee. Nestled between its garden in the front and farm animals in the back, our waiter told us, "We're out of trout—haven't caught any in the past few days. But the gator was just trapped up the road about five miles, so it's fresh." The food was a creative take on Cracker cooking, and it was delicious. Then there's the Florida Cracker Kitchen, which started in Brooksville with an old Florida southern charm—so charming they opened more restaurants, in Keystone and Jacksonville, spreading their creativity with Florida Cracker foods.

From the foothills of the Mountain State to the beaches and backroads of the Sunshine State, little did Jack and I know that both sets of our ancestors of Scotch-Irish descent came to America to fulfill their dreams through hard work and perseverance. Re-creating their heirloom recipes can be challenging, especially when trying to decipher jotted-down notes and a list of ingredients, relying on nonstandard measurements such as "butter the size of an egg." Plus, back in our ancestors' days, eggs were smaller, butter had to be washed and sea salt wasn't as strong as our table salt today. To know that quality ingredients are as important as basic techniques acquired through trial and error is an important part of meal planning. LA (Lower Alabama) memories of sleepovers with Aunt Margaret and Aunt Jo and Granny Mattie in North Florida are only a small part of my childhood memories that have added to my culinary quest to re-create those tastes of the past. From the turn of the last century to another, a remarkable metamorphosis happened in the home kitchen. Hopefully, when I stray from the Cracker cabin kitchen as my condo cooking comes seeping in, I'll keep the recipes polished with memories of Granny Mattie's kitchen.

FLORIDA CRACKER RESTAURANTS

In addition to Florida Cracker Kitchen, Backwoods Crossing and Cracker Barrel, here are a few more Cracker restaurants:

The Blackwater Inn and Williams Landing, along the St. Johns River in Aster: you might find on the menu gator, catfish, frog legs and quail.

The Catfish Place in St. Cloud, serving catfish caught daily from Lake Okeechobee: you might find on the menu the "Florida Cracker Special" of catfish, frog legs, turtle and gator.

The Yearling, established in 1952 near Cross Creek: you might find on the menu gator, frog legs, venison, quail, catfish, collards, okra and tomatoes, cheese grits and sour orange pie.

Chapter 9

CONTEMPORARY CRACKER COOKING

W̲e are still Crackers, but our recipes and tastes have evolved along with our cultures and lifestyles. Over the years, I've continued to use many Cracker recipes that evoke treasured memories, but other recipes have changed with the generations. Here is how I use the best of both in my life today, particularly for special occasions.

The Quick Chicken Stock recipe found on page 45 and the following All Occasion Pie Crusts recipe are two basic recipes I make ahead and store in the freezer up to a few months. Chicken stock is one of the first things I prepare ahead of time and freeze for Thanksgiving dinner. I usually make two or three batches so I have enough stock for the gravy and the dressing. I freeze the chicken meat in plastic bags to use later in chicken salad (also a recipe on page 45) or for adding to the chicken and dumplings, which uses chicken stock and the following pie crust recipe. All of this saves time later in the kitchen, which is especially important around the holidays.

All Occasion Pie Crusts
This recipe makes 2 pie crusts.

2½ cups flour
1 cup cold butter, cut into 1-inch pieces
1 teaspoon salt
⅓ cup ice water

Place flour, butter and salt in a food processor with metal blades and process until it looks like coarse cornmeal.

Add ice water and process until dough begins to clump together. Pulse until dough holds together.

Divide dough into two equal pieces and put each into a plastic bag. Work through the bag to press dough into a ball and flatten.

Refrigerate or freeze for later use. Thaw in refrigerator before using. Roll very cold dough out onto a floured surface to desired size. Fold over and transfer to a greased pie plate. Chill until ready to use.

Bake at 425 degrees for 12 to 15 minutes for a baked pie crust or keep frozen until ready to use as unbaked.

MATTIE'S SUGAR COOKIES AND TRIXIE'S CHOCOLATE DIP

Sometimes Granny Trixie made teacakes with a bowl of chocolate dip for her children when they came home from school, while Granny Mattie made sugar cookies. Since my grannies rarely used recipes, I worked at re-creating them, and GrandMary approved. One easy cookie recipe I've been making for years is homemade cinnamon slice-and-bake cookies, now Jack's favorite. But the biggest treat for me is something I have been doing since my high school days: baking gingerbread cookies to give to friends and family. Later, it was especially fun decorating gingerbread men at Christmastime with Jackson for his elementary school teachers and friends. (I also use the gingerbread cookie recipe to make an old-fashioned West Virginia stack cake to honor my in-laws, as the cookies soften to create cake-like layers when topped with applesauce.) When I pull out my mother's cookie sheet, the one I used all those years ago at home in Parker, it brings those childhood memories back to my heart.

Mattie's Sugar Cookies

1 cup butter, softened
1 ½ cups sugar
1 egg
1 teaspoon vanilla

3 cups flour
2 teaspoons baking powder
Additional sugar for pressing

Beat butter until creamy. Add sugar and beat well; beat in egg and vanilla.
Combine flour and baking powder and add to butter mixture. Mix well.
Chill several hours.
When ready to bake, preheat oven to 375 degrees.
Shape cookie dough into ¾-inch balls and place 2 inches apart on parchment-lined cookie sheet. Flatten cookie dough with bottom of lightly buttered glass dipped in sugar. Dip in sugar each time you press a cookie.
Bake 10 minutes.
Cool on wire racks.
Serve with Chocolate Dip.

Chocolate Dip

1 cup sugar
¼ cup unsweetened cocoa powder
2 tablespoons flour
1 ½ cups whole milk
2 tablespoons butter

In a heavy saucepan, whisk together sugar, cocoa and flour.
Whisk in milk over medium heat. Cook, stirring until thick.
Remove from heat and stir in butter until melted.

~

Cinnamon Slice-and-Bake Cookies

½ cup butter, softened
½ cup brown sugar, packed
½ cup sugar
1 egg
1 ¾ cups flour
½ teaspoon baking soda
2 teaspoons cinnamon

Cream butter and both sugars until light and fluffy. Add egg and mix well. Whisk flour together with baking soda and cinnamon; add to sugar mixture.

Form dough into a roll and wrap in plastic wrap. Place in freezer and chill at least two hours or up to six months.

When ready to bake, preheat oven to 350 degrees.

Remove from freezer, remove plastic wrap and cut into twelve equal slices. Place on parchment-lined cookie sheet and bake 15 minutes.

⌒

Gingerbread Cookies
The fresher your spices, the stronger the flavor.

½ cup butter, softened
½ cup sugar
½ cup molasses
1 egg
3 cups flour
½ teaspoon baking soda
½ teaspoon salt
2 teaspoons cinnamon
1 ½ teaspoons ginger
1 teaspoon ground cloves
Sugar Piping (optional)

Preheat oven to 300 degrees.

Cream butter, sugar and molasses. Beat in egg until light and fluffy.

In another bowl, whisk together flour, soda, salt, cinnamon, ginger and cloves. Stir flour mixture into molasses mixture to make stiff dough. Wrap in plastic wrap and chill.

Roll dough out on lightly floured surface to ⅛-inch thickness. Cut with gingerbread man cookie cutter or desired shape to fit the occasion. Place on parchment-lined baking sheet.

Bake 15 to 20 minutes.

Sugar Piping
2 cups powdered sugar
2 tablespoons milk

2 tablespoons light corn syrup
Food coloring (optional)

Combine sugar, milk and syrup until well blended.
Stir in food coloring, if desired.
Scrape into plastic resealable bag and secure.
Snip off a tiny corner to pipe frosting onto cookies as desired.

~

Mini West Virginia Stack Cakes

The landscape of our surroundings has so much to do with our food choices today, just as it did when our ancestors lived off the land—and that is what Cracker cooking is all about. As a tribute to our West Virginia hillbilly relatives, I created this recipe using my gingerbread cookie recipe and apple butter from a jar. The crisp cookies become soft overnight while wrapped in wax paper, resulting in cake-like layers.

1 batch Gingerbread Cookie dough (see page 135)
1 small jar apple butter

Roll dough very thin and cut with a 4-inch round cookie cutter. Cut 6, 9 or 12 rounds.
Place on parchment-lined baking sheet and bake according to Gingerbread Cookie recipe.
When the cookies are cool, spread apple butter on one-third of the rounds, top with another third of rounds. Spread apple butter on top of each sandwich-like cookie and top with the last of the rounds.
You should have two, three or four mini-stack cakes, depending on the number of rounds you cut.
Wrap each sandwich cookie separately in wax paper and let the apple butter absorb into the layers. They should be ready to enjoy in a few hours or the next day. I keep mine in the refrigerator so they last longer.

GRANNY'S SUNDAY DINNER

A family reunion, or even Sunday dinner at Granny's, was always a feast of food. There were more dishes than I can list, but these are a few of my favorites. They are wrapped in memories of cousins and screen doors slamming, aunts and uncles, chasing lightning bugs and falling asleep in the back seat of the car on the way home. Sliced garden tomatoes were brought in on a platter with flourish and bragging rights, depending on whose garden they came from. The young pods of tender okra were sliced diagonally and coated with cornmeal, then fried in a cast-iron skillet with bacon grease until golden brown. Homegrown creamed corn came from the freezer, thawed and heated with a little bacon and a splash of milk for creaminess. The butter beans and field peas with snaps were also a staple found in the freezer, put up for special occasions and slow simmered with salt pork. The simplicity of summer squash, sautéed with sliced sweet onions in bacon drippings until tender, seemed divine; squash or onions sautéed separately just didn't compare. The greens simmered for a couple of hours with salt pork were only made better with pepper vinegar, which always graced the table. (Note that a swankier recipe for greens appears on page 163 in the New Year's section.) Sweet potatoes were slow roasted at 275 to 300 degrees for about 1½ hours, then topped with fresh, creamy butter. Granny didn't disappoint when it came to dessert, and her layered chocolate cake was prepared just for the occasion. GrandMary told me the number of layers depended on how much batter Granny had; since she didn't measure or depend on a recipe, it was a guessing game.

SWEET TEA
CHICKEN AND DUMPLINGS
DEVILED EGGS (SEE PAGE 130)
SLICED GARDEN TOMATOES
FRIED OKRA
CREAMED CORN
BUTTER BEANS
FIELD PEAS WITH SNAPS
SKILLET SUMMER SQUASH
TURNIPS, COLLARDS OR MUSTARD GREENS WITH HOMEMADE PEPPER VINEGAR
SLOW-ROASTED SWEET POTATOES
TRIXIE'S SEVEN-LAYER CHOCOLATE CAKE

Southern Brewed Sweet Tea

Pour 4 cups boiling water over 2 family-size or 4 regular-size tea bags in a large pitcher and let steep about 10 minutes.
Remove tea bags and stir in sugar to taste, or serve with simple syrup on the side.
Let cool and pour over ice before serving.
In our house, the sweetness of the tea ranges from very to none.

Simple Syrup

Heat equal parts water and sugar in a saucepan until the sugar is dissolved. Store in the refrigerator until ready to use.

~

Easy Chicken and Dumplings

The dumplings are kept frozen until ready to drop into the simmering stock. A recipe for chicken stock can be found on page 45; the pie crust recipe is on page 132.

1 All-Occasion Pie Crust
4 cups chicken stock
½ cup cooked chopped chicken

Roll dough very thin, about ⅛ inch, onto well-floured surface. Use more flour than you would for a pie crust. Using a pizza cutter, cut into 2-inch squares. Let dry on wax paper for 15 to 20 minutes, then freeze until ready to use.
Heat chicken stock to boiling; drop in dumplings one at a time to avoid sticking together. Stir gently while simmering.
Cook 15 minutes, stirring occasionally.
Stir in chicken; continue cooking until chicken is well heated.

~

Homemade Pepper Vinegar

Use enough hot peppers, mostly green with a few red, to fill a sterilized bottle or carafe that has a stopper or cap. Boil enough white vinegar to cover peppers. Slowly pour hot vinegar over peppers and let cool. Replace top and allow to sit for a week or two before using. As the sauce runs low, continue to add vinegar until all the pepper flavor is gone.

⌒

Trixie's Seven-Layer Chocolate Cake

The layers of this cake are made using two flat cast-iron skillets. It takes about three hours from start to finish to complete the cakes. I make three small seven-layer cakes rather than one large cake. Once all the layers are warming in the oven, I make the icing.

2½ cups flour
3 teaspoons baking powder
1 teaspoon baking soda
½ teaspoon salt
1½ cups sugar
½ cup butter, softened
¾ cup milk
3 eggs
1 teaspoon vanilla
Chocolate Icing

Whisk together flour, baking powder, baking soda and salt in bowl and set aside.
In separate bowl, cream together sugar and butter. With an electric mixer, add milk to butter mixture.
Combine flour and butter mixture and beat on low speed 30 seconds. Add eggs; beat on medium speed 2 minutes. Stir in vanilla.
Heat a buttered flat cast-iron skillet on medium-low heat and pour in 2 to 3 tablespoons batter. Cook until edges are done and bubbles on top begin to pop.
Flip cake and cook another minute or two, being careful not to overcook.

Keep layers wrapped in a cloth in a warm oven until all layers are cooked and ready to frost.

Make icing.

Begin with the still warm first layer and ladle about 2 tablespoons of icing on top. Continue with each layer and let some of the icing run down the sides. Pour remaining icing over the top of the cake or cakes.

Chocolate Icing
2 cups sugar
½ cup cocoa
½ cup milk
½ cup butter
1 teaspoon vanilla

In a heavy saucepan, whisk together sugar and cocoa. Whisk in milk.

Cook over low heat and stir in butter until melted.

Bring to boil and cook 1 minute, stirring and watching so it doesn't boil over.

Reduce heat to simmer and stir in vanilla.

Cook for 7 to 10 minutes more, stirring occasionally.

Sunday Dinner in the 1960s

On Sunday morning, GrandMary usually put a roast in the oven before we left for church, and the heavenly aroma permeated the house by the time we got home. Her cooking style changed over the years, and the pot roast went from a basic braised chuck roast with potatoes and carrots to cooked in a bag with onion soup mix. The dressing for the salad came from a bottle and the biscuits were canned, but it was all still very good. The pears with cheese were a simple combination of grated American cheese with a touch of mayonnaise in the cavity of a pear half. But the taste of Harvard beets began my affection for that pretty purple root. Sometimes the meal was topped off with a special dessert of peach cobbler.

Growing up in the piney woods of North Florida, my father still enjoyed the solitude of wooded areas. Out of the cabin for years, after serving in the military and traveling around the world, our family was transferred to Tyndall Air Force Base in Panama City, where he built our home on a lake nestled in the woods. GrandMary's kitchen was a favorite spot for me. With the sparkly Formica countertops, Coppertone appliances and a touch of turquoise to brighten up the already bright white floors, it was my haven from the rest of the world. Looking out the kitchen window, you could see the lonely driveway leading to what was once a gravel road paved with oyster shells and lost arrowheads. The view out the back rarely changed, with moss-covered trees draping over the beautiful, serene lake. It was here that I honed my cooking skills. My tastes were simple, as reflected in my favorite meal of tuna casserole and yeast rolls. Sunday dinner, though, was always the most memorable.

SWEET TEA
OVEN-BRAISED POT ROAST WITH CARROTS AND POTATOES
GREEN SALAD WITH THOUSAND ISLAND DRESSING
CANNED BISCUITS OR BREAD AND BUTTER
PEARS AND CHEESE
HARVARD BEETS
PEACH COBBLER À LA MODE

Thousand Island Dressing

½ cup mayonnaise
2 tablespoons catsup
½ teaspoon chili powder
2 tablespoons sweet pickle relish
1 tablespoon finely chopped green pepper
1 tablespoon white vinegar
1 teaspoon sugar
½ teaspoon salt
¼ teaspoon pepper
Dash hot pepper sauce

Combine all ingredients in a bowl and chill before serving.

⌒

Harvard Beets

2 tablespoons butter
1 tablespoon cornstarch
1 tablespoon sugar
¼ teaspoon salt
½ cup cider vinegar
1 can sliced beets

In a saucepan, melt the butter over low heat. Whisk in cornstarch, sugar and salt.
Add vinegar, continue cooking and whisk until blended and thickened.
Add beets and heat thoroughly.

⌒

Fresh-Baked Peach Cobbler à la Mode

⅓ cup sugar
1 teaspoon cinnamon
2 tablespoons butter
4 cups fresh or canned peaches, peeled, pitted and sliced
1 teaspoon lemon juice

Topping:
1 cup flour
½ cup sugar
1 tablespoon baking powder
¼ teaspoon salt
¼ cup butter
½ cup heavy cream

Vanilla ice cream

Preheat oven to 400 degrees.

Combine sugar and cinnamon. Reserve 2 tablespoons for topping.

Melt the butter in an 8-inch square baking pan; add peaches and sprinkle with remaining cinnamon sugar and lemon juice. Set aside.

For the topping, whisk together flour, sugar, baking powder and salt. Cut in butter with pastry blender. Add cream and stir to form a ball. Drop dough onto peaches a tablespoon at a time, spacing as evenly as possible. Sprinkle with cinnamon sugar.

Bake 40 to 45 minutes or until pastry is golden brown.

Serve with vanilla ice cream.

THANKSGIVING MENU

Shortly before my brother Pat and his wife, Carolyn, evacuated their home in the Panhandle to avoid the wrath of Hurricane Michael, they collected enough Key limes from his trees for me to use in a pie. The Key limes traveled with GrandMary from their yard to Alabama for a few days, where the hurricane followed and knocked out the power. Then they went to Panama City Beach in a crowded rental with extended family and on to Pensacola, where they spent the night with my other brother, Dennis, and his wife, Laurelyn. We picked up the Key limes and GrandMary in Pensacola before heading to her unexpectedly new home in Tampa. The trees are now gone, but Pat's Hurricane Key Lime Pie will always remind us of how thankful we are to have the warmth of family. The sweet tea recipe can be found with Granny's Sunday Dinner

Thanksgiving postcard. The back reads, "Don't eat too much turkey," 1914. *Robert McIntosh postcard collection.*

recipes on page 138. The ambrosia description is on page 105. Orange Blossom Honey Butter is on page 95, and Cranberry Biscotti can be found on page 99. Brown-and-serve rolls and Irish butter are from the market.

SWEET TEA
AMBROSIA
ORANGE ROASTED TURKEY BREAST
CORNBREAD-SAGE DRESSING
THANKSGIVING GRAVY
MAKE-AHEAD MASHED POTATOES
SWEET POTATO CASSEROLE WITH CHEWY TOPPING
PUMPKIN ORANGE BREAD WITH ORANGE BLOSSOM HONEY BUTTER
THANKSGIVING SALAD
BROWN-AND-SERVE ROLLS WITH IRISH BUTTER
SWEET POTATO PIE
PAT'S HURRICANE KEY LIME PIE
SIMPLE PUMPKIN PIE
CRANBERRY BISCOTTI
FALL SPICED COFFEE
NEW SYLLABUB

⁓

Orange Roasted Turkey Breast

After years of grilling a whole turkey outside, our indoor condo turkey is smaller. Using only the turkey breast, sometimes I'll buy turkey legs to roast just for Jack.

1 6-pound bone-in turkey breast
1 orange
1 onion
¼ cup butter, softened
6 to 8 fresh sage leaves

Preheat oven to 325 degrees.
Place turkey breast on roasting rack, skin side up.
Cut orange and onion in quarters, stuff half inside turkey cavity and use the rest to help hold the turkey upright.
Rub butter under the layer of skin, between the skin and breast meat, then place sage leaves under skin.
Roast for 2 to 2½ hours or until thickest part of turkey breast registers 160 degrees on meat thermometer.
Transfer to platter, tent with foil and let rest 20 to 30 minutes before slicing.

~

Cornbread-Sage Dressing

In early November, I do a lot of my Thanksgiving dinner shopping. A sage plant is on the list, using the fresh, fragrant leaves for both the dressing and the turkey. The chicken stock recipe can be found on page 45.

1 cup sweet onion, chopped
1 cup celery, chopped
¼ cup butter plus 2 tablespoons
2 cups chicken stock
2 cups cornbread, crumbled
2 cups bread crust or biscuit, crumbled
1 teaspoon fresh sage leaves, dried and crushed
1 teaspoon salt
1 teaspoon white pepper
1 teaspoon poultry seasoning
4 eggs, beaten well
2 hard-boiled eggs, chopped (optional)

Preheat oven to 400 degrees.
Sauté onions and celery in ¼ cup butter for about 8 minutes.
Pour chicken stock over cornbread and bread or biscuit; add cooked onion and celery.
Mix in sage, salt, pepper and poultry seasoning. Add eggs and mix well.
Place 2 tablespoons butter in 9-by-13-inch buttered baking dish and melt in hot oven.
Put dressing into pan. Bake 30 minutes.

Skillet Cornbread

Skillet cornbread is another make-ahead recipe I store in the freezer for later use in the dressing.

2 cups white cornmeal
1 teaspoon baking soda
1 teaspoon salt
1 large egg, slightly beaten

2 cups buttermilk
3 tablespoons melted butter or bacon drippings
2 tablespoons corn oil

Preheat oven to 450 to 475 degrees.
In a mixing bowl, combine cornmeal, soda and salt.
Add egg to buttermilk and beat until well blended. Add to dry ingredients and mix well. Stir in melted butter or bacon drippings.
Pour corn oil in cast-iron skillet and heat in oven. Pour batter into hot skillet.
Bake 20 to 25 minutes or until cornbread is golden.

⌒

Thanksgiving Gravy

Using butter, I can make this ahead of time without waiting for the turkey to be done.

½ cup flour
½ teaspoon poultry seasoning
½ teaspoon fresh sage leaves, dried and crushed
½ teaspoon salt
¼ teaspoon pepper
3 cups chicken stock (see page 45)
4 tablespoons butter (or turkey drippings drained from roasting pan)

Whisk together flour, poultry seasoning, sage, salt and pepper; whisk in 1 cup stock.
In a saucepan, melt butter and whisk in flour mixture until smooth.
Cook over medium-high heat, stirring often, until thick.
Gradually whisk in remaining stock.
Bring to a boil and simmer about 15 minutes, until flour is fully cooked.

⌒

Make-Ahead Mashed Potatoes

Once frozen, I thaw the potatoes in the refrigerator the night before, then reheat in a 350-degree oven for 45 minutes.

3 pounds Yukon gold potatoes, peeled and chopped, cooked in salted water until tender
2 ounces cream cheese, room temperature
¼ cup butter, room temperature, plus 1 tablespoon for casserole dish
1 cup sour cream
½ teaspoon sea salt
½ teaspoon white pepper

Preheat oven to 350 degrees.
Mash hot potatoes while adding cream cheese, ¼ cup butter and sour cream. Stir in salt and pepper.
Melt 1 tablespoon butter in casserole dish in hot oven.
Place potatoes in buttered casserole dish and bake 45 minutes.
Cool, then freeze until ready to reheat.

Sweet Potato Casserole with Chewy Topping

This is another dish to make in advance and freeze. I thaw the sweet potato casserole, along with the dressing and potatoes, in the refrigerator before reheating on Thanksgiving Day in a 350-degree oven for 45 minutes.

4 cups sweet potatoes, cooked and peeled (about 40 ounces if using canned)
1 cup brown sugar, packed
½ cup sweetened condensed milk
½ cup butter
2 eggs, slightly beaten
½ teaspoon salt
1 teaspoon vanilla
½ teaspoon nutmeg
½ teaspoon cinnamon
Marshmallows or Chewy Topping

Place sweet potatoes in large bowl and mash. Add remaining ingredients except topping and mix well.

Place in buttered casserole dish. Sprinkle marshmallows or topping evenly over potatoes.

Bake at 350 degrees for 35 minutes. Cool and freeze until ready to reheat.

Chewy Topping
1 cup brown sugar, packed
½ cup flour
½ cup butter, melted
1 cup crushed pecans (optional)

Combine all ingredients in a bowl.

—

Pumpkin Orange Bread
Sometimes we fill the pumpkin pie void with pumpkin bread.

1 cup pumpkin puree
2 tablespoons butter, melted
1 egg
1 tablespoon orange juice
1 teaspoon orange zest
1 cup sugar
1 cup flour
1 teaspoon baking soda
1 teaspoon cinnamon
½ teaspoon ground cloves
½ teaspoon ground ginger
1 teaspoon salt
½ cup dried cranberries

Preheat oven to 375 degrees.
Combine pumpkin, butter, egg, orange juice and orange zest.
In separate bowl, whisk together remaining ingredients.
Stir in pumpkin; pour in mini loaf pans, being careful not to overfill. (Filling pans about halfway works well for me.)
Bake 25 to 30 minutes.

~

Thanksgiving Salad

Iceberg lettuce, washed and torn into bite-sized pieces
Dried cranberries
Auntie's Sugar Pecans
Vinaigrette (your choice)
Mandarin orange slices

Combine iceberg lettuce with dried cranberries and sugar pecans to your liking.
Toss with vinaigrette. Garnish with mandarin oranges.

Auntie's Sugar Pecans
1 egg white
⅓ cup sugar
⅓ cup firmly packed light brown sugar
¼ teaspoon cinnamon
3 cups pecan halves

Preheat oven to 350 degrees.
Beat egg white until foamy; stir in sugars and cinnamon.
Add pecans and stir until evenly coated.
Spread pecans evenly on a foil-lined, lightly greased 15-by-10-inch jelly roll pan. (For easy clean-up, line pan with foil, then grease the foil.)
Bake 15 to 18 minutes, stirring once halfway through.
Remove from oven and cool.

~

Sweet Potato Pie

Majority rules here, and with GrandMary on our side, it was 3–1 for sweet potato pie over pumpkin pie. This year, I think this recipe won Jack over to the sweet potato pie side.

1 ½ cups cooked, mashed sweet potatoes
1 cup brown sugar, packed
2 eggs
½ cup butter, softened
1 teaspoon vanilla
⅔ cup evaporated milk
¼ teaspoon salt
½ teaspoon orange zest (optional)
1 unbaked pie crust (see page 132)

Preheat oven to 400 degrees.
Mix together all ingredients except pie crust. Pour into pie crust.
Bake 15 minutes at 400 degrees, then reduce oven temperature to 350 degrees and bake 40 minutes more.

⟃

Pat's Hurricane Key Lime Pie

Before my brother Pat evacuated his property in the Panhandle to avoid Hurricane Michael, he collected enough precious Key limes for me to use in this pie. This recipe is adapted from *Easy Breezy Florida Cooking.*

3 ounces cream cheese, softened
1 (14-ounce) can sweetened condensed milk
1 large egg
½ cup Key lime juice
1 prepared graham cracker crumb pie crust

Preheat oven to 325 degrees.
Beat cream cheese in a medium mixing bowl with an electric mixer until smooth and creamy. Beat in milk, egg and lime juice. Pour into prepared crust and spread evenly.
Bake about 15 minutes. Cool completely.
Freeze, up to 2 hours or 2 weeks, until ready to serve.

⟃

Simple Pumpkin Pie
When I make pumpkin pie for Jack, this is the recipe I use.

1 cup pumpkin puree
1 cup sweetened condensed milk
1 egg
½ teaspoon cinnamon
½ teaspoon ginger
¼ teaspoon nutmeg
¼ teaspoon salt
1 9-inch unbaked pie crust (see page 132)

Preheat oven to 425 degrees. Mix together all ingredients except pie crust. Pour into pie crust.
Bake 15 minutes at 425 degrees, then reduce oven temperature to 350 degrees and bake 35 to 40 minutes more.

⌒

Fall Spiced Coffee
To create an orange simple syrup, I use the orange peels leftover from the ambrosia. Place the orange peels in a container with a lid and cover with sugar, shake and let sit overnight. In the morning, remove the peels and stir. Add an equal amount of water as sugar, then heat in microwave until sugar melts and mixture thickens.

4 to 8 scoops coffee grounds
1 teaspoon cardamom
½ teaspoon vanilla
Orange Simple Syrup

Using an automatic drip coffee maker, place grounds in lined coffee basket and mix in cardamom. Sprinkle with vanilla.
Brew according to your taste.
Sweeten brewed coffee with orange syrup.

⌒

New Syllabub

By substituting apple cider for traditional wine, this old English dessert-like drink quickly became a favorite for the whole family.

1 ½ cups fresh apple cider
½ cup sugar
Pinch of salt
1 cup whipping cream, whipped
1 whole nutmeg

In a saucepan, combine cider, sugar and salt. While stirring, heat the apple cider just enough to dissolve sugar. Remove from heat and chill. When ready to serve, using a large punch bowl, fold the whipped cream into chilled cider and whisk until frothy. Sprinkle with freshly grated nutmeg before serving.

CRACKER CHRISTMAS BRUNCH

Christmas postcard, 1922. *Robert McIntosh postcard collection.*

As we relish the stories of Christmas past, memories such as shooting down clusters of mistletoe (without a word to our parents how we did it) and chopping down a Christmas tree in an open field (without a thought of trespassing) can forever be remembered through the foods we have traditionally served. Steaming black coffee, scrambled eggs with shaved ham, fried leftover sweet potatoes, stone-ground grits and piping hot biscuits with sausage gravy might have graced the early morning table of our Cracker ancestors, but today the Christmas morning meal has gone from a simple breakfast to a holiday brunch for us.

MOCHA LATTE
EGGNOG
HOT MULLED CIDER
SPINACH BITES
HAM AND EGG CUPS
CHEESE GRITS
BAKED BACON
SPICED PEACHES
CUBAN BREAD CINNAMON TOAST

~

Mocha Latte for Two

2 cups freshly brewed strong coffee
½ cup Chocolate Syrup
¼ cup steamed milk
Sweetened whipped cream, if desired

Combine first three ingredients and top with whipped cream.
To add kick of cinnamon: Add ¼ teaspoon cinnamon to coffee grounds before brewing and stir with cinnamon stick.

Chocolate Syrup
½ cup sugar
3 tablespoons cocoa
⅛ teaspoon salt
⅓ cup water
1 teaspoon vanilla

In a medium saucepan, whisk together sugar, cocoa and salt. Add water, bring to boil, then simmer 5 to 7 minutes. Remove from heat and stir in vanilla.

~

Eggnog
"It's like drinking ice cream," says my son, Jackson.

2 cups heavy cream
1 cup milk
2 egg yolks, slightly beaten
½ cup sugar
⅛ teaspoon salt
Freshly grated nutmeg
Kahlua (optional)

Combine cream and milk in a large saucepan.

Whisk together yolks, sugar and salt; gradually whisk into cream mixture.

Cook over medium heat and stir until thickened. Strain and sprinkle with nutmeg.

Serve warm or cold with 1 tablespoon Kahlua, if desired.

⌒

Hot Mulled Cider

1 quart apple cider
1 orange cut into wedges
2 sticks cinnamon
6 whole cloves
¼ teaspoon ground allspice
¼ teaspoon ground cardamom
1 tablespoon brown sugar
Apple slices for garnish

Combine all ingredients in a large saucepan and simmer slowly for 10 minutes.

Strain and serve warm. Garnish with apple slices.

⌒

Spinach Bites

4 eggs, slightly beaten
2 tablespoons milk
1 10-ounce package frozen chopped spinach, thawed and drained
8 ounces Monterey Jack cheese, shredded
¼ cup butter, melted
½ teaspoon salt
¼ teaspoon white pepper

Preheat oven to 375 degrees.
Beat eggs well; stir in milk, spinach, cheese, butter, salt and pepper.
Pour into well-greased 9-by-9-inch baking pan.
Bake 30 minutes. Let cool slightly before cutting into bite-sized squares.

⁓

Ham and Egg Cups
I usually use leftovers from the Holiday Ham recipe for this dish.

4 ¹/₁₆-inch-thick round ham slices, about 5 inches around
4 large eggs
4 ounces shredded cheddar cheese
Salt and freshly ground black pepper
Butter for muffin tins

Preheat oven to 325 degrees.
Butter four compartments of a metal muffin tin. (Cups should be at least 2 inches deep.)
Fold each ham slice into quarters, insert the pointed end in a buttered muffin cup and let it open; it will have a ruffled look.
Carefully crack one egg into the cup. Sprinkle with cheese, salt and pepper to taste.
Bake 15 to 20 minutes, until the egg white looks set but the yolk is still a bit runny.
Remove the ham cups from the muffin tin and serve on individual plates or lined up on a platter.

Holiday Ham
1 fully cooked half ham (spiral sliced or bone-in, 7 pounds)
½ cup brown sugar, packed
¼ cup honey
1 tablespoon cornstarch
1 tablespoon orange juice or pineapple juice

Preheat oven to 350 degrees.

Place ham in a roasting pan. Cover ham with foil and bake for 18 minutes per pound (about 1 hour). Overheating will dry out ham.*

While ham is baking, make the glaze: In a small saucepan, combine brown sugar, honey, cornstarch and orange or pineapple juice. Heat and stir until mixture starts to boil. Reduce heat and simmer 1 minute. Set aside.

With 30 minutes of cooking time left, remove ham from oven and cut off any tough outer skin, if necessary, and discard.

Baste with sauce, return to oven and bake 30 minutes more or until meat thermometer reaches 140 degrees.

*Heating times vary depending on size of ham. Many hams come with heating instructions and should be followed.

Cheese Grits

Jack always prided himself on his great cheese grits recipe: 1 package of instant grits with a spoonful of Cheese Whiz. This one tastes a little better.

4 cups chicken stock (see page 45)
1 cup stone-ground grits
½ teaspoon salt
1 cup cheddar cheese, grated

Bring stock to boil; stir in grits and salt. Return to boil, reduce heat to low and continue cooking 20 to 25 minutes, stirring occasionally. Stir in cheese.

~

Baked Bacon

Preheat oven to 425 degrees.
Place bacon in a single layer on a foiled-lined baking sheet. (The foil makes cleanup easier.)
Bake 10 to 12 minutes or longer for crisper bacon, turning once.

~

Spiced Peaches

4 cups sliced canned peaches (reserve liquid)
½ cup brown sugar, packed
½ cup orange juice
2 sticks cinnamon
1 teaspoon whole cloves

Combine reserved peach liquid with sugar, juice, cinnamon and cloves in a saucepan and bring to a boil.
Boil 1 minute and pour over peaches.
Refrigerate overnight.

~

Cuban Bread Cinnamon Toast

1 loaf Cuban bread
½ cup butter, melted
½ cup brown sugar, packed
1 tablespoon cinnamon

Preheat oven to 400 degrees.
Slice bread crosswise into four equal pieces, then slice each piece lengthwise.

Place bread on baking sheet cut side up.
Brush each side with melted butter.
Combine brown sugar and cinnamon; sprinkle over buttered bread.
Bake 10 minutes.

A merry Christmas
postcard, circa 1920.
*Robert McIntosh postcard
collection.*

HOLIDAY DESSERTS

Once I discovered butter instead of margarine for baking, desserts became my passion. The recipes in this section are some of our family favorites.

GRANNY OWEN'S CHOCOLATE PIE
CHEWY PECAN PIE
TOASTED GINGERBREAD WITH CREAM CHEESE
SPREAD
TRIXIE'S CANE SYRUP PEANUT CANDY

Granny Owen's Chocolate Pie

According to my Aunt Eleanor, you have to use Pet evaporated milk, but for this recipe, I substituted sweetened condensed for the evaporated milk. Both are equally delicious, but this version is a little sweeter. I keep my pie in the freezer covered with plastic wrap, which makes it easier to slice when ready to eat.

*2 cups sugar
¼ cup flour
⅓ cup cocoa
1 12-ounce can sweetened condensed milk
3 egg yolks, beaten
¼ cup butter*

1 teaspoon vanilla
1 prebaked 9-inch pie crust (see page 132)
Whipped cream (optional)

Whisk sugar, flour and cocoa together in saucepan. Gradually whisk in milk. Cook over medium-high heat, stirring occasionally, until mixture boils. Boil 2 to 3 minutes.
Whisk ½ cup hot chocolate mixture into egg yolks until smooth; reduce heat to low and gradually whisk back into hot mixture in saucepan.
Stir in butter until melted. Add vanilla.
Cook over medium-high heat again, stirring occasionally, until mixture boils and continue boiling for 1 minute.
Reduce heat and cook until very thick, stirring occasionally (this may take 20 to 30 minutes).
When completely cool, top with whipped cream.
For whipped cream: Gradually whip in ¼ cup powdered sugar to 1 cup whipping cream, beating until soft peaks form.

⁓

Chewy Pecan Pie

½ cup light brown sugar, packed
½ cup light Karo syrup
1 tablespoon butter, melted
1 cup chopped pecans
½ teaspoon vanilla extract
2 eggs, well beaten
1 9-inch unbaked pie crust (see page 132)

Preheat oven to 350 degrees.
In a medium saucepan, combine sugars, syrup and butter. Cook and stir over medium heat until mixture comes to a boil.
Boil 1 minute. Remove from heat.
Stir in pecans, vanilla and eggs.
Pour into pie crust.
Bake 45 to 50 minutes.

⁓

Toasted Gingerbread with Cream Cheese Spread

Gingerbread Loaves
½ cup butter, softened
½ cup dark brown sugar, packed
½ cup white sugar
I egg, beaten
2 cups flour
I teaspoon baking soda
I tablespoon ground ginger
I teaspoon cinnamon
½ teaspoon ground cloves
¼ teaspoon black pepper
½ teaspoon salt
I tablespoon freshly grated ginger
¾ cup buttermilk
½ cup dark molasses

Preheat oven to 350 degrees.

With an electric mixer, cream together butter and sugars in a large bowl. Beat in egg.

In another bowl, whisk together flour, baking soda, ground ginger, cinnamon, cloves, pepper, salt and freshly grated ginger; set aside.

In a small bowl, combine buttermilk and molasses; stir into creamed mixture, then beat well.

Add dry ingredients to batter and mix well. Scrape batter into five 6-by-3-inch greased and floured loaf pans. (Be careful not to overfill pan or gingerbread might fall in the middle.)

Bake 30 to 35 minutes or until center springs back when lightly touched. Cool slightly, then remove from pan.

Gingerbread Cream Cheese Spread
Slice and toast gingerbread in oven before spreading with this topping.

4 ounces cream cheese, room temperature
2 tablespoons powdered sugar
¼ teaspoon vanilla extract
¼ to ½ cup whipped cream

Whip together on low speed with electric mixer.

~

Trixie's Cane Syrup Peanut Candy

Granny never used a candy thermometer, but you might find it easier to do so. GrandMary reminded me that my Uncle Carl is an expert candy maker, while his two older brothers, Calvin and Alvin, were always entertaining. ("Entertaining" is code for "up to something.") I use a pizza cutter to cut the candy before I dip the bite-sized pieces in powdered sugar, to keep them from being so sticky.

1 ½ cups cane syrup
½ teaspoon baking soda
2 cups parched and pounded peanuts

Cook syrup in a heavy saucepan to the soft ball stage. (When a bit of syrup is dropped into a glass of cold water, it will hold its shape but give when pressed; or use a candy thermometer.) This will take about 30 minutes.
Thoroughly stir in baking soda and cook 1 minute longer.
Stir in ground nuts.
Pour onto buttered, foil-lined baking sheet. Cover with buttered foil until completely cool, then cut into bite-size pieces and dip in powdered sugar.

One-cent postage on 1912 New Year's Day postcard. *Robert McIntosh postcard collection.*

NEW YEAR'S DAY

Ringing in the new year centers on the New Year's Day Outback Bowl at our house. Jack's radio broadcast days go back to its original inception as the Hall of Fame Bowl in 1986 (the same year we were married). But I always try to include Hoppin' John for good luck, ham for good health and collards for wealth. The Hoppin' John and collard greens recipes come from *Easy Breezy Florida Cooking.* I usually purchase a fully cooked, spiral-sliced ham. The recipe for Homemade Corn Chips can be found on page 101; served with pimento cheese is a bonus. Then we have Granny Sheffield's Chess Pie served with café au lait for dessert. Later in the evening, a little potato salad with leftover ham makes a great finish to the end of the day and the beginning of a new year. This year I introduced Florida Orange Coffee Cake to start the first morning of the new year off right.

SPIRAL SLICED HAM
DEEPER THAN DEEP SOUTH HOPPIN' JOHN
COLLARD GREENS FLORIDA STYLE
HOMEMADE CORN CHIPS
PIMENTO CHEESE
NEW POTATO SALAD
GRANNY SHEFFIELD'S CHESS PIE
ORANGE BLOSSOM CAFÉ AU LAIT
FLORIDA ORANGE COFFEE CAKE

Deeper Than Deep South Hoppin' John

8 ounces dried black-eyed peas
8 cups water, divided use (see note)
4 slices bacon
1 medium onion, chopped
1 green pepper, seeded and chopped
1 cup white rice
1½ teaspoons salt

Rinse peas in cold water, taking care to remove any foreign particles. Soak peas overnight in a 3-quart saucepan with enough water to cover 1 inch over the peas (about 4 cups).
Drain peas and add fresh water, enough to cover about 1 inch above peas (again, about 4 cups).
Bring to a boil; reduce heat and simmer, uncovered, about 1½ hours. Stir occasionally.
Cook bacon in a heavy frying pan over medium-high heat until crisp. Drain on paper towels and set aside.

Add chopped onion and green pepper to frying pan and sauté in remaining bacon drippings until tender, about 5 minutes over medium heat.

Add onion mixture, crumbled bacon, rice and salt to the peas. Stir well to combine. Reduce heat to medium and simmer covered, about 30 minutes more.

Note: Water and times are approximate in this recipe. All the water should be absorbed by the final cooking time.

Collard Greens Florida Style

2 slices bacon
1 onion, chopped
1 red bell pepper, seeded and diced
2 cups chicken stock (see page 45)
1 cup water
1 pound frozen, chopped collard greens
1 tablespoon sugar

Cook bacon in a 10-inch frying pan until crisp. Drain on paper towels, crumble and set aside.

Sauté onion and bell pepper in bacon drippings until soft, about 4 minutes.

Bring chicken stock and water to a boil in a large saucepan or 3-quart Dutch oven.

Add collard greens, bacon, onion-pepper mixture and sugar to stock.

Bring to a boil. Cover, lower heat and simmer for 45 minutes to 1 hour. (Another option is to drain the collards after cooking and stir in ½ cup sour cream, ¼ cup butter, 2 teaspoons Worcestershire sauce, 2 teaspoons lime juice, ½ teaspoon salt and ¼ teaspoon white pepper. Stir, heat and serve.)

Pimento Cheese

8 ounces medium cheddar cheese, finely grated
1 4-ounce jar pimientos, diced and drained
¼ cup mayonnaise
½ teaspoon Worcestershire sauce
2 drops hot pepper sauce
dash white pepper

It is easier to grate cheese while cold and then let it come to room temperature.
Mash together cheese and pimientos, then stir in remaining ingredients. Chill.

~

New Potato Salad

2 pounds new potatoes, cubed and cooked
3 hard-boiled eggs, chopped
½ cup mayonnaise
¼ cup mustard
¼ cup dill relish
2 tablespoons apple cider vinegar
1 teaspoon salt
¼ teaspoon pepper

Toss potatoes with eggs. Stir together mayonnaise, mustard, relish, vinegar, salt and pepper. Add to potato and egg mixture and stir gently to coat potatoes.
Chill.

~

Granny Sheffield's Chess Pie

2 cups sugar
1 tablespoon white cornmeal
1 tablespoon all-purpose flour
Pinch of salt
½ cup butter, melted
¼ cup milk
1 tablespoon white vinegar
1 teaspoon vanilla
4 large eggs, lightly beaten
1 9-inch pie crust, unbaked (see page 132)
Sweetened whipped cream

Preheat oven to 325 degrees.
Stir together sugar and next seven ingredients until blended. Add eggs, stirring well.
Pour and scrape the mixture into the pie crust.
Bake 50 to 55 minutes, or until the filling is golden and firm. Let cool to room temperature.
Serve with dollop of sweetened whipped cream.

⌒

Orange Blossom Café au Lait

¼ cup orange blossom honey
¼ teaspoon orange zest
1 cup hot coffee to your liking (French roast made in a French press is my choice)
½ cup steamed milk
1 cinnamon stick

Using the microwave, heat the honey and zest for 20 to 30 seconds. Pour into an extra-large coffee cup; stir in hot coffee and steamed milk with a cinnamon stick.

⌒

Florida Orange Coffee Cake
When making this, I use five disposable mini loaf pans.

1 teaspoon orange zest
2 cups flour
1 cup sugar
½ teaspoon salt
½ cup butter, softened and cut into 1-inch pieces
2 eggs
1 teaspoon baking soda
1 cup buttermilk
Orange Topping
Orange Glaze

Preheat oven to 350 degrees.
Using an electric mixer on low, combine zest, flour, sugar and salt.
Add butter one piece at a time, then beat in eggs one at a time. (Batter will be very stiff.)
Stir baking soda into milk, slowly add to batter. Mix well.
Fill buttered loaf pans half full.
Dollop Orange Topping over batter; as it bakes, this will sink to the bottom.
Bake 30 minutes.
Remove from oven, let cool slightly, then drizzle with Orange Glaze.

Orange Topping
¾ cup flour
½ cup brown sugar, packed
2 tablespoons butter, melted
1 tablespoon orange juice
2 teaspoons orange zest
½ teaspoon cinnamon

Combine all ingredients.

Orange Glaze
1 cup sugar
½ cup orange juice
1 teaspoon vanilla

Combine sugar and orange juice, then heat until sugar is dissolved and mixture starts to thicken. Stir in vanilla.

BIBLIOGRAPHY

Alcott, William A. *The Young Housekeeper*. A facsimile reproduction of 1846 edition. American Antiquarian Society. Kansas City: Andrews McMeel Publishing, 2013.

Bailyn, Bernard. *Voyagers to the West*. New York: Random House, 1986.

Barbour, George M. *Florida for Tourists, Invalids, and Settlers*. A facsimile reproduction of the 1882 edition.

Berolzheimer, Ruth, ed. *The American Woman's Cookbook, New and Revised*. Chicago: Culinary Arts Institute, 1953.

Betz, Myrtle Scharrer. *Caladesi Cookbook, Recipes from a Florida Lifetime, 1895–1922*. Compiled by Terry Fortner and Suzanne Thorp. Tampa, FL: University of Tampa Press, 2012.

Camellia Garden Circle. *Camellia Cookery: Tallahassee's Favorite Recipes*. Tallahassee, FL: Camellia Garden Circle, 1950.

Carlton, Lowis. *Famous Florida Recipes: 300 Years of Good Eating*. St. Petersburg, FL: Great Outdoors, 1972.

Carter, Susannah. *The Frugal Housewife; or, Complete Woman Cook*. A facsimile reproduction of the 1792 edition.

Child, Lydia Marie. *The American Frugal Housewife*. 12th ed. A facsimile reproduction of the 1832 edition.

The Confederate Receipt Book: A Compilation of Over One Hundred Receipts Adapted to the Times. A facsimile of the 1863 edition. Antique American Cookbooks, Oxmoore House, Inc., 1985.

Denham, James M., and Canter Brown Jr., eds. *Cracker Times and Pioneer Lives*. Columbia: University of South Carolina Press, 2003.

Dickinson, Jonathan. *Jonathan Dickinson's Journal*. Florida Classics Library. New Haven, CT: Yale University Press, 1985.

Dull, S.R. *Southern Cooking*. 1941. New York: Grosset & Dunlap, 1968.

English, Marguerite, ed. *Food from Famous Kitchens: The Brand Names Cook Book*. N.p.: Western Printing and Lithographing Company, 1961.

Farmer, Fannie Merrit. *Boston Cooking-School Cook Book*. 1896. Repr., New York: Dover Publications, 1997.

———. *The Boston Cooking School Cook Book*. 8th ed. New York: Little Brown and Company, 1948.

The First Presbyterian Church Miami. *The Florida Tropical Cookbook*. A facsimile reproduction of the 1912 edition.

Fisher, Abby. *What Mrs. Fisher Knows about Old Southern Cooking*. 1881. Historical notes by Karen Hess. Carlisle, MA: Applewood Books, 1995.

Fisher, Marian Cole. *Twenty Lessons in Domestic Science*. St. Paul, MN: Calumet Baking Powder Company, 1916.

Glasse, Hannah. *The Art of Cookery Made Plain and Easy*. A facsimile reproduction of the 1805 edition.

Graceville Garden Club. *Graceville…Country Cookin'*. Memphis, TN: Wimmer Brothers Books, 1985.

Harland, Marion. *Common Sense in the Household: A Manual of Practical Housewifery*. A facsimile reproduction of the 1880 edition.

Harris, Jack. *Jack Harris, Unwrapped*. Tampa, FL: Seaside Publishing, 2005.

Harris, Joy Sheffield. *A Culinary History of Florida*. Charleston, SC: The History Press, 2014.

———. *Florida Sweets*. Charleston, SC: The History Press, 2017.

Harris, Joy, and Jack Harris. *Easy Breezy Florida Cooking*. Gainesville, FL: Seaside Publishing, University Press, 2010.

Hess, Karen, ed. *Martha Washington's Booke of Cookery and Booke of Sweetmeats*. 1749. Repr., New York: Columbia University Press, 1981.

Junior League of Charleston. *Charleston Receipts*. Nashville, TN, 1950. Repr., 2002.

Junior League of Tampa. *The Gasparilla Cookbook*. Tampa, FL: Favorite Recipes, 1961.

Junior Service League of Panama City. *Bay Leaves*. Panama City, FL: Cookbook Marketplace, 1975.

Knight, Charles. *Harris & Co. Cookbook*. Health Craft Inc. Tampa, FL: Depot Press, 1994.

Kollatz, Harry. *True Richmond Stories: Historic Tales from Virginia's Capital*. Charleston, SC: The History Press, 2007.

Kummer, Corby. *The Joy of Coffee*. Shelburne, VT: Chapters Publishing Ltd., 1995.

Lenski, Lois. *Strawberry Girl*. New York: Harper Trophy, 1945.

Lifshey, Earl. *The Housewares Story*. Chicago: National Housewares Manufacturers Association, 1973.

Lowenstein, Eleanor. *American Cookery Books, 1742–1860*. New York: American Antiquarian Society, 1972.

Manning, Jo McDonald. *Seasonal Florida: A Taste of Life in North Florida*. Ponte Vedra Beach, FL: Yardbird Productions, 1994.

Marshall, Phyllis, and Jimetta Anderson. *Myrtle's Favorites: Myrtle Stephens Parkins*. Self-published, 1985.

McCulloch-Williams, Martha. *Dishes and Beverages of the Old South*. A facsimile reproduction of the 1913 edition.

McLean, Alice L. *Cooking in America, 1840–1945*. Westport, CT: Greenwood Press, 2006.

McWhiney, Grady. *Cracker Culture: Celtic Ways in the Old South*. Tuscaloosa: University of Alabama Press, 1988.

Nickerson, Jane. *Jane Nickerson's Florida Cookbook*. Gainesville: University Press of Florida, 1984.

Owens, Janis. *The Cracker Kitchen*. New York: Scribner, 2009.

Plante, Ellen M. *The American Kitchen, 1700 to the Present*. New York: Facts on File, 1995.

Randolph, Mary. *The Virginia Housewife; or, Methodical Cook*. Facsimile reproduction. Mineola, NY: Dover Publications, Inc., 1993.

Rawlings, Marjorie Kinnan. *Cross Creek*. 1942. Repr., New York City: Scribner, 1996.

———. *Cross Creek Cookery*. 1942. Repr., Lady Lake, FL: Fireside Publications, 1996.

Rolle, Denys. *Humble Petition*. Facsimile reproduction of 1765 edition. Gainesville: University Press of Florida, 1977.

Sainte Claire, Dana. *Cracker: The Cracker Culture in Florida*. Daytona Beach, FL: Museum of Arts and Sciences, 1998.

———. "Cracker: Wild Frontier Life." *FORUM: Florida Humanities Council*, Winter 2008.

———. "Many Settlers Were Considered Crackers." *Orlando Sentinel*, January 18, 1998. Articles.orlandosentinel.com.

Seely, Lida. *Mrs. Seely's Cook-Book: A Manual of French and American Cookery, with Chapters on Domestic Servants Their Rights & Duties*. New York: Grosset & Dunlap, 1902.

Simmons, Amelia. *American Cookery*. A facsimile reproduction of the 1796 edition. Mineola, NY: Dover Publications, 1984.

Smith, Andrew F., ed. *The Oxford Companion to American Food and Drink*. New York: Oxford University Press, 2007.

Splint, Sarah Field. *The Art of Cooking and Serving*. Cincinnati, OH: Procter and Gamble, 1929.

Stage, Sarah, and Virginia B. Vincenti, eds. *Rethinking Home Economics: Women and the History of a Profession*. Ithaca, NY: Cornell University Press, 1997.

Stowe, Harriet Beecher. *Palmetto Leaves*. 1873. Repr., Gainesville: University Press of Florida, 1999.

Townshend, F. Trench. *Wild Life in Florida: With a Visit to Cuba*. 1875. Memphis: General Books, 2010.

Tyree, Marion Cabell. *Housekeeping in Old Virginia*. Louisville, KY: John P. Morton & Co., 1879. Repr., BiblioLife.

Voss, Kimberly Wilmot. *The Food Section: Newspaper Women and the Culinary Community*. Lanham, MD: Rowman & Littlefield, 2014.

Wallace, Lily Haxworth. *The Revised Rumford Complete Cook Book*. 1908. Repr., Rumford, RI: Rumford Company, 1939.

Warnock, Alene M. *Laura Ingalls Wilder: The Westville Florida Years*. Mansfield, MO: Laura Ingalls Wilder Home Association, Inc., 1979.

Wellman, Mabel Thacher. *Food Study: A Textbook in Home Economics for High Schools*. Boston: Little, Brown and Company, 1917.

West Virginia Extension Homemakers Council. *West Virginia's Treasured Recipes: A Collection of Early West Virginia Food and Philosophy*. N.p.: West Virginia Extension Homemakers Council, 1974.

Wilcox, Estelle Woods. *The Dixie Cook-Book*. A facsimile reproduction of the 1883 edition.

INDEX

Recipes in **bold** are original to the author.

ABOUT THE AUTHOR

J oy Sheffield Harris was born in Tripoli, Libya, on Wheelus Field
Air Force Base but moved to Florida just in time to attend Humpty
Dumpty Kindergarten and later Florida State University. She was a
home economics and history teacher and a marketing specialist for both
the Florida Department of Natural Resources and the Florida Poultry
Federation. Joy met her husband, Jack, while promoting Florida's natural
bounty on television in the early '80s. After they were married, they briefly
owned a restaurant with friends, called Harris and Company, and in 2010,
they cowrote *Easy Breezy Florida Cooking*. Other books by Joy are *A Culinary
History of Florida* and *Florida Sweets*.

Visit us at
www.historypress.com